ART IN CONTEXT
Second Edition

ART
IN
CONTEXT

Second Edition

Jack A. Hobbs

Illinois State University

HARCOURT BRACE JOVANOVICH, INC.

New York / San Diego / Chicago / San Francisco / Atlanta
London / Sydney / Toronto

Copyright © 1980, 1975 by Harcourt Brace Jovanovich, Inc.

ISBN: 0-15-503470-7

Library of Congress Catalog Card Number: 79-5238

Printed in the United States of America

To
   Marge
   Amy
   Marty

Preface

When the first edition of *Art in Context* was published, the tendency to emphasize the formal aspects of art was still relatively strong, and an introductory textbook that gave so much attention to the emotional and intellectual aspects was something of a novelty. By now, however, the importance of these other considerations in the interpretation and appreciation of works of art has come to be widely recognized; the word *context* seems to play a much larger role in today's critical vocabulary.

This new edition has not made a basic change in approach or priorities, but rather has further refined the ideas that were developed in the earlier edition. A major revision has been made in the selection of works, partly to give the book a broader historical and cultural base and also to keep it up to date. (Twelve of the works dealt with in this edition did not exist when the earlier one was published.) Most of the changes in the text reflect adjustments in organization and emphases that I have found helpful in teaching the course myself. In Part I, the treatment of the visual elements has been expanded, and the discussions of architecture have been combined in a single chapter. In Part II, a new chapter about the works and lives of four great artists of different periods has replaced two of the thematic chapters. In Part III, the historical treatment of the modern period has been expanded in all three chapters.

As in the first edition, each of the three parts deals with a basic context of art. The first examines the perceptual context: the influence of artists' and viewers' cultural backgrounds on what they see, the visual elements, and the various media. Part II presents the human context and is organized around several major themes of art. It demonstrates the reciprocal relationship between art and life by showing, for example, why artists of different cultures depict nature in very different ways, or how artists of different times managed to express their beliefs and ideas in images instead of words. Finally there is the historical context, Part III, in which the process of change in art is examined and the major developments of the modern era are traced by focusing on the evolution of new forms of visual expression.

Organization according to the major contexts and themes of art permits a much freer treatment of each topic and a broader range of examples than does the traditional historical approach. Works from different periods, places, and media can be compared and contrasted in ways that provide readers with a far more vivid sense of the purposes of art. Thus, wherever feasible, works were selected that would serve not only to illustrate a particular point but to offer striking juxtapositions, encouraging students to experience the pleasure of making their own connections and drawing their own conclusions.

Once again, I wish to thank the professors and doctoral students at Illinois State University whose advice I sought while I was writing the first edition, and whose ideas have been carried over to the second. I am especially grateful to George D. Asdell of Glenbrook North High School, Harold Gregor and Robert Stefl of Illinois State University, Lee A. Ransaw of Morris Brown College, and Edward Sturr of Kansas State University for their help with specific chapters; to Hugh W. Stumbo, formerly of Illinois State University, Brent Wilson of Pennsylvania State University, and the late Duane B. McCardle of Hanover Park, Illinois, for their contributions to the development of my ideas.

I also wish to thank editors William Dyckes, Nina Gunzenhauser, and Eleanor Lahn, designers Marilyn Marcus and Dorothea von Elbe, photo researcher Elaine Bernstein, and production manager Robert C. Karpen of Harcourt Brace Jovanovich for their efforts during the critical stages of completing the book.

JACK A. HOBBS

Contents

3 Fine Arts Media

4 Architectural Media

ART IN CONTEXT
Second Edition

PERCEPTUAL CONTEXT

What we see depends in large part on *how* we see. Our perception of even such an ordinary object as a hamburger is affected not only by the visual data of its shape and color but also by our knowledge of hamburgers—which includes such things as their taste, smell, feel, and ability to satisfy hunger.

What we see in a work of art also depends on a combination of visual information and past experience. The ability to perceive images in the lines and shapes that artists put on a piece of paper or canvas is not automatic. We need practice and experience simply to interpret the kinds of pictures that are widely familiar in our own society.

The aesthetic horizons of today are broader than those of the past. Art museums and art books generally show art not only from our own society but from those of the past and those of other parts of the world. Furthermore, the artists around us are constantly trying to develop new forms of art, which further increases the variety of art that we may encounter. The knowledge and perceptual habits we have developed for looking at art in the past may therefore be inadequate for the present.

Part I consists of four chapters that focus on the perceptual context of the visual arts. Here we will deal first with the effects of differences in cultural backgrounds on how art is perceived; then with the visual elements that artists manipulate, and how these elements can be used to affect our perception of artworks; and finally, with the diverse materials and techniques that artists use to create their works—media that can range from pencil and paper to the materials needed to construct a skyscraper.

1
Context

Nonverbal Communication

When we speak of *language*, we ordinarily think of a system of communicating with words and sounds. But language, taken in a larger sense, can mean any system of communicating. For example, one *nonverbal* language that we are all familiar with is the one that has been popularly dubbed "body language." We all use body language every day. Indeed, we use it almost every moment of every day, for we say few things that we do not accompany with a gesture or change in facial expression—consciously or unconsciously—that says the same thing. Very often we can figure out what people are talking about without even hearing their voices. And sometimes we can tell what they *really* mean even though what they say is just the opposite.

Most of the body-language signals people make are conventions that have developed within their particular culture or subculture. The gesture that a Spaniard makes to indicate "come here" is almost the opposite of the gesture that an American makes. Some Asians, it has been observed, are likely to be expressing anger if their eyes open wider, whereas Occidentals usually express surprise that way. So perhaps it would be more accurate to say body *languages*, since they seem as numerous as spoken languages.

Art as Language

The visual arts are also nonverbal languages, but in more ways than one might expect. We all know that paintings communicate, and that we are able to derive some information from them more effectively than we can from words. A great many words would be needed to describe a miracle performed by a saint or what the Rocky Mountains looked like in 1848 with the same degree of detail found in a painted image of such a subject. But few of us are aware of the fact that obtaining information from an image is not automatic—not even from the most realistic picture of a familiar subject. We have to be able to "read" a particular system of distortions that has been used to translate the original three-dimensional scene into a two-dimensional reproduction.

In some ways, learning a visual language is like learning a spoken language. For example, most Americans learn to read the language of cartoons and photographs in very much the same manner as they learn English. Their parents explain the vocabulary and the grammar of comic strips by reading the text and translating the pictures for them ("The little boy is unhappy. See the tears?") and tell them what to look for and how to identify it in home snapshots ("This is your birthday party. See Grandma?"). Learning to read a photograph may not sound like much of a challenge, but in fact there are many people who have never learned to do this. In *The Shape of Time*, art historian George Kubler described an experience with a Peruvian shepherd who had never seen a photograph before.

> . . . when I produced a photograph of him . . . he was unable to orient the flat, spotty paper or to read it as a self-portrait, for want of those complicated habits of translation which the rest of us perform from two to three dimensions without effort.

The Peruvian shepherd, because of a lack of experience with these particular pictorial conventions, could not even identify his own image. But we who have grown up with photography and movies take these things so much for granted that it is hard for us to imagine anyone in the world not being able to grasp their meaning immediately. In order to understand this, let us turn the situation around and look at an image that is not familiar to our own culture.

We would not say that this Alaskan Indian mask (fig. 1-1) has no meaning at all for us. We recognize the image of a face, which immediately generates several associations and ideas. But how well do we actually understand it? Before going any further, let us try to decide exactly what it is we see here. The following description will be simple and objective—that is, limited to statements about the appearance of the mask that all of us could agree with.

To begin with, it is obviously not a very realistic image of a face. Consequently, we may say that it is a ''stylized'' image. The shape of the head and the arrangement of the features are asymmetrical and do not seem very precise or detailed. Most of the mask is convex, but there is a concave area surrounding the main features. One eye is circular, the other almond-shaped. A spiral movement starts along the edge of the scroll-shaped nose, moves around the circular eye, and is carried by the mouth to the other side of the face. There it almost joins with the S-shaped line that forms the eyebrow and the other edge of the nose. The surface of the mask reveals the marks of the carver's tool, and there is a spattering of color around the mouth.

We would probably try to interpret this mask in the same way that we interpret images of faces in our own art. Characteristically, we read an upturned mouth as smiling or laughing. The almond-shaped eye suggests a wink, which reinforces the idea of smiling. Still, there is so little information and so many unusual features that this face is not very easy to understand. For example, we are not accustomed to asymmetry in the representation of a face. Why are the eyes different shapes? Why is the nose twisted and the mouth off to the side? Does the mask represent someone who has been frightened? Or does it represent a simple-minded person, or a madman?

We soon become aware that our cultural background is inadequate for helping us to interpret the mask. And even if we were told that it represents a man-eating mountain demon with a blood-stained face, many things would remain unclear. We still would not know how those people regarded demons. Were all demons alike? Was this one to be feared or pitied? Did the Alaskan Indians represent both their benevolent and malevolent spirits with lopsided faces? Obviously there are many questions that need to be answered before we can begin to understand this particular artwork. We can enjoy looking at it, but we are not able to fully interpret it.

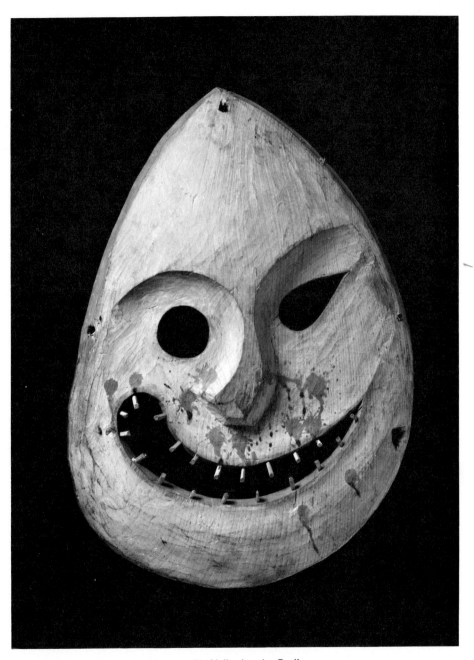

1–1 Alaskan Indian mask. Museum für Volkerkunde, Berlin.

Peanuts   Americans looking at a comic strip of Charlie Brown and his dog Snoopy (fig. 1-2) can understand what is going on and relate it to their own experience, even though it is an improbable situation. If they had never seen the *Peanuts* comic strip before but were reasonably well-informed and three years old or more, they would still understand that this is a picture of a little boy and his pet dog. But if we look at Charlie Brown's face as closely as we did at the Alaskan mask, we will realize that it actually has less detail and is less realistic than the mask. Everything is expressed with extreme economy. When he speaks, Charlie Brown's mouth, like that of the mask, is a simple void. In the final frame, however, it is down-turned, which we interpret as unhappiness. The eyes are no more than a pair of dots bounded by curved lines, but they help us to define his reaction. Charlie Brown's hair is an abstract scrawl above his eyes, and Snoopy's nose is a black dot stuck to the side of his face. But because we are so familiar with these conventions of drawing, we grasp their meaning at a glance.

There is more meaning in *Peanuts* than just the depictions of a boy and a dog. At times it reveals a great many things about the anxieties of growing up in suburban America, public schools, and peer relationships. In order to understand these themes in *Peanuts* one has to have some familiarity with twentieth-century American culture. And it also helps if one is familiar with the ways in which these themes have been treated not only by the cartoon, but by movies, television, and novels. People who lack this knowledge are at a disadvantage in understanding *Peanuts*—just as we are in understanding the image of a mountain demon when we know so little about Alaskan culture.

Picasso   People who are unfamiliar with the work of Pablo Picasso or who are unwilling to accept his personal artistic language usually do not care for paintings like *First Steps* (fig. 1-3). They are apt to criticize such things as the gross hands and feet, the lopsided faces and bodies, the simple eyes, and the abnormally foreshortened head of the mother. Oddly enough, these same people are rarely aware of the radical distortions of anatomy that are committed daily in *Peanuts* and other comic strips. However, the difference between the painting by Picasso and the cartoon by Schulz does not rest only on the fact that the latter uses more familiar conventions. A Picasso painting is not meant to be as easily understood as a frame of a Schulz cartoon.

1–2   Charles M. Schulz, Charlie Brown and Snoopy.
© 1973 United Feature Syndicate, Inc.

Describing *First Steps* is a rather formidable task compared to that of describing the mask or the picture of Charlie Brown, so we will have to concentrate on only its more conspicuous aspects. The dominant feature in the painting is the child's face, especially the eyes, which are wide ellipses staring straight at us. Like the Alaskan mask, the shape of the head and the arrangement of facial features are asymmetrical, but unlike the mask, which was dominated by a spiral form, the face of the infant is made up of lines and shapes that come and go in many directions. The mother's face, which appears smaller than the child's, seems to be looking downward. Her head, neck, and body arch around the infant, while her elongated hand on the right side seems to be both prodding and supporting his hand. Although we recognize the forms of two different people, the many shapes and lines within the picture tend to confuse their separateness so that, in places, the bodies of mother and child and the space around them become a single shape. This effect can be seen at the top of the painting, where the arched lines of the mother's head, eyes, and breasts complement the lines in the child's head; at the right and left sides, where the stubbier lines of hands interpenetrate; and at the bottom, where legs, feet, and ground are all warped in similar ways.

We can identify the subject of Picasso's painting because it is close enough to forms of representation that we already understand—in particular to the forms of *Peanuts*. (And this is largely because Picasso's art influenced artists who draw cartoons, not the other way around.) We can also appreciate some things about the way *First Steps* is presented because elements of it—the archlike protective shape of the mother, for example—are simple and direct enough for us to grasp. But most people run into problems if they try to go beyond the subject matter and these few elements. Why, for instance, does the child's face look the way it does? Someone unfamiliar with art might rightly guess that there is some relationship between these distortions and those of children's paintings. But *First Steps* also contains references to such things as Christian Madonnas of the Renaissance, Greco-Roman sculpture, African masks, and Picasso's own Cubist experiments (figs. 1-4 through 1-7). The fact is that without some knowledge of the language of Western art and the themes that have been important in the past, we cannot appreciate the richness of this painting or grasp much of its meaning.

1–3   Pablo Picasso, *First Steps*, 1943. Oil on canvas, 51¼″ x 38¼″.
Yale University Art Gallery, New Haven, Connecticut (gift of Stephen C. Clark, B.A. 1903).

1–4   Pablo Picasso, *Head of a Woman,* 1909.
Gouache, 24¼″ x 18¾″. The Art Institute
of Chicago (Edward E. Ayer Fund).

1–5   *Constantine the Great, c.* 330 A.D.
Marble, approx. 8′6″ high.
Palazzo dei Conservatori, Rome.

The meaning of Picasso's *First Steps* is more than the simple
act that the title helps us discover in these shapes and colors—a
mother helping her infant son take his first steps. So to stop at this
level of meaning is to seriously impoverish an exceptional work of
art. First steps are, after all, a major moment in the life of any
human being—''a moment of crisis in which eagerness, determi-
nation, insecurity, and triumph are mingled,'' as museum director

1-6   Fra Lippo Lippi, *Madonna and Child*
(detail), 1437. Galleria Nazionale
d'Arte Antica, Rome.

1-7   African Negro Mask, *c.* 1775.
Wood, 14" high. Itumba region, Africa.
Collection, The Museum of Modern Art,
New York (given anonymously).

Alfred Barr once wrote of this painting. Picasso used a particular
artistic language to express this deeper meaning, and we can find it
there if we know how to read his work. It is in the way the child's
face is distorted, in the radiating lines of his clothing, the awkward
balance of his body, the protective domelike shape of the mother,
and at least a dozen other details. All of these help to convey the
emotions of this extraordinary moment.

Summary   The problems of understanding unfamiliar art might be summed up effectively with an analogy drawn from sports. Most Americans would probably be at least as puzzled by an English cricket match as they would be by an Alaskan mask. Our lack of knowledge of an Alaskan Indian's feelings about mountain demons is comparable to our lack of knowledge of a Yorkshire fan's feelings about the traditional rivalry between his team and that of Lancashire; and our ignorance of the reasons for carving a lopsided, spiral face can be equated with our ignorance of terms like ''no ball'' and ''wide.''

The point of this discussion is not that one group of people is more sophisticated or more primitive than another, but that each group develops different ways of seeing. Environment and past experience affect the way people see things, and the *way* that people see affects much of *what* they see. Each group also develops different languages of art, and, in a complex society like our own, there are many languages. Knowledge of an art language— the conventions used and the cultural context—can help us to understand a particular artwork better.

2

The Visual Elements

A painting like Georges Seurat's *Bathing at Asnières* (colorplate 1) is—to us—obviously a picture of boys gathered along a riverbank on a summer day. But let us imagine for a moment how it might appear to the Peruvian shepherd of Chapter 1. If he were to describe what *he* saw as precisely as he could, he might tell us that it is a flat, rectangular surface covered with patches of color.

What is interesting about this is that Seurat himself would probably have described this painting in very much the same way. For the fact is that he was more concerned with arranging the *visual elements* of the painting—colors, shapes, lines, textures, and space—than he was with the re-creation of a particular scene. Artists of any sort, whether they make paintings, design buildings, or weld scraps of iron into sculptures, are always basically concerned with the visual elements. This is true whether the work is intended to look like a group of swimmers on a riverbank or an abstract collection of shapes and colors.

By the same token, the viewer must understand something of the workings of the visual elements in order to fully appreciate and enjoy a work of art. To be unaware of the ways that Seurat meticulously organized the visual elements in *Bathing at Asnières* is to miss a great deal of what the painting has to offer. In the following pages, therefore, we will examine these elements in some detail and try to establish a fairly precise and useful set of definitions for them.

Color   The problems of definition begin almost with the first sentence one writes. So many writers on art have approached the visual elements in so many different ways that there is often great disagreement over exactly what the elements are and how they should be dealt with. For example, many people consider *light and dark* to be a separate element. Others use it, as we will do here, to refer to one property of color.

If we accept the idea of black, white, and gray as being part of color, then we may say that color is basic to all things. Not only that; color is basic to the other visual elements. It is through variations of color that we distinguish shapes, lines, textures, and space.

In order to understand the role of color in art and vision, we must analyze it in terms of three basic properties: *hue, value,* and *saturation*. Although all three are continually and inseparably present in normal vision, they can be separated in theory and isolated for the purposes of this analysis.

Hue   Words like *red* or *green* refer to hues, the qualities that differentiate one color from another. Our perception of them is affected by the frequency of the light waves reflected to our eyes from the surface of an object, whether it be a green leaf, a poster printed with red ink, or particles in the atmosphere that deflect the sun's rays and make the sky seem blue. Hue can be established with great precision by measuring light waves with scientific instruments, but for everyday purposes this is certainly not necessary. The words for color that everyone learns in childhood are quite sufficient for communicating to other people what we mean. Yellow, red, blue, green, purple, and orange are rarely confused by Americans with normal vision.

Three of these hues—yellow, red, and blue—can be combined to create any of the others. We can mix yellow and red to produce orange, yellow and blue to produce green, and red and blue to produce purple. Combining all three at once produces dull versions of the hues, or browns and grays. (The aspect of dullness in color will be discussed under the heading of saturation.) The three basic hues are therefore known as the *primary colors*, while the other three—green, purple, and orange—are called the *secondary colors*. These relationships can be illustrated with the use of a *color wheel*—or color circle, as it was called by Isaac Newton, the man who originally designed it—a circular chart on which each secondary color is placed between the two primary colors of which it is composed (colorplate 2). Most color charts also include *tertiary colors*, which are those that lie between the primaries and secondaries and are created by making unequal mixtures of any two of the primaries; many variations are possible. The names of these colors are somewhat arbitrary and often exotic—such as cerulean, aqua, and turquoise, to name but a few of those that lie between blue and green.

Hues that are situated alongside one another on the color wheel are called *analogous*, while those that are directly opposite each other are called *complementary*. The former tend to relate to each other, while the latter tend to contrast with each other. Seurat made use of this characteristic of complementaries in *Bathing at Asnières*. He painted many of the surfaces that received the direct light of the sun in variations of orange and the shadows in variations of the complement of orange—blue or blue-violet. He further employed complementaries to make figures stand out from the background—a combination of adjacent colors that is sometimes referred to as *hue contrast*. The orange cap of the bather on the far right contrasts sharply with the background blue of the water. Less vivid are the variations of the mahogany red of the dog and those objects on the bank that are roughly complementary to the green grass.

Seurat often used an unusual method for producing different color effects. Rather than blending hues before applying them to the canvas, he would apply them unmixed in separate little strokes, allowing them to blend in the viewer's vision—provided the viewer is standing at a normal distance from the canvas. This effect is known as *optical mixing*, and it is the opposite of hue contrast (in which relatively large areas of color are made to appear more separate). We can see the principle at work in the blue-green of the water, which Seurat painted by daubing several hues—mostly blues, greens, and whites—directly on the canvas rather than physically mixing them beforehand. (The same principle was later applied to color printing, with only the three primaries and black ink used to re-create even as complex a subject as this painting.)

Value   The range of light and dark in color is called *value* (colorplate 2). Had Seurat chosen to paint *Bathing at Asnières* with just a single hue—say, red—we would still be able to distinguish the riverbank and the boys and the water because of the different values of red. We could easily make out the shapes of figures and details on the basis of their differences in light and dark, for we could read the all-red visual field essentially the same way that we would read a black-and-white photograph.

The range of light and dark that we experience in everyday vision is much more relative than we often realize. We tend to think that a white sheet of paper is always the same white, whether it is in bright light or shadow. This effect is referred to as *color constancy*. Normally, we see the color of an egg (fig. 2-1) as a uniform off-white over all of its curved surface. Yet if we look at the image in this photograph as a pattern of lights and darks, we can easily see a great difference in color—specifically the values of the color—between the top and bottom of the egg. Color constancy, then, points up one of the discrepancies between optical data and the mind's interpretation of that data in the everyday business of viewing our world.

Artists, aware of the factor of color constancy, use different values when they want to make an image of something appear three-dimensional. The method for picturing the effect of reflected light as it plays across a surface—whether that of an egg or a person's body—was developed several centuries before the time of Seurat. Called shading or, technically, *chiaroscuro* (from the combined Italian words for light and dark), the method is admirably demonstrated in a study of the boy wearing a straw hat that Seurat drew in preparation for his painting (fig. 2-2). Using broad strokes of crayon on rough-grained paper, the artist skillfully suggested the volumes of the boy's body and clothing.

Like hue contrasts, *value contrasts* were used in *Bathing at Asnières* to help set off the figures from their surroundings. We can see the adjustments of color in the river where it forms the background of the central figure. The values of blue touching the shaded parts of the boy—his face, neck, and back—are lighter; those touching the sunlit portions are darker. The artist also adjusted the values around the figures in the water. By so doing, Seurat helped to make these two figures stand out from their surroundings.

2–1
Example of
color constancy.

2–2   Georges Seurat, *Seated Boy with Straw Hat,* 1883–84. Conté crayon on paper, 9½" x 11⅞".
Yale University Art Gallery (Everett V. Meeks, B.A. 1901, Fund).

As is the case with hue, values are subject to optical mixing. Black and white lines or brushwork set side by side can appear to be shades of grey. In the woodcut *The Four Horsemen of the Apocalypse* (fig. 2-3) we see a masterful use of chiaroscuro: the sixteenth-century German artist Albrecht Dürer used only black ink and the white of the paper, yet the work appears to have a wide range of *middle values*, or greys. If we look closely, we can see that any of these middle values is actually the result of optical mixing caused by the closely-spaced black lines.

Similar to optical mixing is an effect referred to as the *assimilation effect*, in which a pattern of small units of one color superimposed over a different background color seems to cause the color underneath to shift its value and hue somewhat toward that of the pattern. The red of the background in *All Things Do Live in the Three* (colorplate 3) is actually the same throughout, but it appears to be two or three different reds forming subtle but clearly distinguishable diamond-shaped patterns across the canvas. The artist, Richard Anuskiewicz, accomplished this illusion by overlaying the red with a system of uniform dots of blue, green, and yellow.

Saturation

Saturation refers to the relative purity of a color on a scale from bright to dull (colorplate 2). Most paints are intense to start with; thus an artist who desires a strong blue uses the paint straight from the tube. A less intense, or "muted," blue can be made by mixing blue with brown or with its complement, orange. Some colors are so muted—such as most browns and grays—that they are sometimes called *neutrals*. Typically, most of the colors in a painting are intermixed and, as a result, tend not to be bright. Seurat, however, did not always mix his pigments; he preferred to use bright colors applied in individual strokes. In colorplate 1, the river, in addition to blues and blue-greens, contains dots of orange that, had they been mixed with the other paint, would have produced a dull, grayish blue. Instead, the orange interacts in our vision without sacrificing the intensity of either. We see a vibration of color, an appropriate equivalent of sparkling water.

Expressive Use of Color

Although some knowledge of color theory is very helpful in understanding works of art, the effect of color on human feelings is no doubt more important. Color does affect us emotionally, but questions still exist as to exactly why and in what ways. Without attempting to deal with these questions in detail, we can summarize some general tendencies of human response to color.

2–3
Albrecht Dürer,
The Riders on the Four Horses
from the Apocalypse,
c. 1496. Woodcut, 15¼″ x 11″.
Metropolitan Museum of Art, New York
(gift of Junius S. Morgan, 1919).

Color qualities are often identified with thermal qualities—that is, they are said to be "warm" or "cool." Reds, yellows, and oranges are considered warm; blues, greens, and violets are considered cool. Correspondingly, we usually regard warm colors as stimulating and cool colors as relaxing. There are probably associations between this way of thinking of color and the colors of such things as fire, blood, and water. But there may also be a physiological reason to account for human responses to the different hues. Light consists of energy waves of different lengths, and warm colors have longer wavelengths than cool colors.

Warm colors give the impression of advancing toward the viewer, while cool colors seem to recede. This effect is also achieved by the other properties of color—darker values seem closer than lighter values, and brighter intensities seem closer than duller intensities. Reasoning from this, one could assume that a red—the warmest hue—with a dark value and high intensity would advance the most. And indeed, this seems to be true. When one looks at a crowd of people in a stadium, for instance, one is invariably more aware of those who are wearing bright reds.

However, it must always be remembered that colors do not operate in isolation from each other or from the shapes to which they belong. Their effects are functions of their contexts, of their interaction with one another, and of other associations that may not even have anything to do with the work of art. The colors we perceive in Seurat's painting are not necessarily the colors that he actually used, but they may be the colors that we normally associate with people and landscapes. On the other hand, the colors in Anuskiewicz's painting are obviously deprived of such associations, since the artist has eliminated most of the factors except those of color interaction. It is an art that depends not on cultural norms, symbolism, or the observer's past experiences but on the physiology of the human eye and on the brain's ability to respond to pure color and pattern.

Shape

It was pointed out earlier that, technically, we cannot perceive shapes or anything else without color (or, in the case of black-and-white photography or of someone who is colorblind, the value aspect of color). But we certainly can *conceive* of shapes independent of their color, and we tend to see ourselves and the objects we live with in terms of their characteristic shapes. Indeed, in our everyday commerce with the world, shape may be more important than color.

Two-Dimensional Shapes

We live in a three-dimensional world, surrounded by infinite space in every direction and filled with three-dimensional objects. Originally, human beings did not think in two-dimensional terms. Indeed, it took at least a million years for them to begin drawing images of any kind on cave walls. But after that, making marks on a flat surface—whether they functioned as images, symbols, or patterns—became one of the most common types of communication.

In order to survey the nature of shape perception in two dimensions, it would be helpful to review two principles developed by Gestalt psychologists. The first of these, the *figure-ground principle*, has to do with our tendency to divide a visual pattern into two kinds of shapes—figure and ground. A figure appears to stand out, to be "on top of" a ground; a ground, on the other hand, appears to be underneath and surrounding a figure. Printed letters, for example, usually are figures while the white page is the ground. As

2–4
Ellsworth Kelly,
Untitled, 1960.
Oil on canvas, 86" x 49".

a general rule, smaller and darker shapes are figures while larger and lighter ones are grounds. (Artists sometimes use the terms ''positive shapes'' and ''negative shapes.'') Figures, however, do not have to have solid colors. The outlined shapes of Charlie Brown and Snoopy (fig. 1-2) function as figures.

When we look at the world around us, we normally see objects and people as figures and their surroundings as the ground (or ''background,'' as we usually say). This habit of perception applies as well to the way we perceive Seurat's riverbank scene; indeed, realistic pictures like this can be likened to windows. But whether something is figure or ground can also depend on its circumstances and how we are attending to it. The reclining man in Seurat's picture usually functions as a figure, but if we concentrate on just his ear, then he becomes the ground and the ear alone becomes the figure.

Although abstract paintings lack the familiar visual cues of realistic paintings, we tend to perceive their patterns as figure-ground relationships. However, these relationships may not always be so obvious or stable. At first view, one is likely to see the white shape—the single, unbroken form—of Ellsworth Kelly's painting (fig. 2-4) as the figure and the black shapes around it as the ground. In other words, it looks like a black canvas with a large white shape painted on it. Yet with very little effort, one can also see this painting in exactly the opposite way, as a white canvas with four separate black shapes painted on it. This reversal of figure and ground—a flip-flop that one can almost feel when changing from one way of looking at it to the other—is virtually impossible to accomplish with a realistic work such as Seurat's. On the other hand, with one of M.C. Escher's fantastic illustrations (fig. 2-5), figure-ground reversal is not only possible; it is almost impossible to avoid and is an essential part of the work.

The second principle of perception that is helpful for us to understand is *closure*, the tendency for incomplete figures to be perceived as complete. Closure occurs, for example, when a person sees a square in an arrangement of four dots—the mind's eye fills in and completes the latent connections along the side of the figure (fig. 2-6). Gestaltists reason that a person's mind searches for the

2–5   M.C. Escher, *Day and Night,* 1938. Woodcut, 15½" x 26¾".
Courtesy Vorpal Gallery, New York.

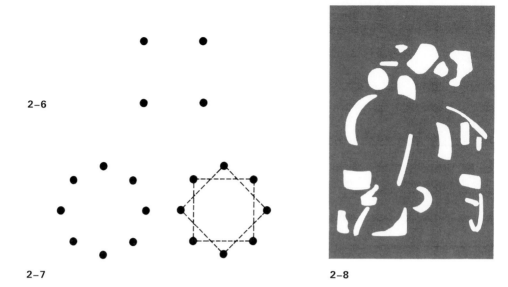

2-6

2-7

2-8

simplest and most stable form in a complex optical situation. A square, therefore, is more satisfactory than four separate dots; similarly, a circle (fig. 2-7) is a more satisfactory form than two overlapping squares.

But there is also reason to believe that experience plays an equal if not a more important role in the process of closure. This can be demonstrated through the use of "completion figures" that are designed to confuse the beholder. The white patches on a black background in figure 2-8 seem to resist any particular arrangement other than that of an abstract pattern. If, however, the viewer is told that the picture represents a train, the image of an approaching steam locomotive is apt to surface. Once it does, this interpretation of the completion figure becomes virtually irresistible.

Representing Three-Dimensional Shapes

The constancy of perception is an important factor in any discussion of three-dimensional—solid—shapes. If we perform the simple act of turning the cover of a book, we can witness the paradox of *shape constancy*. As the cover swings toward us, its rectangular shape goes through a series of distortions (fig. 2-9). It changes to a trapezoid that grows progressively thinner, until at one point it becomes nothing more than a line that is the thickness of the cover material—its ultrathin shape contrasting with that of the rest of the unopened book. But what we perceive is an unchanging rectangular cover swinging on the hinges of the book's binding.

The phenomenon of shape constancy, like color constancy, has to be dealt with by artists who try to represent the third dimension in a flat picture. In a sense, they must distort a form in order to make it appear undistorted. The drawings in figure 2-9 are a good example. The artist radically shortened the width of the cover in those drawings where it was necessary to make it appear to be a tilted plane in three-dimensional space. This is called *foreshortening*. In a natural-looking scene the use of foreshortening is much more complicated. In Seurat's painting of the bathers it is manifested in numerous places—for example, in the bodies of the dog and the man lying down in the foreground. Actually, foreshortening is present wherever any object—a forearm, a finger, or the brim of a hat—has to be represented in depth.

A related phenomenon that artists must deal with is *size constancy*, the tendency to perceive objects as being a certain size no matter how far away they are. A striking demonstration of this phenomenon is seen in a photograph of a row of posts that stretches away from the camera (fig. 2-10). The last post in the row has been exactly duplicated alongside the nearest one, but the contrast between them appears so great that we are almost forced to measure and compare the two. Were it not for the duplicated image, we would assume that the last post is more or less the same size as the first one.

As proof of the power of this phenomenon and the difficulty that artists have in dealing with it, one might cite the fact that it was not until a few hundred years ago that painters began to represent the world of three dimensions on a two-dimensional surface with any real success. Apparently it was very difficult for them to understand that by making something smaller in a picture, they could make it appear to be farther away rather than simply smaller in size.

2–9

2-10

Three-Dimensional Shapes   Solid shapes, width, height, and depth are the bases of the sculptor's art. The crucial difference, visually, between a painting and a piece of sculpture is that the latter offers more than a single point of view. Each vantage point reveals a different shape. Yet, as was pointed out earlier, the factors of shape constancy and size constancy tend to fuse the viewer's different perceptions into a single perception. This is usually true of realistic sculpture, but in the case of a more abstract work that employs unfamiliar shapes in a novel composition, these factors are likely to play a less important role. Picasso's concrete *Bust of Sylvette* (fig. 2-11) does not allow itself to be easily understood because of the difficulty of establishing in the mind's eye a single configuration for the whole work.

Expressive Use of Shapes   Just as colors are spoken of as warm and cool, shapes are habitually grouped by artists into "organic" and "geometric" categories. Organic shapes, those with curved surfaces and contours, are usually found in nature, while geometric shapes are generally associated with objects made by human beings. This division of shapes is accompanied by a set of associations, such as nature versus technology, human beings versus machines, or even life versus death. The contrast between curved and straight (or round and rectangular) also inspires analogies of soft versus hard, feminine versus masculine, or affection versus indifference.

But again, human feelings toward particular shapes cannot be isolated from the other elements present in a work of art. As with colors, the expressiveness of shapes is a function of complex inter-relationships. Jean Arp frequently expressed the theme of a life force in the undulating and organic shapes of his abstract sculptures. *Growth* (fig. 2-12), a smooth compound of botanical and human anatomy, suggests life and procreation. But because of the unbroken envelope of its surface, it seems to be a self-contained and reticent type of life. Moreover, its twisting form and shiny surface tend to suggest coldblooded rather than warmblooded growth.

2–12
Jean Arp, *Growth,* 1938.
Bronze, 31½" high,
Philadelphia Museum of Art
(gift of Curt Valentin).

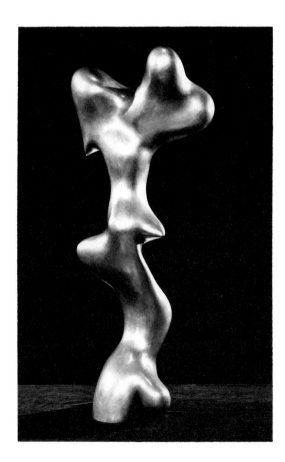

◀ 2–11
Pablo Picasso,
Bust of Sylvette, 1967.
Concrete and black Norwegian
basalt aggregate, 36' high.
Courtesy of New York University.

Line
In a sense, lines can be considered another species of the category of shapes—that is, very thin shapes. Practically speaking, however, lines are normally distinguished from shapes and can be perceived virtually anywhere: in the wrinkles of a person's face, in the veins of a leaf, in the spiny ridges on a seashell, or in the wind-etched surface of a sand dune.

But we come across lines probably most often on paper, in the form of drawings, diagrams, printed words, notations, doodles, and so on. People begin very early in life looking at drawings made with lines, such as those in storybooks and comic strips. People also begin making lines themselves at an early age—at first in the form of random scribbles inspired by the pride of being able to leave a personal mark on paper (or a wall), and later in the form of rudimentary images or symbols, when the child begins to name the scribbles (fig. 2-13).

In art, lines can be used to represent objects in a very simple, direct way—by describing their outer contours. The cartoon characters Charlie Brown and Snoopy (fig. 1-2) and the opening book

2–13
Martin Hobbs,
Mommy and Daddy, 1973.

2–14   Albrecht Dürer, *Barbara Dürer*, 1514.
Charcoal drawing, 22″ x 23″. Kupferstichkabinett, Berlin.

(fig. 2-9) are two examples in which lines function primarily as outlines. The images are very flat, having little more depth than that afforded by the most basic kind of figure-ground relationship. But lines can also be employed to represent a subject in far more complicated ways, even going so far as to suggest texture and three-dimensional shapes. In the drawing of his mother (fig. 2-14), Albrecht Dürer described the bony structure of the brow, nose, cheeks, mouth, and chin of the face, and the tendons of the neck as these are both revealed and concealed by leathery, sagging flesh. He also showed the heavy-lidded, protruding eyes, the wrinkled forehead, and a few strands of hair as well as the folds and gatherings of the veil. In places the artist employed fine, closely spaced lines to indicate shadows or touches of chiaroscuro, but he accomplished the effects of depth—the many bumps and hollows—mostly by means of single lines that are light or dark, thick or thin.

Unlike the drawing of Barbara Dürer, *Bathing at Asnières* conveys the sense of depth by use of chiaroscuro rather than line. Indeed, going by the definition of lines being very thin shapes, one might have a hard time locating any lines in Seurat's paintings. But lines can be inferred from the boundaries that separate objects from one another or from their surroundings—such as the edge of the riverbank and the contour of the man lying down. They are also implied, as in the horizon. Although it is far from being a single, unbroken line, we still can, with the help of some closure, see the horizon extending from one side to the other.

Expressive Use of Line

Lines do not have to be used descriptively. In the twentieth century, abstract art liberated line from the need to represent things. In *No. 3* by Jackson Pollock (fig. 2-15), the convoluted lines suggest movement and energy rather than describing the shapes of objects, and the lines' alternating thickness and thinness are qualities in their own right rather than means of conveying an impression of depth.

Whether intentionally used for expression or for description, lines are, in one sense, inescapably expressive. This claim is based on the belief that gestures such as the drawing of lines reveal something about personal behavior. Like handwriting, they are a fairly direct reflection of an artist's thinking and feelings.

Käthe Kollwitz made a number of works dealing with suffering, death, and human vulnerability. In *Death Seizing A Woman* (fig. 2-16), the intensity of feeling is evoked by the starkness of the lines and their abrupt shifts in direction as well as by the familiar symbol of death, the struggling woman, and the look of terror in the mother's face. Compare Kollwitz's bold and forceful strokes with Picasso's flowing, leisurely line in the portrait of the composer Igor Stravinsky (fig. 2-17). The vast difference between the two works is due to the different personalities of their lines as much as it is to their different subject matter.

2–16　Käthe Kollwitz, *Death Seizing a Woman,* 1934. Lithograph, 20″ x 14½″. The Museum of Modern Art, New York (purchase).

2–15　Jackson Pollock, *No. 3,* 1951. Oil on canvas, 56⅛″ x 24″. Collection of Robert U. Ossorio.

2–17　Pablo Picasso, *Portrait of Igor Stravinsky,* 1920. Private collection.

2–18
Ivan Albright,
*Into the World There Came
a Soul Called Ida,*
1929–30.
Oil on canvas,
56⅛" x 47".
The Art Institute of Chicago
(Collection of
Mr. and Mrs. Ivan Albright).

Texture
The term *texture* is used to refer to the surface qualities of things—for example, the hard, smooth feeling of an egg or the soft, smooth feeling of velvet. The best way to find out about the texture of something is by touching it. Yet most of our day-to-day information about texture comes from looking at things.

Visually, information about texture is transmitted by the way in which different materials affect the light that falls on their surfaces. A surface rough with bumps or pores will cast many little shadows; a matte surface will absorb light; and a glossy one will reflect it. In other words, these textures can be perceived by the eyes in essentially the same way that color and shape are perceived.

In painting, texture actually can take two different forms. In representational works it can be simulated with patterns of light and dark. It can also be a characteristic of the materials them-

2–19
Jean Dubuffet,
Tree of Fluids (*Body of a Lady*),
1950. Oil on canvas,
45⅝″ x 35″.
Secrétariat de Jean Dubuffet.

selves—the paint, the canvas, or some substance that is attached to the surface or mixed with the paint. Usually one or the other of these forms predominates. In Ivan Albright's *Into the World There Came a Soul Called Ida* (fig. 2-18), the simulated textures of a wicker chair, a vanity, cosmetic jars, clothing, and, especially, middle-aged flesh do much of the work in suggesting the process of human aging and deterioration. In Jean Dubuffet's *Tree of Fluids* (fig. 2-19), it is the paint itself that seems to be deteriorating. Here the material existence of the art object participates symbolically in a statement about the universal fate of biological and spiritual decay.

Texture is even more fundamental in sculpture than it is in painting. For many centuries, many of the best sculptures have highlighted the textures both of the materials used in them and the materials in the objects they were made to represent. As the art historian Herbert Read once pointed out,

> For the sculptor, tactile values are not an illusion to be created on a two-dimensional plane: they constitute a reality to be conveyed directly, as existent mass. Sculpture is an art of *palpation*—an art that gives satisfaction in the touching and handling of objects. That, indeed, is the only way in which we can have direct sensations of the three-dimensional shape of an object.

Read went on to lament the fact that visitors to a museum are not allowed to touch the artworks. But he would no doubt concede that human visual perception, assisted by past experience and a little bit of imagination, is enormously capable of appreciating the tactile values of a piece of sculpture without actually touching it. It would certainly be a pleasant experience to pick up the Barbara Hepworth carving (fig. 2-20) and experience its surfaces directly. But though we cannot touch the object depicted here, the photograph provides enough cues for us to compare the sculpture with our memories of other wooden objects and to imagine its smooth surfaces, subtle contours, weight, and perhaps even its smell.

2–20 Barbara Hepworth, *Pendour,* 1947. Painted wood, 10¼" x 27¼" x 9".
Hirshhorn Museum and Sculpture Garden, Smithsonian Institution, Washington, D.C.

Space   Space can be thought of as the "empty shape" that exists around solid shapes. Can we see space? To the extent that air, or atmosphere, is not really empty, space can be seen under certain conditions, and painters are able to depict it. (More will be said about this under the topic of aerial perspective.) Under most conditions, however, space is relatively transparent. Yet we are aware of it at all times, and, like solid shapes, it can be described and measured. Space is really seen by its boundaries—where it touches objects and other solid shapes. The space of a room, for example, is defined by the ceiling, floor, walls, and objects in the room. By looking at these things we can see the space well enough to describe it. Outdoor space is defined by the land, trees, and buildings it touches (while its outer limits may be the horizon and the dome of the sky). The complementary relationship between solid shapes and space in our perception of the three-dimensional world is similar to that between figure and ground in our perception of two-dimensional pattern.

We also experience space through our *kinesthetic sense*—our feeling of the position and movement of our own bodies. If we were blindfolded, the only way we could perceive and get to know the space of a strange room would be by moving about in it—perceiving it with our kinesthetic sense (along with our tactile sense). But although we see, we still sense a space surrounding us by how it feels to move around in; and we probably do this in our imagination when not actually moving. Like texture, for which the eyes are aided by the sense of touch, the element of space is experienced cooperatively by vision and movement.

Architecture and Sculpture   Space is a very important element for the architect, who is concerned about designing it for human use. Michelangelo, who is famous as a sculptor and painter, also undertook several architectural projects, including the redesigning of Rome's Capitoline Hill (fig. 2-21). His solution was to redesign the front of one of the two buildings already on the hill and add a third building to create a symmetrical, trapezoidal public square. To accent the shape of the square and to set off the statue of Marcus Aurelius in its center, Michelangelo provided a strikingly decorative oval pavement. Most squares of the time were closed on all four sides by buildings, but Michelangelo chose to leave this square open on one side, with a low balustrade to define the limits of the square there. Today's visitor to the Capitoline Hill experiences not only the majesty of the

2–21
Michelangelo,
Capitoline Hill,
Rome,
designed *c.* 1537.

ancient buildings but the drama of being inside an ordered, symmetrically balanced, and partly closed space.

Another very dramatic space that is entirely closed is the inside of New York's Guggenheim Museum (fig. 2-22), designed by Frank Lloyd Wright. There is no question that the spiralling, multilevelled interior appeals vividly to both the visual and the kinesthetic senses. To see the artworks, which are displayed on the outer walls of all the levels, a visitor takes an elevator to the top level and then must descend a gently sloped spiral ramp on foot. The spectacular interplay between the solid shapes and spaces of the complex structure is experienced directly.

The interplay between shape and space is a primary concern of most modern sculptors, who, like Hepworth, tend to include openings in their work for space to flow through. Traditional sculpture was usually a solid, relatively uninterrupted shape with few openings. The forms of today's abstract sculpture, such as Richard Hunt's *Drawing in Space No. 1* (fig. 2-23), are usually very open, allowing for a maximum of shape-space interplay. For the viewer, this alternation between closed and open creates a continually changing perception of shape and space relationships when viewing the piece from different vantage points.

2–22
Frank Lloyd Wright,
The Solomon R. Guggenheim Museum,
New York, 1943–59.
View of interior from dome.

2–23
Richard Hunt,
Drawing in Space, No. 1, 1977.
Welded steel, 34" high.
Collection of the artist.

Representing Space
in Painting

In his painting of bathers, Seurat created the illusion of depth in a variety of ways. Two of them already discussed, chiaroscuro and foreshortening, were used to make individual objects and people appear three-dimensional. Seurat also employed several methods to make the people and objects appear to exist in space—that is, nearer to or farther away from the viewer.

One of the most obvious methods is the *placement* of things higher or lower in the picture, because we tend to think of the things that are higher as being farther away. Another is *overlapping*—one thing being set in front of another, such as the dog and the man—which also strengthens the impression of nearness or farness. Another set of cues is provided by the artist's use of *aerial perspective*, a method that simulates the effects of color in the atmosphere. Sometimes air contains high amounts of particulate matter—as with the smoke in the distance in Seurat's painting—which can be easily seen. But even without the presence of smoke, air is dense enough to affect the appearance of objects: the farther away from us they are, the softer their outlines and the more subdued their colors. We can see how Seurat has imitated this effect if we compare the colors of the people and objects in the foreground with those of the buildings and bridges on the distant horizon. *Gradient of texture and detail* is still another system for suggesting depth. Gradients can be seen in the grassy bank of the Seurat painting, where the blades of grass gradually turn into a generalized texture as they go farther back in the picture.

The most traditional system of spatial representation that Seurat employed is *linear perspective*, which dictates the relative sizes of things according to their distance from the viewer. This technique was not completely developed until the fifteenth century, when it became widely used in nearly all painting, but it continued to be used extensively until the twentieth century. Its basic principles can easily be demonstrated in a set of drawings of a football field. The simplest form of linear perspective is single-point perspective (fig. 2-24), in which all the lines going away from

2-24
Single-point
perspective.

the viewer meet, or would meet if continued, at one point—the *vanishing point*—on the horizon. Note that the yard lines and the crossbars of the goalposts, if extended, meet at the vanishing point. The same is true for the dotted lines connecting the tops of the goalpost uprights and the light poles. (Indeed, the heights of these things are established by means of lines extended to the vanishing point.) The remaining lines are either vertical, such as the light poles and uprights, or horizontal, such as the sidelines. Accustomed to this system of representation since childhood, we are able to interpret the yard lines as being at right angles to the sidelines, and, as long as the vanishing point is on the horizon, we think of them as being level with the plane of the ground.

Pictures that use two or more vanishing points (fig. 2-25) are able to accommodate more complicated views of things. Whereas

2–25
Multiple-point perspective.

the single-point system works only for a line of sight that is perpendicular to the horizontal lines of the things being viewed, the two-point system works for all other lines of sight, including one that might occur if the viewer were sitting at the corner of the field. Note that the sidelines are not horizontal and, if extended, would meet at their own vanishing point. And anything else, like the bandmaster's platform, that sits at an angle to the field would have to have its own set of points. The final illustration (fig. 2-26), showing a single-point perspective of one end of the field, demonstrates the effect of lowering the horizon (or eye-level) line.

2–26
Single-point perspective from a low angle.

Although Seurat's painting presents a somewhat more complicated problem than that of a football field, we can still see that the sizes of the people in the picture are progressively reduced according to their relative distances. The eye level is on an implied line somewhere just under the distant bridge line that is intersected by the head of the central figure. Specific vanishing points are difficult to locate, because the few linear features of the picture are almost all on the horizon.

Composition

So far we have discussed each visual element separately. But in order to understand how they function in a work of art we must also examine how these elements work together. *Composition* is the term that is used to describe the organization—the working together—of the visual elements.

Seurat composed *Bathing at Asnières* to create a convincing illusion of people and objects in spatial depth, but at the same time he was very concerned about composing the picture in such a way that the various parts harmonized with one another and made it pleasing and interesting to look at. Under the headings of *unity* and *balance*, the discussion that follows will present some of the principles and methods involved in creating a successful composition.

Unity

Unity has to do with integrating everything in a work of art to make it a single, indivisible whole. The greater the variety of things in a work, the more difficult it is to achieve unity. *Bathing at Asnières*, for example, contains several people, all dressed differently and doing different things, together with a river, sailboats, buildings, trees, and a dog.

One way in which Seurat managed to unify this variety was by *grouping* many individual things closer together so that they form fewer units for the eye to contend with. (We do this when we "straighten" a messy desk by organizing a hodgepodge of separate papers, writing tools, books, and coffee cups into larger and tidier-looking units.) This practice can be seen, for example, in the grouping of the three boys on the right to make them seem to form a single, almost triangular shape.

Individual things—even those that are far apart from one another—can also be connected by *similarities* of shape, color, or other elements. For example, the dome shape of the large bather's head is repeated in the head and the hat, respectively, of the boys

2-27 Georges Seurat, *Bathing at Asnières.*

in the water, in the hats of two of the men on the bank, and in some of the treetops. Triangular shapes can also be found throughout the composition: in the way three of the figures are sitting, the bend of a pair of legs, the upper back of the man lying down, and the way the bather at right holds his hands to his mouth. A major color similarity connecting different parts of the picture consists of the red-orange found in the hair and trunks of the large bather, the hat and trunks of the bather in the water, the dog, the pillow underneath the boy with the straw hat, and even the band of the hat itself.

Emphasizing *continuity* is another way an artist can unify a composition. Continuity has to do with a single element or a series of elements that continues relatively uninterrupted throughout a large part of the composition. The edge of the riverbank is a prime example of continuity in this painting, even though it appears to be broken by the bather. (Actually, the lighter value of his skin blends in generally with the river, while the darker value of the shadow on his legs and trunks picks up and continues the contour of the riverbank edge.)

Another example of continuity is the horizon line that extends across the whole picture and, like the riverbank, is relatively unbroken. But unlike the riverbank, this line is made up of several barely visible vertical units—trees, bridge supports, buildings, smokestacks—that comprise a *rhythm*, or repetition of similar elements. (In other works by Seurat, rhythms such as this often play very prominent roles.)

The last major method Seurat used to achieve unity was that of making one part of the picture the *dominant feature*—in this case, the head of the central bather. This single feature serves as a major cohesive factor and the main focal point of the whole composition. The dominance of the head is established by a number of things: its centralized location, its isolation from other well-defined shapes, the strong contrasts between its dark value and the lighter values that surround it, and the fact that it intersects the horizon. When scanning the scene our eyes tend to return to this head, and it is probably the image we will remember most when we are not looking at the work. It is very influential, both visually and psychologically. Its shaded stillness affects all other aspects of the painting and underscores the general quality of summer torpor.

Balance   Seurat was particularly concerned about *balance.* Normally, we think of balance as having to do with equalizing the physical weights of things supported by something like a seesaw or balance scales. In art it is a matter of equalizing the visual and the psychological weights of things. Visual weight has to do with such things as the relative size, brightness, or amount of contrast of one or more of the visual elements. Psychological weight usually has to do with the relative importance of a person or object in the picture.

Among the ''heaviest'' things in visual weight in Seurat's composition are the following: the man lying down, because of his size and the value contrasts of his white towel and smock set against the dark colors of the hat, trousers, and dog; the central bather, because of his size and location; the central bather's white towel, because of its extreme lightness; and the bather on the right, whose orange hat in combination with the blue background provides the strongest hue contrast in the painting. Unlike real weights, visual weights cannot be accurately measured, so it is difficult to determine exactly how a large figure with a white smock balances a small one with an orange hat. However, considering everything with visual weight (including the boy with the straw hat, whose size and color are also relatively prominent), it would seem that there is more weight on the extreme left than on the right. But in a representational picture, one cannot overlook the importance of psychological weight. In this case, the right side is favored because, for one thing, a river has more psychological importance than a riverbank; for another, almost all of the people are facing to the right; and, finally, the most important figure—the large bather—is slightly to the right of center. Thus we could probably say that the slightly heavier visual weight on the left is counterbalanced by the heavier psychological weight on the right.

The general feeling when looking at *Bathing at Asnières* is that of stability (and this feeling may be a better test of balance than that of trying to add up all the visual and psychological weights and to compare the two halves of the picture). Seurat was a very methodical artist, and he consciously sought both unity and balance in all his work and wanted to generate an impression of harmony, repose, and stability in the viewer. But unity and balance are not the only attributes that make a work of art great, and harmony, repose, and stability are not the only expressive qualities that works of art are capable of producing. Indeed, many great works of art are not particularly outstanding in these attributes and qualities. Seurat's paintings were, and *Bathing at Asnières* is a good example for illustrating them.

Summary It was said at the beginning of the chapter that while Seurat's painting was obviously a picture of boys gathered along a riverbank, it was also a rectangular surface covered with patches of color, and that Seurat had to deal with the visual elements to make his painting. The rest of the chapter was devoted to explaining the visual elements and their role in everyday seeing as well as in works of art, both two-dimensional and three-dimensional. It also presented several artistic methods—different ways of manipulating the visual elements—used to make us see works in certain ways. An artist working with the visual elements can create illusions and even evoke certain emotions in the viewer.

Much is made of the fact that it takes a lot of learning to make art; it is equally true that it requires learning to see art. This chapter was intended to give some insight into the ordering processes of the artist as these relate to what the viewer perceives; insight that will enhance appreciation and enjoyment of works of art.

3
Fine
Arts
Media

The materials with which a work of visual art is created affect its appearance as much as any of the visual elements discussed in the preceding chapter. A sculpture will not look the same in marble as in wood or bronze, not only because of the appearance of each material, but because each material requires the artist to work in a different way.

The materials and techniques with which a particular artwork is created are known as the *medium*. Oil paint is considered a medium, as are marble, bronze, and photography. Traditionally, the visual arts were limited to relatively few media, but in the twentieth century, new materials and techniques—as well as new concepts of art—have expanded this number; and many of the new media cannot be easily classified.

Painting
There are a variety of media that come under the heading of painting, but all of them consist essentially of applying colors, made of *pigments* mixed with a *vehicle* (a liquid such as water or oil), to a *support* (a surface of some kind, such as canvas or wood).

Fresco   To make murals (wall paintings) for a chapel in the early 1300s, the Florentine artist Giotto di Bondone employed *fresco*, a technique of painting on fresh, wet plaster with pigments mixed with water. The advantage of working directly on the plaster is simply that the picture is more permanent; painting over dry plaster is likely to cause flaking. The thin layer of plaster intended for the paint must be applied day by day, and Giotto therefore had to plan carefully to ensure that the day's work would end at the edges of a figure or other prominent feature in the composition. He was unable to make corrections or repaint an area without removing the old plaster and entirely redoing the unsatisfactory portion on a new base. Because of its nature, fresco is best suited for murals, like Giotto's *Meeting at the Golden Gate* (colorplate 4), that stress large, well-defined images. But the nature of the medium did not prevent Giotto from representing such delicate emotions as that expressed in the tender embrace of Joachim and Anna (who have just been told that Anna will give birth to Mary, the mother of Jesus). Fresco was a popular medium during the late Middle Ages and the Renaissance, and especially in Italy, for the decoration of churches and monasteries.

Tempera   For smaller, movable works, such as altarpieces, artists in Giotto's day used wood as a support. They painted with *egg tempera*, a medium of pigment mixed with eggyolk and water. However, this also dried rapidly and did not blend easily, so that color mixing had to be accomplished by painting in short, fine brushstrokes that allowed the painting layer below to show through.

Oil   By the 1400s, artists had begun to combine pigments with oil. When specially treated canvas was introduced as a support to replace wood, oil painting on canvas soon became the principal painting medium, overtaking in popularity both fresco and tempera. One reason for its popularity was the lighter weight of canvas. But the main breakthrough was the flexibility of the oil medium itself. Unlike fresco, oil paint dries slowly enough that an artist may take up or leave off wherever convenient and may change an area without having to start over. Unlike tempera, the proportion of pigment to liquid is not fixed. This allows greater control over degrees of transparency and thickness of paint layers and makes possible the subtlest variations of light and color. To catalogue the different ways oil can be used and the effects that can be obtained from its use would be virtually to recite the history of European painting from the fifteenth century to the present. The nineteenth-century French artist Eugène Delacroix employed many effects to arouse the romantic imagination of his public. He portrayed his exotic subjects in an impetuous, colorful style that at times was almost electrifying, and took great pains to keep the surface of his pictures alive with rich, thick strokes of paint (colorplate 5).

Acrylic   Today's abstract artists share with Delacroix the appreciation of paint and its expressive capabilities, but they carry this a step further by eliminating the subject matter of their pictures. Some artists are now using *acrylic paint*, a synthetic medium developed since the Second World War. While acrylics can be used to imitate almost all the effects of oils, they are even more versatile and durable. Their qualitative differences in surface appearance may be negligible to the average observer, but the differences to the artist in "working" texture are often crucial. Oil offers far more resistance to the brush. Acrylic can be mixed with water and is much faster drying, traits that can be considered either advantages or disadvantages depending on what the artist is trying to do. Sam Gilliam turns the water-soluble characteristic of acrylic into an aesthetic advantage by soaking the paint directly into raw canvas— something he would be unable to do with oil, since oil decays cloth. (For oil paintings, canvas has to be treated by *sizing*—applying a material such as glue to seal its surface—prior to the application of the paint.) In a work like the one shown in colorplate 31, the paint permeates the canvas, staining it rather than lying on the surface in layers of varying thicknesses.

Airbrush   Another modern technique that has enabled artists to achieve effects that were previously impossible is the *airbrush*, a type of miniature spray-gun that can be adjusted from a narrow, pencil-thin jet to a broad mist of paint (fig. 3-1). The instrument never touches the canvas and can be used to produce an absolutely smooth, evenly shaded surface on the painting. The first group of artists to make serious use of it was the Photo-Realists of the late 1960s, most notably Chuck Close, who adapted it to a technique similar to the color printing process. Working from photographs that separated the primary hues, Close re-created each area of the face three different times to produce a full-color picture (colorplate 32).

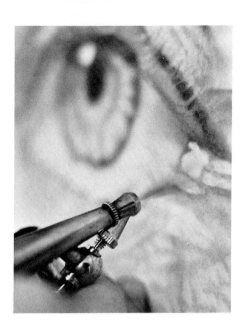

3–1
Painting with an airbrush.

Drawing

Drawing consists of making marks—usually of a single color—on a support—usually paper—and including the color of the support as part of the work. Since a drawing is usually simpler to make than a painting, it is typically used for recording quick descriptions or planning another work such as a painting. But it is also recognized by many as being more spontaneous and reflective of the artist's thinking. And for this reason, many drawings are admired as works of art in their own right.

Such media as pencils and sticks of charcoal, chalk, or crayons are probably the most common and convenient tools for making drawings. The artist makes marks or lines directly on the paper. Chiaroscuro and variations of value are created by different degrees of pressure or by the close or wide spacing of small lines; the color of the paper mixes optically with the color of the marks. The various ways in which charcoal lines have been applied to the page in Edgar Degas's *After the Bath* (fig. 3-2) serve not only to indicate the outline of the woman's body, but also the volumes of her back and even the soft texture of her skin. But in many places the drawing is ambiguous, requiring some help from the viewer's imagination. The spontaneity of the marks in those places makes them reminiscent of the brusque movements the woman would need to dry her hair.

Ink is another common material for drawing. Typically, black or brown colors are used with pen brush. The ink is fluid and generally opaque (not transparent). But it can be made relatively transparent by diluting it with water. A transparent layer of ink applied

3–2 Edgar Degas, *After the Bath*, 1890–92. Charcoal drawing on pink paper, 19¾″ x 25⅝″. Fogg Art Museum, Harvard University, Cambridge, Massachusetts (bequest of Meta and Paul J. Sachs).

with brush to a support is called *ink wash*. When handled skillfully, ink washes are capable of producing the subtle varieties of shades needed to suggest the misty spaciousness of a mountain landscape (colorplate 8). Diego Rivera, who was not interested in subtle variations when he made *Mother and Child* (fig. 3-3), used a brush loaded with opaque ink to create bold lines rather than delicate ink washes. Yet he skillfully varied the widths of the lines to emphasize the three-dimensional character of the stocky woman and child and to provide accents throughout the composition.

Printmaking
Prints of all kinds are usually produced on paper, like drawings, but differ from them in that prints involve the production of numerous identical copies of a single work by means of partially mechanical methods. (Another difference is that the ink used in printmaking is thick and oil based rather than fluid and water based.) Not surprisingly, this art began to be developed at about the same time as book printing. The dissemination of knowledge was facilitated by

3–3 Diego Rivera, *Mother and Child,* 1936.
Ink drawing on paper, 12⅛" x 9¼".
San Francisco Museum of Modern Art
(Albert M. Bender Collection).

the labors of artisans who translated drawings and paintings into the various printmaking media, which were then used to make hundreds of reproductions. The technology of printmaking was also adapted by some artists as a tool for personal expression.

Woodcut

3–4
Relief printing.

The *woodcut* is the oldest of the major techniques, a form of *relief printing* (fig. 3-4) made by drawing an image on a block of wood and cutting away the areas that are to remain white. After the image has been rubbed with ink, it can be printed under moderate pressure. Albrecht Dürer was well known in the sixteenth century for his extraordinary woodcuts. Today we are still awed by his mastery of the medium, by the precision and control that made possible such complex and fine-lined pictures (fig. 2-3).

Intaglio

3–5
Intaglio printing.

Intaglio printing (fig. 3-5) is the opposite of relief printing. The image is cut into a metal plate (usually a sheet of cold-rolled copper) and, after ink has been rubbed into the lines, transferred to a sheet of paper under extreme pressure. The metal plate may be

3-6
Rembrandt van Rijn,
Christ Healing the Sick,
c. 1649. Etching and drypoint
(second state), 11" x 15½".
The Art Institute of Chicago
(The John H. Wrenn
Memorial Collection,
bequest of Ethel Wrenn).

cut with special gouges (*engraving*), scratched with a needle (*drypoint*), or dissolved with acid (*etching*). In etching, the most popular of these three methods, the plate is covered with a wax-based material and lines are drawn in this coating with a needle. When the plate is placed in acid, the exposed parts are eaten away. Shadings can be achieved by allowing some lines to be "bitten" deeper by repeated immersions in the acid.

In Rembrandt's etchings, the velvety blacks were usually the result of denser, more deeply bitten masses of lines (fig. 3-6). Gerardo Aparicio's etchings take advantage of the medium's capacity to produce incisive lines (fig. 3-7).

3-7
Gerardo Aparicio,
Design for a Tranquil State, 1975.
Etching, 9¾" x 12¼".
Collection William Dyckes.

Lithography

3–8
Planographic printing.

Lithography is a *planographic* system of printing (fig. 3-8). It involves drawing or painting directly onto the flat surface of a special form of limestone or a zinc or aluminum plate with a greasy crayon or liquid. The working surface is then treated with chemicals that make the area with the image resist water. During the printing process the stone is dampened, and the uncovered areas, being wet, will not accept the ink. Lithography allows more freedom and directness in the drawing phase, and a great variety of line, texture, and shading is possible. Henri de Toulouse-Lautrec, who emphasized the spontaneous and witty, found lithography perfectly suited to his uninhibited approach. He also furthered the medium's possibilities through his own technical experiments and unorthodox style (fig. 3-9).

3–9 Henri de Toulouse-Lautrec, *Jane Avril, Jardin de Paris,*
1893. Color lithographic poster, 49⅝″ x 36⅛″. The Museum
of Modern Art, New York (gift of A. Conger Goodyear).

3–10   Victor Vasarely, *Triond,* 1973. Silkscreen, 31⅛" x 31⅛".
Collection Victor Vasarely, Annet-sur-Marne, France.

Silkscreen   *Silkscreen*, or *serigraphy*, the most recently developed of the popular forms of printmaking, consists of silk, organdy, or similar open-
meshed material stretched tightly over a frame. Parts of the screen
can be blocked out by glue, plastic strips, or even photographic
emulsions, leaving the rest open for ink to pass through. Printing is
accomplished by placing the screen on the surface to be printed
and pushing viscous ink across the mesh with a squeegee. The
materials used in silkscreening are less expensive than wood blocks
and copper plates, and the techniques used are faster and less
complicated than other techniques. These are the principal reasons
why silkscreen has become a popular medium, but the fact that it
also lends itself very nicely to precision-edged shapes has proved
an important attraction to artists like Victor Vasarely (fig. 3-10).

Photography *Still photography*, even more than printmaking, involves mechanical processes and chemistry, and, like printmaking, is capable of producing identical editions. A virtually unlimited number of "prints" can be made from a single film negative, an item that is to the photographer what an etched plate is to the printmaker.

Photographers, however, instead of making images mostly by hand, select subjects from the environment and capture the light reflected from those subjects on chemically treated, light-sensitive film. This is done with a camera—essentially a dark box with a lens in the front that projects the light onto a film. Making the image visible (and permanent) calls for immersing the film in certain chemicals, a process known as developing. The result is a translucent negative image in which the blacks are clear and the whites are almost opaque. A positive print, the photograph itself, is made by passing light through the film negative onto sensitized paper, again producing a latent image that has to be developed. Exposing the print and then developing it—a job done in a darkroom—often involves such hand methods as manipulating the amounts of light exposure over different areas of the print and controlling the effects of the chemical bath.

The creative problems of producing photographs have to do with gaining control of a mechanical process by making a series of selections every time one takes a picture. Among other things, the photographer must choose the type of film, subject, lighting, camera distance, and point of view; and, depending on the type of camera, the focal length of the lens, width of the lens opening, and shutter speed. The photographer also has the option of controlling aspects of the exposure and development of the print in the darkroom. These are some—perhaps the most important—of the variables in making a photograph, but certainly not all of them.

The many variables—the numerous possibilities for different results even when using the same subject—might call into question the popular notion that a photograph is a true record of something seen. Nevertheless, a photograph does have a special relationship to its subject that a painting, no matter how realistic it may be, can never attain. As critic Susan Sontag explained, a photograph "is not only an image . . . it is a trace, something directly stenciled off the real, like a footprint or a death mask." It is doubtful that Dorothea Lange's *Migrant Mother* (fig. 3-11) would convey the same sense of a real person existing at a certain place and time if it had been a painting instead of a photograph. And, since this

3-11 Dorothea Lange, *Migrant Mother, Nipomo, California,* 1936. Photograph. Dorothea Lange Collection, The Oakland Museum.

picture was part of a report on California workers that Lange was commissioned to do in the 1930s, authenticity was an issue. But the effectiveness of the picture in evoking a story about family life and conditions in general during the Great Depression reveals that Lange was able to use the medium's variables for expressive ends as well as reporting.

Jerry Uelsmann's purposes are purely expressive. But the power of his photographs rests in large part on the medium's aura of believability. In one of his works (fig. 3-12), we see the union of a tree and a gigantic leaf—a compelling and disturbing image that violates our common-sense perception of the world. The veins of

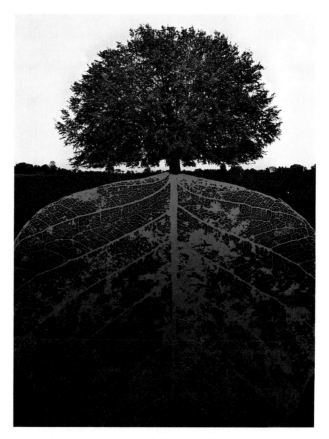

3–12   Jerry N. Uelsmann, *Untitled,* 1964.
Photograph. Collection the artist.

the leaf can be seen as the tree's roots (as if we were looking at an X-ray photograph). Or the leaf can be seen as the tree and the real tree as the roots, if we turn the photograph upside down. The symmetry of nature is made surprisingly visible in this photograph. Uelsmann creates a print like this one by integrating the images of two or more negatives in the darkroom. (Light exposures can be controlled to make parts of the print lighter or darker, according to the desires of the artist.) Uelsmann calls his method "post-visualization," because the greater part of the creativity does not take place in the camera—which he uses more or less conventionally—but in the darkroom.

Sculpture Unlike the images made by the media described earlier, images in sculpture are three dimensional. They may be *in the round*— independent, free-standing objects—or *relief*—forms that protrude from a background. With the exception of some sculptural media introduced in the twentieth century, the materials of sculpture have generally been of harder, more permanent substances than those found in the media reviewed so far.

Carving Gianlorenzo Bernini's life-sized in-the-round sculpture of David (fig. 3-13), showing the hero as he is about to pivot and hurl the stone at Goliath, is carved out of a single block of marble. *Carving*— sometimes called the subtractive process—calls for removing material from a block of wood or stone with a knife, gouge, or chisel. Carving requires the artist to have a very well defined idea of how the piece is to look. Bernini probably began by making a small model in clay and then having the shape roughly cut in the marble block by an assistant. Further cutting and refinements, using progressively finer tools, were done by the artist. Unlike oil painting, carving in stone permits very little room for changes and in-process modifications. The mental anxiety and the physical exertion of chipping away at an obstinate block no doubt discourages many artists from working in this medium. Judging from his output, it appears that Bernini was rarely discouraged; indeed, looking at individual works, one gets the impression that marble carving was, for him, easy. Few other sculptors of stone have been able to imbue their works with such a degree of realism. Bernini so carefully articulated and refined the textures of the flesh, hair, and cloth that one can easily forget that this figure was carved from stone. But the most innovative aspect of the work is its suggestion of movement. *David* is not a static form that merely represents a Biblical figure, but a fascinating study in potential motion and energy. David's slender body is caught in the very act of hurling the sling; its position, balance, and violent twisting force the viewer to move almost all the way around the sculpture in order to understand it.

Modeling Not all sculptural methods are as difficult as carving, and not all materials are as hard as stone. *Modeling*—sometimes called the additive process—involves forming three-dimensional shapes out of a pliable material such as clay or wax. These materials can be manipulated with the hands or shaping tools such as knives. It is

3–13
Gianlorenzo Bernini, *David,* 1623.
Marble, life-size.
Galleria Borghese, Rome.

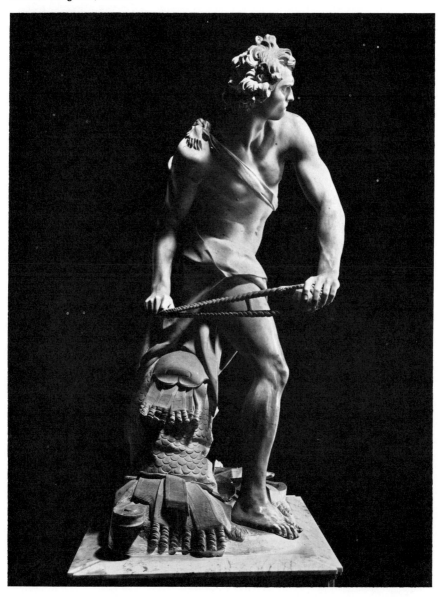

not surprising that sculptors like Bernini used modeling for the same purpose that painters use drawing—to make preparatory "sketches" for their finished works. The disadvantage of the medium, or course, is that figures made in clay or wax are not permanent and therefore not satisfactory for finished works. Clay, however, can be changed into a relatively hard material called *ceramic* by baking it at a high temperature in a special oven called a *kiln*. Both clay and wax can be copied in more durable materials by a technique called *casting*.

Casting   Casting includes several methods of making exact copies. The artist covers the original form with plaster, which hardens and becomes a mold when it is removed. The inside of the mold is a negative shape that corresponds to the positive shape of the original. Into this cavity a substance such as molten metal or polyester is poured or pressed. After the filler hardens, the mold is removed.

   The *cire perdue* or *lost wax* process, used for bronze casting, consists of applying a layer of wax of the same thickness desired for the metal (usually around three-eighths of an inch) to the inside of a mold. The wax-coated cavity is then filled with a plaster core and the whole mold is baked. The wax melts and runs out, leaving a thin space for the molten bronze, which hardens into a lightweight, hollow cast. Lorenzo Ghiberti used bronze casting to make a series of reliefs for the doors of the Baptistry of the Cathedral of Florence that are known as the Gates of Paradise. A close look at one of the reliefs, *The Meeting of Solomon and the Queen of Sheba* (fig. 3-14), reveals that the greatest relief is in the lower portion, where some figures are almost in the round, while the upper third—the most distant part of the scene—is very flat. In the flat part, Ghiberti

3–14
Lorenzo Ghiberti,
The Meeting of Solomon and the Queen of Sheba,
detail of the
Gates of Paradise door,
Baptistry, Florence,
c. 1435. Gilt bronze,
31¼″ x 31¼″.

3–15
John de Andrea,
Clothed Artist and Model, 1976.
Cast vinyl, polychromed in oil,
life-size cast.
Collection William Jaeger.

employed one-point perspective to help suggest the depth of the background.

Casting in polyester resin and fiberglass is popular with many sculptors today. A versatile medium (and also far less costly than bronze casting), polyester resin is a heavy, syrupy liquid before it is hardened by the addition of other materials. It is extremely durable when reinforced with flexible sheets of fiberglass. John de Andrea casts with this and other plastics in molds made directly from bodies. After they have been painted with oils, the images are incredibly accurate likenesses of the actual person—right down to goosebumps (fig. 3-15). De Andrea, an exception to the general run of modern sculptors who emphasize abstract forms, takes advantage of new technologies and materials to focus once again on the old problem of verisimilitude. Even Bernini, who was remarkably successful at making marble look like flesh, would be impressed by the possibilities that are now available to artists.

3–16
Julio González,
Head, 1936.
Wrought iron, welded, 17¾" high.
The Museum of Modern Art,
New York.

Other Methods   Long before de Andrea began to make his realistic sculptures in
polyester, other sculptors had experimented daringly with new
technologies. In the late 1920s, Julio González pioneered the use
of *welding*, the joining of pieces of metal by heat, as an art technique. At the time, this represented a radical break from what were
considered the appropriate media for sculpture. González made
crude constructions of scrap iron, rods, and nails. The textures,
shapes, and spaces of a work like his *Head* (fig. 3-16) are stated in
a completely modern sculptural language. The piece is not built up
from a lump of clay or cut down from a mass of stone, but pieced
together around empty space—an early example of what is known
as *open sculpture*.

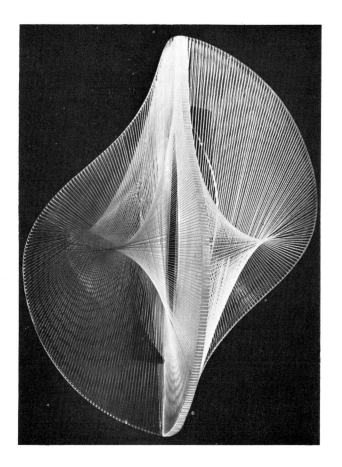

3-17
Naum Gabo,
Linear Construction, 1950.
Plastic and nylon, 15" high.
Private collection.

Open sculptures can be constructed out of virtually any material. Naum Gabo used a two-piece plastic frame and nylon thread to put together *Linear Construction* (fig. 3-17). Entirely removed from traditional sculpture's attachment to human or animal forms, constructions such as Gabo's reflect the preoccupation of many twentieth-century artists with abstract shapes, lines, and spaces. Gabo, who had been trained as an engineer and mathematician, was attracted to the beauty of the forms of analytic geometry, and in the early 1920s, he began to translate these forms into open sculptures made from lightweight materials. One of his later works, *Linear Construction* is a keen blend of art and mathematics as well as a gently curving, transparent image.

3–18 Lee Bontecou, *Untitled,* 1960. Welded metal, canvas, wire, 55″ x 58″. Private collection, New York.

Lee Bontecou's untitled work (fig. 3-18) also reflects twentieth-century approaches to sculpture. Like the works of González and Gabo, it is an abstract form pieced together rather than modeled or carved. But unlike theirs, it is a closed form, highly reminiscent of relief sculpture. Bontecou made this work by building a metal armature—much like the frame of a ship or airplane—and stretching canvas and other materials over it. The relief proceeds in steplike intervals to the rim of an abyss before plunging into the black void near the center of the form. The spatial sensation is reinforced with the use of lighter and darker shadings, a chiaroscuro method that makes some intervals appear steeper than they really are. Some viewers see works like this one as mysterious

3-19 Alexander Calder, *Sumac,* 1961. Sheet metal, metal rods, wire, 49¾" x 94". Courtesy Perls Galleries, New York.

caverns, but others find they suggest some kind of mechanical volcanoes or even the cowlings of jet engines.

Kinetic Sculpture Sculpture's possibilities have also been expanded to include movement. *Kinetic sculpture* is the name applied to those works that, through motors, wind, or other energy sources, escape the static state of ordinary sculpture. But even though kineticism was in large part inspired by machines, the first really successful works of this kind were not motorized at all. Alexander Calder's hanging *mobiles* (fig. 3-19) depend on a system of precise balances to make their metal vanes respond to movements of the air. The drifting and dipping of the abstract color shapes continually transforms the

3-20
Jean Tinguely,
Homage to New York,
1960.
Kinetic assemblage
of machinery,
fireworks, piano.
In the sculpture garden
of The Museum
of Modern Art, New York.

appearance of the sculpture. Motorized kinetic sculpture was re-
vived in the late fifties, but for all the technological means it makes
available to sculptors today, it has still not produced any series of
outstanding works. Oddly enough, the most interesting of the
artists in this area is one whose whimsical vision of the machine is
anything but scientific. Jean Tinguely's sculptures are constructed
of odds and ends and have nothing of the polished discipline and
sense of purpose of the machine. His most symbolic construction of
all was the huge *Homage to New York*, the ultimate purpose of
which was to destroy itself—which it did, with fire, noise, a fitting
degree of confusion, and the applause of New Yorkers, in the
garden of that city's Museum of Modern Art (fig. 3-20).

Mixed Media   Jean Tinguely's *Homage to New York* could as easily be included in
this category as in sculpture, for the term *mixed media* covers all
those works of art that break away from traditional uses of methods
and materials. Typically, they combine two- and three-dimensional
approaches, or, like Tinguely's inspired conglomeration, bring together disparate, almost incompatible materials.

3-21
Romare Bearden,
Pittsburgh Memory, **1964.**
Collage, 9¼" x 11¾".
Private collection.

Collage

Collage consists of pasting fragments of paper or other relatively flat materials against a flat surface. Although its history goes back to around the First World War, it has become quite popular in recent years. Romare Bearden who is noted for his collages, pieces together fragments of ''found images'' from photographs and other pictures. His ideas are drawn from the broad spectrum of black life in America—city and rural, North and South, old and young—and his found images include facial features, fragments of clothing, parts of buildings, and even bits of African masks. In his hands, these originally unrelated fragments magically combine to create a new whole (fig. 3-21). Although the visual patterns are interesting, it is the capacity to generate mental associations that gives Bearden's multiple images their unusual strength.

Assemblage

An outgrowth of collage, *assemblage* differs from that medium in that it is not restricted to flat materials. Typically, an assemblage employs fairly substantial, three-dimensional things—oftentimes ''found objects'' such as stuffed birds, plaster casts, and clocks. As the name implies, this art calls for assembling these things with glue, nails, rivets, or any other means. There is no limit to the kinds

3-22 Arman, *Brush Off*, 1978.
Accumulation of paint brushes, 27" x 25" x 9".
Courtesy Andrew Crispo Gallery, New York.

3-23 Colo, *Artifact for Keeping Secrets*, 1977. Mixed media, 17" high.
El Museo del Barrio, New York.

of things eligible to be incorporated in an assemblage or the ways they can be put together. Most assemblage makers tend to use eccentric materials or found objects as abstract forms, treating them as indifferently as individual brushstrokes. Few artists have risked using the objects for what they are, and of these only the French sculptor Arman has been consistently successful. Arman has found a perverse beauty in the refuse of the technological age. He has capitalized on this in striking compositions that often take the form of repetitions of similar items—as if imitating the assembly lines that created them (fig. 3-22).

Colo, a Puerto Rican artist, has taken a simpler and more direct approach to assemblage, combining everyday objects in a provocative image. His *Artifact for Keeping Secrets* (fig. 3-23) is a sculpture that both attracts and repels the viewer, for he has taken a small, chrome-plated cashbox and penetrated the coin slot with a long, sharp knifeblade that points threateningly upward. This unusual marriage of alien objects produces a variety of ambiguous connotations—sex, money, mystery, and danger.

Environments

Environment is a relatively new term in art, created to describe experiments that began in the late 1950s and that attempted to literally bring the spectator into the artwork. Environmental works are not hung on a wall or placed on a pedestal; they surround the viewer on all, or nearly all, sides. The concept, however, is an old one, with precedents in such other areas of the arts as theater, landscaping, and architecture.

Colored Light

One of the best examples of early environmental art is the interior of the huge Gothic cathedral at Chartres, France. The thirteenth-century builders erected a structure with a masonry ceiling that

3–24
Nave of
Chartres Cathedral,
1194–1220.

spans 53 feet of the main part of the church at a height of 118 feet from the floor (fig. 3-24). This cathedral is like an enormous open sculpture, its interior spaces interrupted by massive piers and archways on the main level and smaller arcades and columns on the upper levels. The outer walls, especially the area just below the ceiling, are penetrated by large windows of stained glass that transform the sunlight (colorplate 6). The rays of intense color, whether seen directly through the glass or indirectly as they pierce the dark interior, are a significant part of the experience of being inside the cathedral.

To make stained glass, color has to be added (by introducing certain minerals) when the glass is in a molten stage. Pressed into sheets and allowed to cool, the glass is then cut into smaller pieces according to a previously prepared design. Details such as facial features are usually painted on with oxides and made permanent by firing in a kiln. The fragments are then joined together with lead strips by a technique called leading.

The environmental art of Dan Flavin in our own day is related to that of the windows of Chartres Cathedral, although Flavin uses colored fluorescent light fixtures rather than stained glass (colorplate 7). The nature of the room in which the work is displayed obviously plays a crucial role in the appearance of the work. As the color reflects off the room's surfaces, it is affected by such factors as the size and shape of the room and the color and texture of the walls—as well as by the other lights. Flavin was not the first artist to have used real rather than reflected light, but none had ever tried to actually make it the very *substance* of a work.

Merzbau   A major precedent for much twentieth-century environmental art was the *Merzbau*, a name given by the German artist Kurt Schwitters to a series of interior spaces he altered by installing constructions made of all sorts of odds and ends. The first of these, begun in 1924 in the artist's home in Hanover, was an assemblage of rusty tin cans, newspaper and pieces of broken furniture. He called it *Cathedral of Erotic Misery* and filled it with secret panels that hid other objects or tiny scenes that reflected his own erotic misery and that of his time. Eventually, however, he replaced the chaotic collection of junk with abstract forms made of wood. Although the later creation may not have been as richly suggestive as the earlier one, it did focus more attention on the spaces and their importance in an environment (fig. 3-25).

3-25   Kurt Schwitters, *Merzbau,* 1924–37
(destroyed). Mixed media. Photo Kunstmuseum
Hannover mit Sammlung Sprengel, Hannover.

3-26   Allan Kaprow, *18 Happenings in 6 Parts,* 1959.
Photo by Fred W. McDarrah.

Happenings   The *Happening*, which began as something like a cross between a temporary Merzbau and improvisational theater, attracted a number of painters and sculptors in the early sixties. The first use of the term *Happening* appears to have been in a 1959 article by Allan Kaprow, in which he included a brief script for a related series of events called *18 Happenings in 6 Parts*. He later produced a version of this work (fig. 3-26) in a New York gallery, which he outfitted with plastic partitions, Christmas lights, slide projectors, tape recorders, and assemblages of junk. ''Performers'' spoke doubletalk, read poetry, played musical instruments, painted on the walls, squeezed orange juice, and executed other similar acts. The gallery patrons had to be given instructions on how to move through this potpourri, becoming in a sense performers themselves—a role that was developed in Kaprow's future works.

Happenings differ from theater in a number of important ways, although these are becoming more difficult to distinguish because of the influence that such works have had on experimental theater. The spectator-participant is involved in a work that may take place anywhere, indoors or out, viewing it on a picturelike stage. Sight and hearing are not the only senses addressed. There are no actors separated from the audience by fictitious roles. Usually there is no plot and no focused structuring of sequence. Instead, there is a series of separate, often overlapping, sometimes unrelated events. Despite the apparent randomness, however, many Happenings are carefully scripted and rehearsed—though unpredictable occurrences are accepted as integral parts of the total experience.

Earth Art For some artists, a canvas, a room, or even an entire building is not enough space—they set about rearranging the landscape itself. Michael Heizer, one of the principal figures of the Earth Art movement, did a number of pieces in the desert. His *Double Negative* (fig. 3-27) is an enormous rectilinear gash in the earth, at the edge of a canyon; a sculpture that consists of both real and imaginary (where the canyon eats away the earth it is cut from) space, a geometric shape constructed by a human being contrasted with an organic one created by nature. Although the work may appear no more complex than any other hole in the ground, it inspires many observations. Among these are the fact that the use of a negative form makes the space itself the work, and that the immense scale allows for radically different perceptions of the form of the work depending on the vantage point, including that of someone in an airplane. Another important point is that this work is far more vulnerable to the erosions of time and weather, so that it will disappear in a relatively short time. A hundred years from now all that will remain are the photographs that document it.

Summary The complexity of today's art seems to be unlimited. In the past few decades, the boundaries between the arts, which once seemed so secure, have been challenged and overrun by experimental artists bent on discovering new forms in the combination of two or more areas. Such hybrids as assemblage, environment, and Happening have gained respectability and must be considered part of art. The traditional limitations concerning the materials of art have also been challenged. One can no longer say that a sculptor is an artist who works with marble, wood, or bronze, for any substance is

3-27 Michael Heizer, *Double Negative,* 1969–70. Two-hundred-thousand-ton displacement in rhyolite and sandstone, 50′ x 1500′ x 30′. Collection Virginia Dwan.

likely to be suitable, even water and air. Finally, the concept of the art object itself has been challenged. Performances, environments, and the use of perishable materials have raised fundamental questions about art's relationship to its audience.

The lack of solid definitions does introduce an element of unpredictability, if not chaos, but this is the inevitable price of freedom. The advantage of this uncertainty is that it allows artists to expand the possibilities of their work and viewers to enlarge their own experience.

4

Architectural
Media

Architectural objects are utilitarian—places where people live, work, and congregate. This is not to say that they cannot also be aesthetic, but that is not their main purpose. Because of its utility and its intimate involvement in everyday human affairs, architecture, more than the fine arts, is closely affected by the values, needs, and technologies of the society it serves.

In this chapter, we will be studying architecture from two perspectives: principles of construction and levels of architecture. The first has to do with the methods and materials, both traditional and modern; the second has to do with the ways in which we experience architecture in our daily lives.

Principles of Construction

As we saw in the previous chapter, the form of an artwork is affected very much by its medium. Similarly, the form of a building is affected by the principles of construction used to create it. Although there is an almost infinite variety of architectural forms, there are relatively few principles of construction underlying those forms.

4–2 Temple of Horus, Edfu, Egypt, 237–212 B.C.

Post and Lintel

4–1
Post and lintel.

The simplest and most ancient method of spanning a space is the *post and lintel*, in which horizontal lintels—often called beams—are supported by vertical posts or walls (fig. 4-1). This method has been used with a variety of materials throughout the world.

The oldest buildings still in existence are *masonry*, that is, made of stone or bricks. The hall of an Egyptian temple dedicated to the god Horus employs a post-and-lintel system of carved stone (fig. 4-2). The masonry roof is carried by heavy beams which in turn are supported by massive posts (columns) and walls. The interior is dark and appropriate for its original function as a sanctuary. But this is also due to the limitation of stone as a building material. It is heavy and lacks the necessary tensile strength (the ability to withstand stress) for spanning large distances. Thus much of the floor space in a masonry building like the Temple of Horus is taken up by thick posts or walls needed to support the short, heavy lintels.

Arch

The disadvantage of masonry construction can be reduced by using the *arch* (fig. 4-3), which spans a space with a number of small stones or blocks in a curve rather than with a single lintel. In an arch, the blocks are wedge shaped and press against one another without falling, the force of gravity being diverted outward toward the walls. The same principle is involved in the *barrel vault*

4–3
Arch.

4–4
Vault.

4–5
Cross vault.

4–6
Pointed cross vault.

4–7
Flying buttresses.

(fig. 4-4), which is simply a kind of continuous arch used to cover a rectangular area. A vault has the disadvantage of requiring heavy walls for support along its entire length. The *cross vault* (fig. 4-5), formed by two intersecting barrel vaults, is an improvement because it permits the support to be focused at just four points. Arch systems of construction were used extensively from the time of the Romans through the nineteenth century. But it was the Gothic builders of the twelfth through sixteenth centuries who carried these systems to their fullest architectural and aesthetic expression.

One of the major contributions of Gothic builders was the *pointed arch,* which proved far more versatile than the round arch in building vaults (fig. 4-6). A round arch is a semicircle; thus its height is strictly governed by its width. A pointed arch, which is more like a triangle, allows the ratio of width to height to vary simply by changing the angle of the arch. This in turn allows intersecting vaults of different widths to have the same height—an advantage that was very important to the Gothic builders. The sharper angle of the pointed arch also serves to divert the force of gravity more direcly toward the ground, thereby requiring less bracing on the sides. The bracing problem was also dealt with by another important contribution of the Gothic builders, the *flying buttress* (fig. 4-7). This is a system of half-arches outside the walls that reinforces the vaults and walls at key points by absorbing some of the outward thrust of the ceiling. (Many vanelike flying buttresses can be seen grouped along the outside wall of Chartres Cathedral in fig. 4-8.)

4–8 **Chartres Cathedral, France, twelfth through sixteenth centuries.**

4–9
Balloon-frame construction.

Frame Although post-and-lintel and arch systems continued to be used into the nineteenth century, they were challenged by new technologies brought about by the needs of the Industrial Revolution. In the 1830s, the wooden *balloon frame* (fig. 4-9) was developed to answer the demand for a rapid means of building houses, to keep pace with the growth of Chicago and other settlements of a rapidly developing America. Two-by-four boards were nailed together to form a lightweight framework to support the exterior siding and interior walls. This method of construction coincided with the improvement of sawmill machinery and the mass production of nails. Today it is called studs-and-joints construction and is so commonplace that we have difficulty appreciating its once-revolutionary importance. Prior to the balloon frame, wooden buildings in America were either log cabins or post-and-lintel constructions, the spaces between the posts filled with such materials as stone, bricks, plaster, or earth. The balloon frame, on the other hand, was not only lighter in weight, but also capitalized on the standardization of parts to speed construction. Two-by-four boards and machine-produced nails could be converted to a building in two weeks by two men who were handy with saw and hammer.

In 1851, a vast building called the Crystal Palace was erected in London. A single structure of iron and glass that allowed the light of day to flood the interior, it was the site of the Great Exhibition, a world's fair that featured industrial and agricultural products from many countries. Despite its size—a ground plan of over 800,000 square feet—the Crystal Palace was built in less than six months. To accomplish such an engineering feat, its designer,

4–10
Joseph Paxton,
Crystal Palace,
London, 1851.
Nearly 2000′ long.

Joseph Paxton, designed structural units that could be partly pre-fabricated. Planned around the largest standard sheet of glass (which at that time was only four feet square), the wood and iron members were manufactured in Birmingham and fitted together into a framework on the site in London (fig. 4-10).

Although it was a remarkable tour de force—both as a technical accomplishment and as a spectacular sight—the Crystal Palace was not considered architecture by the people of the time. They thought of it as a functional structure built for a particular job and suited for rapid construction (and perhaps equally rapid dismantling)—a kind of super circus tent. But the main reason it was not considered architecture was that it was made of iron and glass. Other iron buildings of the nineteenth century had more permanent uses—railroad stations, warehouses, factories—but they too were looked on merely as functional "sheds." To be called architecture, a building had to use solid stone, not a lightweight framework of iron posts and girders bolted together. Few observers had the foresight to realize that the Crystal Palace would inspire radical changes in architecture. Its principle of construction—a metal framework that freed the walls of their load-carrying function—eventually came to be the basis of twentieth-century public and commercial building.

The revolution launched by the Crystal Palace spread to America in the last two decades of the nineteenth century, when a colony of high buildings began to rise over Chicago's downtown district. These first *skyscrapers* were born of new industrial technologies including that of steel-frame construction, an outgrowth of the Crystal Palace's iron framework, and the elevator. They were also the result of a growing need for office space in a commerical hub where real-estate costs were extremely high. It was a case of simple economics: using the free space of the sky instead of the costly space on the ground. The principle of construction was the same as that of the balloon frame: a skeletal framework—this time iron and steel rather than wood—constructed prior to the walls.

Early skyscrapers were sheathed with outer walls of stone. Even though the practical need for this kind of construction no longer existed, there appears to have been a psychological need to make a building seem heavy and solid. It was an addiction that continued to some degree until the early 1950s, when architects began to design buildings with steel skeletons covered with a nonstructural skin of glass and metal. The freedom to create a simple geometric shape and sheathe it with any material for the ''curtain'' was inspired in large part by the work of Mies van der Rohe. His bronze and glass Seagram Building in New York (fig. 4-11), designed with Philip Johnson, is one of the classic examples of a style that has since become commonplace in American cities.

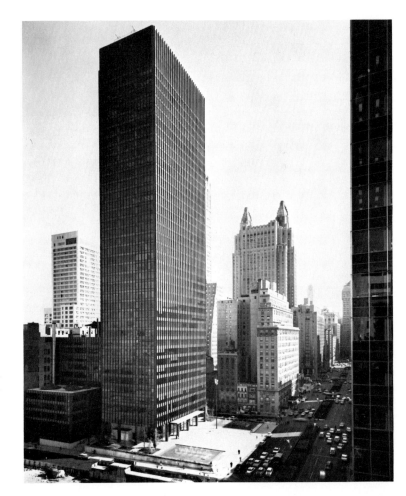

4-11
Ludwig Mies van der Rohe
and Philip Johnson,
Seagram Building,
New York, 1956–58.

4-12   Jörn Utzon, Sydney Opera House, Australia, 1959–72.

Ferroconcrete   Construction in concrete is one of the more recent techniques to find a place in the modern world of architecture. This material, like the methods of construction employed with it, constrasts vividly with steel. A blend of cement, water, sand, and small stones is poured into molds that correspond to the shape required by the construction. When this mixture has hardened, the molds are removed. Unlike steel, which lends itself to the geometry of sharp angles and flat surfaces, concrete can assume almost any shape. By itself, however, concrete is weak in tensile strength. (A slab of concrete spanning a given area will not support as much weight as will the same thickness of steel.) But this handicap can be overcome by imbedding stretched steel rods or cables in the concrete, a combination called *ferroconcrete* or *reinforced concrete*. The dual advantage of plasticity and strength makes ferroconcrete an extremely versatile medium. Jörn Utzon made excellent use of these qualities when he designed the curving vaults of the Sydney Opera House in Australia (fig. 4-12). Looking at the building, one is reminded of gull wings, swelling sails, or breaking waves—all of which are appropriate to the site, on a peninsula in Sydney's

4-13   Buckminster Fuller, United States Pavilion, EXPO 67, Montreal, 1967.

harbor. The repetition of the vaults, together with their slightly varied axes, gives the whole ensemble a sense of movement. With the highest shell rising nearly two hundred feet, the Sydney Opera House forms a striking landmark both for approaching ships and for the residents of the city.

Geodesic Dome   Buckminster Fuller's invention, the *geodesic dome*, uses a method of assembly related to that of Paxton's Crystal Palace and the balloon frame of the previous century, but it involves a different principle of construction. Rather than a grid system, as with a wood or metal frame, the geodesic dome employs a system of hexagonal pyramids constructed of triangles; the repetition of the pyramid module eventually forms a spherical enclosure. The dome used for the American Pavilion at EXPO 67 in Montreal (fig. 4-13) employed an additional supporting system of triangles that bridged the apexes of all the pyramids. Each side of the triangle is part of a line that encircles the dome's surface. The pavilion was slightly higher than the Sydney Opera House, yet its weight was only a fraction of the weight of that building, for it was constructed of nothing more complicated than steel pipes and panels of transparent acrylic. Fuller's dome seems to be unlimited in its capacity for interior space, possibly capable of spans even several miles wide. It may well be the most rapid and efficient construction method presently available. What remains to be seen is whether or not the geodesic shell will play as significant a role in answering future social needs as the balloon and steel frames did for the past and present.

Levels of Architecture

We will now observe some of the ways in which architecture affects the spaces we live in. The twin considerations of *lived space* and *architectural space* will help define this topic. Lived space refers to that which we physically occupy, move through, and use for various purposes, and in which we encounter and interact with objects and other people. But we also interpret this space with our minds and feelings. Architectural space consists of the solids and openings and places and paths that shape lived space.

An architectural writer, Christian Norberg-Schulz, identified different levels of what he called "existential space." Three of these levels—landscape, urban, and house—are convenient divisions with which to classify and review some varieties of lived space and their counterparts in architectural space.

Landscape Level

The scale of space at the landscape level might be likened to that which we can see in a landscape painting or in the view from a tall building or a low-flying plane. At this level the relationship between community and site can be examined.

Historically, major settlements such as San Francisco were formed on sites where a number of favorable natural features were found, especially waterways. Because of the large bay and fine harbor and the location on the western coast of a new continent, early San Francisco had the potential of becoming an international city. With a little help from historical events—such as the 1849 gold rush—the great city has lived up to the promise of its location. In addition, the Bay Area has the natural endowments of a rich and fertile peninsula in a setting of sea water and foothills. It has the double blessing of a harbor for trade and a varied topography that gives it an aesthetic identity of its own (fig. 4-14).

San Francisco's builders have both complemented and detracted from the natural beauty. The exceptional Golden Gate

4–14
View of
Lombard Street,
San Francisco.

Bridge, which is the visual keynote of the area, and the historic personality of the waterfront and cable cars have contributed to San Francisco's reputation. However, the regularity of the street layout, unrelated to the natural contours of the hills, and the insistence on putting up tall buildings threaten to obscure some of the qualities that gave San Francisco its landscape identity in the first place.

Landscape in a modern city receives its most visible transformation in the city's spiritual center, the commercial district. There, the man-made monuments of office buildings, hotels, and department stores, along with a network of elevated freeways and bridges, give the original site a metropolitan identity. In other times, the central or most prominent part of a city was transformed instead by architecture intended for religious purposes.

4–15 View of the Acropolis, Athens.

Probably the most venerated city landscape in the world is the Acropolis of Athens (fig. 4-15). To Athenians living in the fifth century before Christ, this hilltop was the spiritual focus of their world—the showplace of their artistic glory and the rallying point of their civic and religious ceremonies. With the help of famous artisans from all over Greece, a great popular effort during the time of Pericles crowned the Acropolis with a sacred city overlooking the *agora*, or marketplace, of the city below. The hierarchy of sacred and profane was therefore confirmed by landscape elevation. The landscape's potential was further utilized in the city's ceremonies, in which processions starting in the agora wound their way up the rocky slopes, through the majestic gate of the Propylaea, and onto the exalted plateau of the Acropolis. One of the main legacies of Greek art and architecture is the concept of the heroic, and the heroic qualities of the gateways and temples on the Acropolis can best be understood in the context of their heroic landscape setting.

4–16　Safdie, David, Barott, and Boulva, Habitat, Montreal, 1967.

Less dramatic but equally important is the role of landscape in residential living, where attention is given to the selection of sites for family homes and to how the buildings can be accommodated to the land. Unfortunately, the sites of many American homes— especially those in non-hilly areas—lack variety. The general practice of developing new subdivisions consists of laying out a grid of asphalt roads, clearing the trees, and leveling each lot.

Habitat, a dramatic grouping of apartments designed by architect Moshe Safdie for EXPO 67, may be an answer to the monotony found in so many suburban developments (fig. 4-16). It provides a great deal of variety of level and direction even though it is built on a flat site. An even greater variety of levels, directions, spaces, and textures is afforded by a Dogon village in Africa (fig. 4-17). This richness is due to the fact that the architecture— mostly houses and granaries— is organically related to the natural shapes and contours of the hillside.

4-17 Dogon village, Mali, West Africa.

Urban Level   The ways in which architecture accommodates social interaction are the focus at this level. The physical elements of space that define our urban world are determined by a complex network of history, beliefs, customs, and available technology.

VILLAGE AND TOWN   Bandiagara, capital of the Dogon people, is not far from the legendary city of Timbuktu in Mali. It has recently become, along with other settlements of the Dogon people, an object of absorbing interest to sociologists and architects.

The hand-built architecture of the Dogon has the same sensuous qualities as sculpture. And, as we noted earlier, the organic arrangements of their buildings create a pleasing variety of levels. The design of the homes and the community is determined by symbol and tradition rather than geometry. A house is built in the

A – STORAGE

B – CHILDREN, ANIMALS OR STORAGE

A – RAISED BED

B – STORAGE & SMALL ANIMALS

C – KITCHEN

4–18   Plans of a Dogon house.

image of a human being, with the entrance representing the vulva, the cooking area the lungs, and the kitchen itself the head. The proportions are based on the sexual symbols of 3 (male genitals) and 4 (female labia) multiplied by 2; thus a house is always 6 by 8 paces (fig. 4-18). This anthropomorphic symbolism is extended to the village. Individual family complexes are grouped to form various parts of the total village, which represents a man's body lying down in a north-south direction.

The symbolic interlocking of house parts, groups of houses, and village parts reflects a reciprocal interlocking in the social structure. Families of a village are linked by a complex patrilineal system that is recognized by marriage customs and a system of individual and collective ownership. Each person is linked emotionally to a network of houses, which in turn is linked both socially and symbolically to the village.

CITY PLANNING   Perhaps the unity and togetherness of a Dogon community can only be provided in a small village in a preliterate society. The larger towns and cities of advanced societies cannot always depend on inherited symbols and traditions to furnish the order needed to conduct their daily business.

The name most associated with city planning of ancient times is Hippodamus of Miletus, who allegedly introduced the gridiron scheme to the cities of Greece and Asia Minor in the fifth century B.C. (fig. 4-19). Regardless of his actual role in planning cities, the

4–19
Simplified ground
plan of the city
of Priene, Greece.

use of parallel streets intersecting at right angles in later Hellenistic and Roman communities came to be known as the Hippodamic system. Such a system, of course, facilitated the flow of commerce that was so important to Greek cities, but it also provided order and regularity in contrast to the chaos of older cities, whose streets were determined by the dictates of custom—old footpaths and ceremonial parade routes—rather than by people's needs.

Modern city planning is intended to satisfy the same needs; however, the enemy of order and regularity in this case is not just a loose pattern of streets but also crowded living conditions and their attendant social problems.

Ebenezer Howard, who is considered to be the earliest city planner of the modern era, was not enthusiastic about modern cities. Disliking what he saw, heard, and smelled in late-nineteenth-century London, Howard proposed to stop the city's growth and surround it with smaller cities combining the "best of town and country." His "garden cities" were to be encircled by agriculture, with industry, schools, and housing in planned preserves, and with culture and commerce at their centers (fig 4-20). In essence, his proposal was anti-city in both its rationale and intended effects. It helped to start people thinking about the problems of urban living and consider decentralization—thinning out the population of the city and spreading it across the land—as the best way to solve those problems. The concept was furthered by two men who were also probably the most influential architects of the twentieth century. Both became engrossed with their own conceptions of urban living—each of which in some way reflected Howard's garden cities.

Frank Lloyd Wright, like Howard, was no lover of cities. "To look at the plan of a great city," he said, "is to look at something like the cross-section of a fibrous tumor.'' A dramatic and forceful person, Wright was a passionate promoter of decentralization; he equated centralization (symbolized by the evil skyscraper) with antidemocracy, the antichrist, and the gravestone of capitalism. On the other hand, Wright included the automobile as an essential element of his utopian vision. The private citizen with a car was likened to a bird freed from a cage; he could ''go where he may enjoy all that the centralized City ever gave him, plus the security, freedom, and beauty of the Good ground....'' In 1934 he proposed a model for this ''good ground.'' The *Broadacre City* plan—a sort of updated version of Howard's garden city—gave recognition to and relied heavily on the automobile.

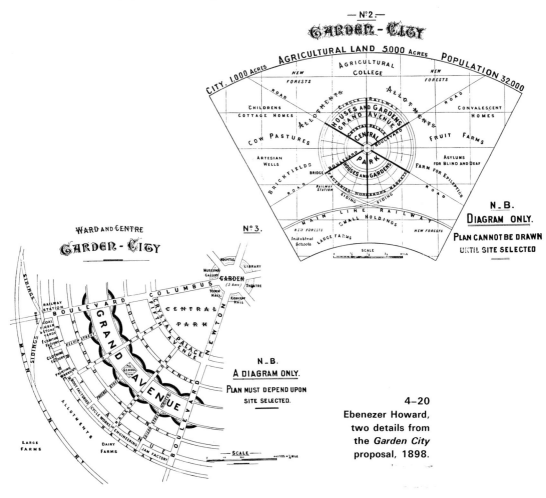

4-20
Ebenezer Howard,
two details from
the *Garden City*
proposal, 1898.

4-21 Le Corbusier, sketch from the *Ideal City* proposal, 1922.

Le Corbusier, a Swiss architect based in France, was as enthusiastic about the city as Wright was opposed to it. Yet Le Corbusier did not like cities in their present state, which he perceived as "bulging with human detritus, with the hordes of people who came to them to try their luck, did not succeed, and are now all huddled together in crowded slums." The *Ideal City* proposal (actually twelve years earlier than Wright's plan) consisted of wide avenues that crisscrossed to form large city blocks—the Hippodamic system on a grand scale (fig. 4-21). Many of these superblocks were to be topped with skyscraper towers—for residential or work purposes—surrounded by large parks as well as light and air. Although it appalled disciples of the garden city concept, it was in fact a garden city in a different form—a "vertical garden city," in Le Corbusier's own words. Although his scheme called for twelve thousand inhabitants to an acre, high-rise quarters would only take up 5 percent of the ground. His ambitious idea, unlike Wright's, made extensive use of the skyscraper, but like Wright's, made ample provision for automobile thoroughfares and parking.

Le Corbusier's later versions of his *Ideal City* plan for the reconstructions of Paris and Moscow were never accepted, but his dream city has had immense influence on American city planners. In 1948 his towers and superblocks were embodied in New York's Alfred E. Smith Houses (fig. 4-22). His concept, in its basic essentials, underlay the thinking and planning of many urban renewal projects. The clarity, simplicity, and glamorous visibility of Le Corbusier's drawing-board city has, directly or indirectly, captured the imagination of architects, zoning officials, mayors, and even university regents. Wright's *Broadacre City*, meanwhile, has been translated (and sometimes vulgarized) into the spacious spread of suburbia—the post-World War II explosion of "greenbelts" surrounding even our smaller cities.

Today many urbanologists are questioning the value of these developments that reflect the thinking of famous city planners. The solutions of Howard, Le Corbusier, and Wright are no longer viewed as answers to our problems. The vertical solution of centralizing people in high-rise housing usually produces bleak skyscrapers surrounded by parking lots rather than greenery, or worse, destroys old neighborhoods, with catastrophic results. The horizontal solution of dispersing the population, which is aimed at helping families fulfill their dreams of green grass and clean air, usually turns into expensive and inconvenient strips of housing neatly laid out with roads that go nowhere and end nowhere. The enthusiasm of both Le Corbusier and Wright for the automobile

4-22   Alfred E. Smith Housing Project, New York, 1948.

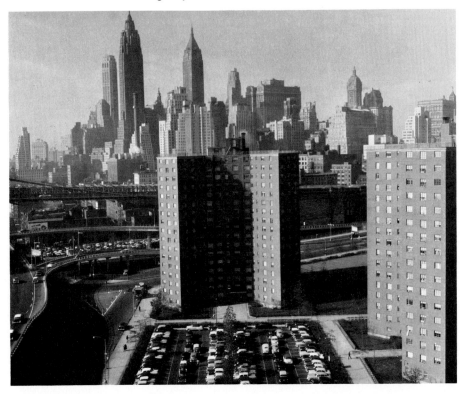

seems especially misplaced. "Our fast car," Le Corbusier exclaimed, "takes the special elevated motor track between the majestic skyscrapers." Today, however, our automobile-clogged urban and suburban streets are looked upon more and more as a disease of modern life rather than as a panacea.

PLANNING FOR PEDESTRIANS   If social interaction is to take place at the urban level, cities must also provide for pedestrians.

Italy is a country famous for its public walkways, from winding medieval streets to dramatic squares like the Capitoline Hill (fig. 2-21). Even there, the Galleria of Milan is unequalled in its own way (fig. 4-23). It is a covered street housing numerous shops and a permanent gallery of industrial products in one of the richest commercial cities of Europe (and, of all the Italian cities, the one most like an American city). But the Galleria is more than a shopping center; its arcades contain bars, cafes, and restaurants, and its marble streets are a place for dining and leisure as well as business.

4–23
The Galleria
of Vittorio Emanuele,
Milan, 1865–1867.

4-24
Vaults of
Trajan's Market,
second century A.D.

It is a square for informal seminars and a promenade for strolling, where artists and members of the entertainment world can mix with ordinary people. Add a few pickpockets, prostitutes, and tourists, and the mixture is complete. But most of all, the Galleria is a focal point for the citizens of Milan.

Precedents for the Galleria go back to Imperial Rome. Little remains today of Trajan's Forum—a large square formed by colonnades on three sides and an immense covered building called a *basilica* on the fourth—except parts of the large market on the east side of the square (fig. 4-24). But it was once an important center of the capital. In addition to being a place for shopping and leisure, like the Galleria, the forum was a combination civic center, financial exchange, sacred area, and sculpture gallery. Legal cases were tried in the basilica or in an open-air court where crowds of listeners could admire the legal eloquence.

Surprisingly, the automobile is responsible for a creation that could be considered a revival of the Forum of Trajan and a partial rival to the Galleria. Americans, who often feel compelled to drive a car just to mail a letter, are now encouraged to stroll for their shopping because of a commercial solution to the parking problem in downtown areas of the city. Obviously serving fewer functions than a forum, an American shopping center is, nevertheless, a unified complex of retail stores, eating places, and malls for strolling; larger centers even have movie theaters, skating rinks, and sculpture courts. The Woodfield Shopping Center in Schaumburg, Illinois, even has a Greek-style amphitheater (fig. 4-25). Some two hundred attractive shopfronts face the main courts and entryways to catch the attention of passersby. Several balconies, crossovers, ramps, and staircases, together with gleaming sculptures, give the shopping center the appearance of a futuristic Emerald City. But for all its attractions, few people go there for the purpose of social contact. Woodfield was not intended to provide for civic gatherings, nor is it conducive to informal seminars. Most shopping centers are connected to suburbia by the expressway and are therefore extensions of its culture. Shoppers buy and go home. They keep up on public affairs by watching the six o'clock news and receive their spiritual nourishment from the evening T.V. movie.

4-25   Woodfield Shopping Center, Schaumburg, Illinois, 1971.

4–26
Paley Park,
New York,
1967.

Meanwhile, the open square is experiencing a revival in the downtowns of many cities, both large and small. Blocking off the traffic for two or three blocks converts a street running through a major commerical area into a pedestrian mall. Such a practice provides more opportunities for human contact as well as a little architectural variety. Also, refurbishing old stores, restaurants, and theaters, and perhaps adding some new ones along with a parking ramp, may draw some customers away from the shopping centers.

Paley Park, a ''vest-pocket park'' in New York City, was created from empty space between buildings just off Fifth Avenue (fig. 4-26). It was not necessarily intended to attract trade, but it certainly provides some relief from an unbroken urban environment and is a popular place with office workers in the area, who go there at lunchtime to talk, eat, and relax.

House Level   The urban level is characterized by public places where people gather and paths where people move about. Private spaces within the urban environment are classified as the house level. The essence of the house level is interior space, intimately proportioned by and related to the human being. It is a center of personal activity, a place someone goes to or comes from, and most important, a place in which a man, woman, or child establishes a feeling of personal identity.

SINGLE-FAMILY DWELLING   The formal directness and material economy of Japanese art has long been an influence on some of the modern art in the West. And Western interest in Eastern art has been especially visible in the area of domestic architecture.

The smaller scale of Japanese houses is due to social conditions and lack of space rather than to the size of the average Japanese adult. On a chain of mountainous islands supporting a huge population, every habitable and arable bit of land has been put to human use. The vacant lots and other patches of idle ground so common in America are simply unknown. And the same radical economics applied to the countryside carry over into the design of Japanese houses. Architectural space in Japan is, perhaps more than anywhere else in the world, closely and economically related to the human body.

The basic ordering unit for a Japanese house is the *tatami*, a tightly woven rice-straw mat that is spread on the floor. Conveying the size and function of Japanese rooms, the meaning of these six-by-three-foot mats has so penetrated the Japanese language that the phrase ''four-and-a-half-mat novel'' (suggesting an intimate nine-by-nine-foot-square room for a man and woman) is a familiar slang expression for a romantic book.

Japanese rooms, which serve different functions depending on the occasion, do not correspond to rooms in American homes (fig. 4-27). For one thing, the nature and arrangement of rooms is profoundly affected by the Japanese custom of removing one's shoes before entering the house proper. The combined entrance hall (1) and anteroom (2) used for this purpose has thus become a very important space, which in the smallest of houses may consist garden design for residence of 20 tsubo = 66.1 sq.m = 720 sq.ft. with tea-hut   mizusawa komuten · ca

**4–27
Plan of
a Japanese house.**

of 10 percent of the entire floor area. The act of taking leave of the outside world by removing one's shoes symbolizes the first stage of shedding the indifference and estrangement of the outside and assuming the peace and harmony of the inside. The second stage of integration with the inner environment comes in the adjoining anteroom. It is here that the wife welcomes her husband, and here that the host and guest meet and bow. Now a person is ready for full integration into the house. The anteroom is usually adjacent to all of the other rooms; however, a guest would be directed into the reception room (3). Roughly equivalent to an American living

4–28   Old Samurai's House, Miyagiken, Japan.

room, it is the most important space in a Japanese house (averaging at least eight mats in size). Containing a revered and ornamental alcove, called a *tokonoma*—a sort of private-home sanctuary—and bordered by a broad veranda that leads to a lovingly cultivated garden, this room is the spiritual core of the house.

Chief among the admired aspects of Japanese architecture is the outdoor-indoor relationship (fig. 4-28) and the concept of continuous or "flowing" space. A small garden, even under the limited conditions of city living, is considered a minimum requirement, and it is linked with the interior by a veranda that serves to visually and psychologically bridge the gap. In addition to the continuity between exterior and interior, movable partitions and the modular coordination of rooms lend to the Japanese house a sense of uninterrupted flow between interior spaces.

Yet any wholesale application of Japanese principles of architecture to Western architecture would be superficial. The differences in life style related to the custom of entering the home have already been mentioned; basic occidental attitudes toward physical comfort and hygiene require an assortment of furnishings that would suffocate a Japanese interior. Even more fundamental are the traditional differences in personal philosophy that always operate as underlying premises in domestic architecture. A Japanese interior, with its small scale and thin walls, is not conducive to the unfolding of individual personality.

Frank Lloyd Wright successfully assimilated into his early homes some elements of architecture that could be attributed to Japanese inspiration (fig. 4-29). Ground-hugging horizontal lines accentuated by exaggerated overhangs, indoor-outdoor relationships occasioned by floor-to-ceiling glass, and the opening up of interior spaces are hallmarks of the Prairie Style that he began to develop in the first decade of this century. But the elegant, romantic sensation of luxury is strictly American in spirit. Way beyond the pocketbook of the average American, the prairie house has nevertheless left its indelible mark (and thus a Japanese touch) on every suburban ranch house with its familiar overhanging eaves, picture window, and "scientific" floor plan.

4-29 Frank Lloyd Wright, Robie House, Chicago, 1909.

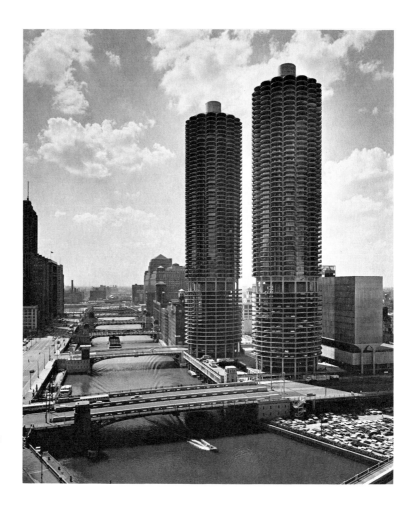

4–30
Bertrand Goldberg,
Marina City, Chicago,
1964.

CONCENTRATED-FAMILY DWELLING   The single-family dwelling is too expensive for most Americans, let alone people of other parts of the world. And if the $100,000 ranch house on an 80-by-150-foot lot were multiplied to keep up with a population that increases by 2 percent every year, the whole country would soon be suburbanized. Clearly, there is a need for forms of concentrated living that will permit large numbers of people to occupy relatively small surface areas.

High-rise projects like Chicago's Marina City (fig. 4-30) have been the most popular approach to the problem. These tall, airy buildings, located beside the marina and within walking distance of shopping and work, are comfortable and convenient for the upper-middle-class people living there. Even the parking problem has been solved by turning over eighteen floors to the residents' automobiles. But for average families, high-rise projects are not always as comfortable and convenient. The dream of a vertical garden city can become the nightmare of a vertical slum. One of the most notorious examples is the Pruitt-Igo project in St. Louis, which eventually became a ghost city. Among the reasons for its troubles was the fact that outdoor play areas were inadequately small, unsupervised, and relatively inaccessible for the children. Hallways and elevators soon became the play areas and eventually the targets of vandalism, leading to the complete disruption of family living.

The high-rise apartment is not the only type of high-density housing available. One alternative consists of individual units linked together, with each unit having a patio, if not its own ground space. Called "urban low-rise group housing," this scheme is a solution that is attracting architects and urban planners today. Yet this type of housing is not new. It existed in the Western Hemisphere before the time of European settlers and long before land started to become scarce. The Anasazi Indians of the Southwest, for example, began living in concentrated settlements as early as the first century A.D. The Cliff Palace in Mesa Verde National Park (fig. 4-31) was a multistoried, masonry-walled community contain-

4-31 Cliff Palace, Mesa Verde National Park, Colorado, c. 1100 A.D.

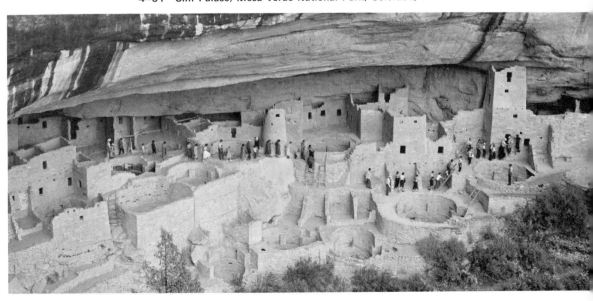

ing over two hundred dwelling rooms. In Africa, the Dogon style of living resembles that of low-rise group housing (fig. 4-17). Although each house is separate, the complete unit of house, plot of ground, and granary bins is connected with those surrounding it.

The experimental apartment complex, Habitat, which succeeds in looking like a hillside town without the benefit of a real hill, is a contemporary example of high-density group housing (fig. 4-16). The nearly identical modular units were ingeniously designed so that they could be attached to each other in enough different ways to lend a degree of individuality to each unit and prevent the whole complex from looking monotonous. (The lack of central hallways and elevator shafts, however, makes garbage disposal and access to the apartments very difficult.) In Europe, where lack of space is more of a problem than it is in America, there are already many interesting but less radical examples of new apartment complexes. Terraced, staggered, linked, and patioed, they retain many of the advantages of detached single-family dwellings and the attractive qualities of garden-house life (fig. 4-32). Surprisingly, low-rise urban housing was found to be almost as economical as high-rise housing, both with regard to site requirements and to cost of construction. Further, it was found that concentrated living, if effectively designed, can contribute to the quality of life rather than detract from it.

Summary

The first part of this chapter surveyed some basic principles of architectural construction while providing one or two examples for each. Post and lintel was the method used for much of the world's architecture for centuries, but with that method, people were able to make buildings as different as an Egyptian temple and a frontier house. A few new methods have been developed within the last 150 years, giving architects considerably more freedom. Using ferroconcrete, they have been able to make structures as different as Habitat and the Sydney Opera House. But, although today's architecture can take a variety of forms, it is still not as free as today's fine art. To erect a roof over people's heads, architects—no matter how experimental they may be—cannot afford to ignore certain laws of nature and the practical matters of function, materials, and technological know-how.

The second part of the chapter reviewed some different levels on which architectural environments affect the ways people live and function. Some of the examples, such as the Athenian Acropolis, qualified as being distinguished architectural monuments, while others, like the pocket park, were unpretentious pieces of people's daily surroundings. All of them exist as examples of humankind's constant and unceasing alteration of the physical environment. It is an enterprise that satisfies practical needs, but also, sometimes, gives pleasure and inspiration.

4–32
Low-rise housing units,
Bern, Switzerland.

HUMAN CONTEXT

Artists who work with images use them as writers use
words—to interpret the human experience of the time and
place in which they live. In primitive societies, where groups
of people share a common history and set of beliefs, their
conceptions of the world are interpreted in their art, their
ceremonies, their ritual objects, and even in the ways they
build and decorate their houses. In a society such as
contemporary America, where religious, educational,
regional, class, and ethnic differences divide the population,
such a degree of unity is impossible; the pluralism of beliefs
and values is reflected in the pluralism of artistic
expressions.

Nevertheless, certain themes seem to be present in the
artistic expressions of all periods and cultures, whether
primitive or modern, simple or complex. These themes
usually have to do with such basic questions as: What is the
nature of the world? Who are we? What is our place in the
world? Part II presents some of the ways that artists in
different times and places have responded to some of these
themes and how they have dealt with them in their art.

5

Images
of
Nature

"Almost every Englishman," Kenneth Clark once said, "if asked what he meant by 'beauty,' would begin to describe a landscape . . . ." The same might be said of a Japanese, or an American, or, in fact, almost any citizen of a modern society. To the average person, the art of painting is often identified with the landscape—despite the fact that relatively few serious artists these days make landscape paintings.

This popular conception of art is reinforced by the endless number of cheap reproductions of landscape paintings sold in department stores for the decoration of American living rooms. Perhaps the proliferation of these images in our culture has led to their self-cheapening and has reduced them to little more than pleasant ornaments. If this is so, it obscures the fact that landscape painting is a sophisticated product of art and human consciousness. It is the result of a long artistic evolution linked to a history of changing human attitudes toward the natural environment. The varieties of attitudes toward nature and how these have been expressed in art (not only in terms of landscape) are the subject of this chapter.

Paleolithic Painting

Animals appear to have been the very first subject matter of art. So far as we know, the earliest image makers were members of a hunter-gatherer society that existed more than fifteen thousand years ago. The Paleolithic (Old Stone Age) culture left in its painting and sculpture an artistic record of all the larger fauna—mammoths, bison, horses, rhinoceroses, boars, wolves, and reindeer—that inhabited Europe at the time. Ever since the discovery of this art about a century ago, observers have been impressed by the evidence it provides of an extraordinary level of artistic observation and image-forming ability.

Although some of the species painted on the walls of the caves near Lascaux in southern France may no longer exist, the artists made their images so vivid that we have no trouble recognizing them as various types of grazing animals (fig. 5-1). The outlines and proportions seem to have been based on fairly accurate observations of the profiles of real beasts.

We can only guess at what the artists used for paints and brushes. They may have mixed pigments of red ocher and manga-

5-1 *Hall of Bulls,* Lascaux, *c.* 15,000–10,000 B.C. Dordogne, France.

5-2 Bellowing bison and fragments of another galloping bison, Altamira, *c.* 15,000–10,000 B.C. Altamira, Spain.

nese with animal fat, and then used reeds or animal tails for transferring this mixture to the walls. There is also reason to believe that hunter-artists painting at some other sites used blowpipes to spread the mixture. The images in the caves of Font-de-Gaume and Altamira (fig. 5-2) are even more lifelike than those of Lascaux, mostly because of a chiaroscuro effect—not unlike that in a modern picture made with an airbrush—that brings out the bulky qualities of the animals.

Not all subjects were treated with as much sophistication as the animals. Representations of people are mostly stick figures; the rare references to landscape features such as rocks, plants, and streams are more like schematic symbols than images. Likewise, the arrangements of the animals (with or without other images) reveal none of the sophisticated methods—overlapping, vertical placement, variations in size, and linear perspective—that are now employed by artists to suggest spatial depth. Indeed, few of the arrangements seem determined by any identifiable logic. Randomly placed, sometimes overlapping but usually unrelated to one another in size or narrative, the images are, in this respect, reminiscent of modern graffiti. The impressive realism of Paleolithic art is restricted almost entirely to the portrayal of individual animals.

But if we speculate on the kind of lighting (or lack of it) that was available in these caves, we can guess that prehistoric people probably could not have viewed more than one painting at a time anyway. Imagine what it must have been like to see one of these beasts leap into view as a torch was waved in front of it. This intriguing mental image leads us to wonder about what an animal picture meant to these hunters. It requires both research and imagination to piece together the few bits of evidence and guess the purpose and meaning of prehistoric art. The awkward locations of many of the murals and the poor ventilation of the various chambers make it seem unlikely that these caves were used as art galleries or dwellings. This, plus the fact that many of the images of beasts show the marks—real or painted—of weapons, suggests that they did not serve purely aesthetic purposes.

The best guess may be that the awkward locations served as privileged sanctuaries for religious rites and that the images of beasts contained within served magical purposes. Animals, which the Paleolithic hunters depended on for survival, must have been at the center of their religion.

There are parallels with the art and crafts of Paleolithic cultures to be found in some modern African societies (fig. 5-3). And totem-

5-3 Bushmen defending their herds from a band of Zulus, rock painting.

ism, a belief that animals are ancestrally or spiritually related to human beings, has continued to thrive in many places in the world. The mythologies of preliterate peoples are filled with stories of humans turning into animals, and vice versa. Accordingly, it seems likely that Paleolithic societies probably also believed in some form of totemism.

In such societies, distinctions were not made between the natural world and the spiritual world. Since Paleolithic life was totally bound to animals, art depicting animals must have had awesome significance. Its magic not only was important for ensuring success in the hunt but was part of the very structure of belief and social continuity. In a sense, these paintings were not images but real spirits, occupying the same magical stage as the hunter-dancers.

Egyptian Tomb Art

Human beings—and the dead rather than the living—were represented in most Egyptian art, for one of the principal uses of paintings was the decoration of tombs. Here, too, art had a magic function. The image served to provide a home for the spirit of the deceased, especially if the mummified remains should deteriorate. The tomb of Ti, located at Saqqara, provides an excellent example of this custom. Ti, who lived around 2400 B.C., was an important bureaucrat, the overseer of the pyramids and the Sahura temple. Consequently, his remains were privileged to reside in a *mastaba* (a type of tomb) in a special burial ground for deceased officials.

One of Ti's earthly privileges was that of fishing and hunting in the marshes down by the Nile, and in order to ensure this pleasure in the hereafter he commissioned a major mural depicting it (fig. 5-4). Along with his own image, magical images for servants, boats, animals, and plants were also needed. Other painted reliefs in his mastaba illustrate the many needs of his rich estate in eternity: workers polish his statues, cooks and bakers prepare his food, craftsmen build boats for his favorite sport, and peasants harvest his grain and care for his cattle.

In order to guarantee that an image would be an adequate home for a soul, the Egyptian artist was compelled to follow certain rules. Ti's body, for example, which seems pinned in an upright position to the corrugated thicket of reeds, has its head, legs, and feet shown in profile while one eye and the trunk of the body are shown frontally. This formula, called *fractional representation*, was applied

5–4 *Hippopotamus Hunt,* tomb of Ti, Saqqara, *c.* 2500 B.C.
Painted limestone relief, approx. 48″ high.

to almost all human figures, whatever their activity. Had the artist shown the back rather than the front of the nobleman's head, or one of his arms hidden behind his body, or his feet hidden inside the boat, then according to the rules of magic, he would have tragically omitted some of Ti's anatomy, leaving him literally without a face, two arms, or two feet. The artistic solution was to provide the most adequate and characteristic full view, not only of Ti, but of the people and creatures that were to serve him forever.

The same type of thinking that considered anatomy a sum of the parts was applied to the organization of the picture. Although various elements of nature, people, and animals are logically connected (to an extent never achieved in Paleolithic art), they are not at all integrated in the realistic sense that we are accustomed to associate with landscape art. Divided into tidy zones, the relief clearly spells out the proper neighborhood of each figure. The aquatic animals are relegated to their own environment, which is symbolized by neat rows of vertical ripples. The scarcely broken line on top of the water is the base line for the boats. Overhead is another clear zone of fowl and smaller animals among the papyrus tops. Little if any overlapping is permitted, even where there are swarms of animals.

In the rigid structuring of this mural we can also perceive the symptoms of a highly organized agricultural society (where hunting was pictured as a sport) that was physically and emotionally dependent on the Nile. Although the river and its banks provided much of what they needed to live—fish and game, papyrus to write on, clay for pottery—the vital and abiding resource was the annual overflowing of the Nile, which irrigated and enriched the fertile valley with silt. All Egyptian agriculture, hence Egyptian survival, depended on this event. So regular was the flooding— between July 19 and 21 at Heliopolis (now Cairo)—that the river imposed its rhythms on the life and thinking of the people. Thus the dependable fluctuations of the Nile, sanctified in Egypt's mythology as well as its law, helped produce what was perhaps the most rigid and stable society ever seen on this planet. This conservatism was exemplified by Egypt's art—an art that changed very little over a period of three thousand years.

Roman Wall Painting

It is believed that Greek landscape painting developed out of Greek theater sets, the word "scenery" coming from the Greek word for "stage." Yet we can only guess about the origin and development of

Greek landscape art from pottery painting or from written sources because almost no Greek painting still exists. We can, however, obtain a secondhand reflection of the later forms of this art from Roman frescoes and mosaics, which frequently were imitations of Greek works. Indeed, Greek artists were sometimes imported to Italy to decorate the walls of wealthy Romans' homes.

In a painting on a wall of a Pompeii villa (fig. 5-5), we see a few trees and buildings on a gentle hillside, a quietly romantic setting

5-5 Wall painting transferred to panel, from the Villa of Agrippa Postumus, late first century B.C. Portion shown approx. 26" high. Museo Nazionale, Naples.

for strollers and a little herd of goats. This view of nature, as well as the feeling it inspires, represents an enormous leap from Egyptian art. The separate figures and objects are lighted by the sun; some even cast shadows. The temples and the bases of monuments, unlike the Egyptian boats in figure 5-4, expose two of their sides instead of one (although their oblique angles do not always create a consistent perspective). The people and animals are not restricted to their profile views but are free to stand or relax in any natural position. Everything—trees, architecture, creatures, and the ground on which they rest—is integrated into a single visual event. A pervasive light blends the elements by de-emphasizing edges and boundaries. But this integration is also achieved by some of the logic and controls of optical space. We interpret an Egyptian picture vertically or horizontally, like a floor plan, but we can view the Roman picture—because of overlapping, relative sizes, and other visual cues—in much the same way as we see real objects in space.

The Romans, delighted by the illusionistic potential of a more realistic form of painting, decorated their walls with numerous false architectural features such as collonnades, bays, and cornices, perhaps to tease their guests into seeing nonexistent courtyards and temples (fig. 5-6). Landscapes were often framed by false window mouldings to give the impression of seeing beyond the wall.

Paradoxically, the mental attitude that allows one to view an illusion as a surrogate of a real scene is the product of a more scientific approach to reality. The awakening of the intellect that began with the Greeks, and to which the Romans were heirs, introduced scientific explanations not shared by other ancient cultures. Eventually this more objective attitude drove totemism out of nature. Image-making, liberated from taboos and its primitive magical function, was free to be used to represent natural appearances. But hand in hand with science and the art of appearances came an attitude of detachment from nature, signifying that the Greeks and Romans were no longer *participants* in but *witnesses* to the drama. The primitive hunters and the Egyptians were so much a part of nature that they were incapable of detachment—that is, of standing apart to view the world scientifically and artistically.

On holidays the traffic of our freeways, jammed with cars and campers, is headed mostly away from the city. The view of nature as being not only beautiful but a place to escape to is, in our day, taken for granted. Roman citizens, especially those who could afford wall paintings, seemed to have held a similar view. They, too, were urban dwellers, enjoying public services—water, sewage, markets, courthouses, theaters, and public baths—that were remarkable for a preindustrial society. But despite the amenities, city dwelling then, as now, must have exerted a psychological pressure. The idea of "opening up the wall" to imaginary porticoes and parks was probably intended to satisfy a need to be in closer contact with nature—even though it was only an unreal paradise.

5-6 Architectural wall painting from the bedroom of the Villa Boscoreale, first century B.C. Metropolitan Museum of Art, New York (Rogers Fund, 1903).

Chinese Landscape Painting

To the Chinese of the Sung Dynasty (960–1279), landscape art was much more than a stage prop. Nature itself was the protagonist of a drama in which humans were merely minor actors. By the tenth century, Chinese artists had translated their feeling for nature into a pictorial language that produced glowing images of landscape.

With only ink on paper, Tung Yuan evoked a sensation of boundless space in *Clear Day in the Valley* (colorplate 8). The faint indications of human life—the fisherman, strollers, and houses—are almost completely absorbed into the magnificent natural panorama. The artist did not evoke the sense of this vastness by means of any single identifiable vanishing point. Instead, through the sensitive control of ink diluted with water, he managed to suggest overlapping layers of rocky or forested hillsides and the misty spaces in between. In places, empty paper is used to hint at the deepest areas of mist and the plane of the lake. These effects were not mere artistic devices; Tung Yuan's openness was also characteristic of the Oriental intellectual attitude that favored cooperation with, rather than subjugation of, nature. Also, by not forcing an image of nature on the viewer, the sense of realism was, if anything, enhanced. But *Clear Day in the Valley* is more than open space filled with vapors. The ink washes were given form by a structure of lines and figures. The feeling of distance and altitude suggested by the washes was increased by the device of placing small trees and pavilions at the bottom of the picture. (The sensation of potentially falling into the scene is due perhaps to this ''plunging'' perspective.) Lines also complement the tonal areas in defining the craggy land formations and the textures of leaves and rocks.

In addition to providing realistic information, the lines create intricate patterns to complement the broader ink-wash patterns. This sensitivity to the subtleties of abstract rhythms, especially as demonstrated in the use of line, can be explained by the fact that Chinese artists received extensive training in handwriting, or *calligraphy*. Calligraphy was looked on as a fine art just like painting. Chinese painting was nurtured by the freedom and fluency of Chinese script and by the cults that refined the art of calligraphy over the centuries.

Rather than directly copying a section of nature, Chinese artists gathered impressions while walking. They absorbed the subject matter from many angles, in the process savoring its different aspects and mentally translating this information into the forms for trees, water, and mountains that they had learned from their masters. Everything was stored in the memory, to be released later during an act of creativity. Like a stage performer, the artist felt the need for mental preparation before the act. According to documents of the time, some Chinese artists depended on wine for this creative release. But the artist Kuo Hsi (fig. 5-7), who lived in the eleventh century, relied on a private ritual that was described by his son.

> Whenever he began to paint he opened all the windows, cleared his desk, burned incense on the right and left, washed his hands, and cleansed his ink-stone; and by doing so his spirit was calmed and his thought composed. Not until then did he begin to paint.

The absorption and filtering of reality before transferring it to paper was an artistic habit that was founded on a philosophy of life. The goal of the Chinese artist was to reveal the essentials of nature rather than to record its outward appearance. The twelfth-century Confucian philosopher Chu Hsi compared the ultimate knowing of anything to the act of peeling an orange: an artist who

5-7 Kuo Hsi, *Clearing Autumn Skies over Mountains and Valleys* (detail), eleventh century. Ink and light color, 81⅜" x 10¼". Freer Collection, Washington, D.C.

merely imitated outer appearances was one who stopped at the peel. Educated artists, like the philosophers who meditated on religion and philosophical subjects until these became engraved on their inner consciousness, studied nature from all angles until they could internalize its universal character. Central to this philosophy of art was the concept of *Ch'i*—life force, or energy. *Ch'i*, to which artists had to attune themselves, became not only the source of their creativity but the measure of the value of their work.

Ideas connecting nature and human beings run deep in Chinese thought. By the time of the Sung painters, a cult of nature had arisen out of elements of all three of China's religions (Buddhism, Confucianism, and Taoism). Both Taoism and Ch'an Buddhism, the sect to which most painters and intellectuals belonged, involved the search for an escape from reality, an escape that took the form of a withdrawal to nature. This was motivated by more than purely religious insights and metaphysical speculation, since at that time China was being divided by internal upheavals and barbarian attacks on its borders. Artists, however, received salaries from the government or rich patrons and were insulated from the mainstream of Chinese living, free to fulfill their wishes of withdrawal. Their art was not shared with the average Chinese but was circulated among a cultural and economic elite. Love of nature and *Ch'i*, it seems, were a privilege of the wealthy.

Christian Manuscripts

At the time Tung Yuan and other Sung painters were glorifying nature, Christian artists in Europe were glorifying the gospels. *Christ's Entry into Jerusalem* from the *Gospel Book of Otto III* (fig. 5-8) is a fair example of medieval landscape at the time—which serves to show how far European art had retreated from Greco-Roman realism by the year 1000 A.D. Christian artists, totally committed to the spiritual world, translated their message of salvation with an art of symbols. Theologians held that nature, like the human body, was ultimately sinful, and were therefore essentially hostile toward artistic imitations of nature as well. Not that nature was entirely excluded. Illustrations of animals, for example, were often used to decorate gospel texts, but they were turned into emblems for beings or ideas other than themselves: the ox, the lion, and the eagle, for example, were symbols of the Evangelists Luke, Mark, and John. Nature, downgraded in medieval Christian life, was used in art largely for symbolic or ornamental purposes.

5–8. *Christ's Entry into Jerusalem* from the *Gospel Book
of Otto III, c.* 1000. Bayerische Staatsbibliothek, Munich.

An anecdote about mountains illustrates the great difference
between the Chinese and Christian attitudes toward nature. The
Alps, so attractive to tourists today, were not considered a fit
subject for human attention in the Middle Ages. Petrarch, a famous
fourteenth-century scholar, talked his brother into accompanying
him on a climb of Mt. Ventoux. In those days, climbing a mountain

for aesthetic reasons was almost unheard of. But when they reached the top, Petrarch read a passage from Saint Augustine that made him feel guilty about enjoying himself and forgetting the needs of his immortal soul. "I turned my inward eye upon myself," he says, "and from that time not a syllable fell from my lips until we reached the bottom again."

Leonardo   Five hundred years after Tung Yuan's *Clear Day in the Valley* and the *Gospel Book of Otto III*, a Florentine artist named Leonardo da Vinci painted the portrait of the young wife of Francesco del Giocondo (fig. 5-9). Since then, she has become the most famous woman in the Western world; her famous smile has fascinated every generation. The fact that it was possible to make such a portrait in 1503 shows the vast distance that European art and intellectual life had come. The intellectual interest of Europeans was shifting, as suggested by the expression on Mona Lisa's face,

5-9
Leonardo da Vinci,
Mona Lisa, 1503–05.
Oil on panel, 30" x 21".
Louvre, Paris.

5–10
Giovanni di Paolo,
Saint John in the Wilderness
(detail), *c.* 1450.
Tempera on wood,
27″ x 14¼″.
The Art Institute of Chicago
(Collection of Mr. and Mrs.
Martin A. Ryerson).

away from the mysteries of the Church and beginning to focus on the mysteries in themselves. Even before Leonardo, artists had experimented with the problems of expressing the human spirit in more secular terms. People's interest had also turned from the heavens to the earth. And it is the form of the landscape behind Mona Lisa, as well as its newly discovered human meanings, to which we must now turn our attention.

As might be expected from Petrarch's experience, Europeans' historical lack of rapport with the land appears to have made it difficult at first for their artists to incorporate land features into their pictures. Early attempts, especially with mountains (fig. 5-10), were naive or fantastic (not unlike the papier mâché concepts of moon scenery that appeared in movies before the days of space travel). The mathematically minded Florentines perfected linear perspective (see Chapter Two) in their search for a logical system to use in coping with the problem. This method worked well for representing a room or the shape of a building, but hills and valleys and forests and streams did not submit as readily to the controls of vanishing points and straight, diminishing lines. Renaissance artists before Leonardo also seemed to have a difficult time fitting their people into continuous landscapes. Either the people were the wrong size, or the foreground was discontinuous with the background, or both.

5–11
Leonardo da Vinci,
detail of
the upper-right
background of the
Mona Lisa.

Leonardo, who was a scientist as well as an artist, was more observant and less restricted to abstract formulas in his approach to landscape than were his contemporaries. He solved the problem of reconciling the subject with the background by placing her on a high ledge overlooking a landscape (fig. 5-11). The networks of cliffsides and valleys, roads and riverbeds, jagged mountains and sky, join forces to make a single environment, one that is held together by a pervasive atmosphere. (Leonardo also perfected the technique of *sfumato*—blurred outlines and smoky atmospheres that tend to fuse figures and objects.) But his landscape images were a product of strong emotions as well as scientific research. It is no accident that the geological forms behind Mona Lisa seem to throb like a living organism. Leonardo believed that a life force, not unlike that of the Sung concept of Ch'i, courses through all things of the earth. Yet there is an unmistakably forbidding quality in Leonardo's mountains and valleys that borders on hostility toward creature life—a touch of the apocalypse that is totally absent in Chinese art (fig. 5-12). Nature, as he once observed in his notebooks, ''often sends forth pestilential vapours and plagues upon the great multiplications and congregations of animals, and especially upon mankind.'' Some of the chill of medieval art survived the Renaissance thaw and lingered in Leonardo's landscapes.

5-12   Leonardo da Vinci, *Alpine Mountain Peaks*, 1510–11.
Red chalk on brick-red paper. Royal Library, Windsor Castle.
Reproduced by Gracious Permission of Her Majesty Queen Elizabeth II.

5–13 Nicholas Poussin, *Landscape with the Burial of Phocion,* 1648.
Oil on canvas, 47" x 70½". Louvre, Paris.

Constable The landscape of cool trees and distant meadows in the nineteenth-century English painting *The Hay Wain* (colorplate 9) radi-
ates serenity and optimism. The countrysides of John Constable
show a debt to earlier work by Dutch artists and their art of low
horizons with scudding clouds and moving shadows, and also to
his studies of the tree-lined, classical stillness of French landscape
paintings (fig. 5-13). But even though he was a thorough student
of the techniques of other artists, he was also a keen observer of
nature itself. Constable's dedication resulted in his extending the
vocabulary of outdoor art to perhaps its finest manifestation in the
Western world. His particular contribution was that of capturing the
transient phenomena of nature's ''dews, breezes, bloom and freshness'' by means of brighter color, broken touches of paint, and

flecks of pure white applied with a palette knife (fig. 5-14). Such effects were not simply a matter of facile painting technique. Constable's fresh vision was a result of both his closeness to nature and continual experimentation with the oil medium. His belief that painting should be pursued as an inquiry into the laws of nature is reminiscent of Leonardo da Vinci's attitude. And as was the case with Leonardo, Constable's reliance on careful observation was enhanced by a reverent passion for his subject.

5-14   John Constable, *Willy Lott's House near Flatford Mill, Suffolk,* *c.* 1816. Oil on paper, 9¼" x 7". Crown copyright, Victoria & Albert Museum.

A variant of nature worship had infected all of Europe since the eighteenth century. On the Continent, Jean-Jacques Rousseau had challenged the hearts and minds of Europeans by championing the virtues of primitive simplicity over the vices of civilization. In England, the Romantic poetry of Wordsworth (which was read by Constable) extolled the spiritual revelations of nature in even its most humble aspects. Literature and art reflected an intellectual revolution that seemed to be bringing Europe around to an outlook like that of eleventh-century China—the common ground being a mystical feeling for nature. (One symptom of this shared state of mind was the mutual taste, in China and nineteenth-century England, for large, informal gardens.) Constable's temperament and personal religious views coincided perfectly with this cultural movement. The natural universe, in which the philosophers of the time believed the highest moral feelings were revealed, was considered to be the handiwork of God. And this handiwork extended to every last thing—mill dams, willows, old rotten planks, shiny posts—that Constable revered in the English countryside. His finest landscapes, like *The Hay Wain*, were painted in the East Anglian countryside around the river Stour where he grew up.

Ironically, the works of Constable, the artist who most successfully expressed the moral, philosophical, and visual ideals of the people of England at that time, were more popular in France than in his own land. English artistic tastes, which favored a more finished-looking and idealized product, had not as yet caught up with English spiritual values. But in France, *The Hay Wain* received a prize in the Salon of 1824 and profoundly influenced many French artists, including the Impressionists, who based an entire style on the technique of breaking up color. But Constable had his greatest effect on the artists of the movement known as *Romanticism*. The extremes of Romantic painting either sank into sentimental depictions of rustic life or soared into extravagant visions of idealized nature. But Constable's complete respect for nature seems to have enforced an artistic honesty that helped him to resist the seductions that so tempted other artists of his generation.

After Constable

Landscape art and nature worship have declined since Constable's time. The French Impressionists of the latter half of the nineteenth century helped set in motion the separation of art from many of the social and spiritual values necessary to a landscape tradition. Nature, no longer felt to have any religious significance, became a source of color sensations and patterns and a stage for portraying the newly developing middle class. After the Impressionists, a preoccupation with color and the formal elements of art became a more central concern, and nature became less and less important, even as a point of departure.

Perhaps it is possible to extol nature without realism or images of nature. Throbbing colors and vivid patterns can correspond to the ways that we experience the sensations of nature or act as metaphors of creative energy. According to Robert Wolff, a twentieth-century teacher of design, ''Nature is not the sight of the forest, it is the sap in the tree.'' In its most general forms, nature has been and still is a motivation for some abstract art, but a look at the whole story of art in our century would show that a concern for nature has been minor at best.

The general public, however, still likes to visit the countryside, favors exhilarating natural backgrounds in the movies, and hangs landscape pictures in the living room. But nature, despite this token sentimental recognition, has not benefited at the hands of the general public; instead, it has had its relevance diminished by buildings of concrete and steel and its very existence threatened by pollution. Meanwhile, there is great opportunity in our time—in terms of both motives and means—for artists to deal with nature. The possibilities of ecological disaster may be reason enough for many to begin dramatizing an awareness of that prospect. For others, the possibilities of new images of nature may be the main inspiration. Before now, our view of the world was limited not only by our eyes but by our position on earth. One extreme is represented by Leonardo's portrait of Mona Lisa, the other by Tung Yuan's distant view of mountains. Now the limits have been considerably extended, permitting us, with the help of such tools as the electron microscope, to get a look at the inner world of matter, and, with the help of space travel and television, to see our own planet from a separate vantage point.

Some artists are already dealing with nature in ways very different from the oil-on-canvas methods of people like Constable. *Earth Art* calls for these artists to expand the scale of their work to that of their subject, using the land itself as material. With such tools as picks, shovels, trench-hole diggers, and earth-moving equipment, Michael Heizer transformed large areas of the landscape into works of art (fig. 3-28). By creating interesting shapes and spaces on a large scale, he brings our imagination into a contact with nature that may cause us to discover new aspects and beauty where they might be least expected. Thus his function as an artist is not very different from that of such older landscape artists as Constable, Leonardo, and Tung Yuan.

6

Men
and
Women

The human figure has always been a very popular subject in art, which should not be surprising. After all, what could be more interesting to us than ourselves? However, the kinds of human beings found in many paintings and sculptures do not always resemble ordinary mortals like us. Human figures have often been transformed or idealized to represent gods and goddesses, angels, heroes and heroines, and so forth. Yet regardless of their special status, these images usually resemble us in at least one respect: they are either male or female. The sexual distinction can be very important—especially if the figure is that of an idealized naked adult—because it is an essential and fascinating dimension of our lives.

In the first part of this chapter we will consider images of men, and in the second part, images of women, concentrating on works of art that particularly reflect the sexual ideals of different cultural periods. This focus is, in large part, intended to demonstrate how the aesthetic object has played a role in creating a set of standards for the sexual object. Finally, in the third part, we will consider images of men and women *together*. The examples will trace the

6-1
Kouros, c. 615–600 B.C.
Marble, 7'2" high.
Metropolitan Museum of Art,
New York
(Fletcher Fund, 1932).

development in Western art of the depiction of the human body and examine some of the ways in which it has been used for the expression of ideas.

Men In our contemporary American culture, physical beauty is usually associated more with the female body than with the male body. The ancient Greeks, however, were preoccupied with male beauty and developed a cult around idealized portraits of the god Apollo. Sexual interest was not the primary impulse for creating these statues, but sexual connotations are present in the religious legends about the god, and are reflected in images of him.

The Greeks The Greek interest in competitive athletics, particularly the Olympic games, was one of the origins of this type of sculpture. At least as

6-2
Mycerinus and Queen,
from Giza, *c.* 2500 B.C.
Slate, 4'8" high.
Museum of Fine Arts, Boston
(Harvard-M.F.A. Expedition).

early as the sixth century B.C., athletes competed at those events in the nude. A stereotyped notion exists today that nakedness, the "natural" state of people, occurs only in primitive societies. But nudity to the Greeks, who by this time were emerging as an important Mediterranean civilization, was a factor setting them apart from the surrounding "barbarians." The nude body, far from being considered scandalous, became an expression of the essentially human concern in Greek philosophy. Early sculptures of nude males, which may be statues either of Apollo or of athletes (*Kouroi*), display an alert self-confidence characteristic both of young athletes and a young culture (fig. 6-1). But they also have a marked stiffness, a result of the influence of Egyptian sculpture, that diminishes their naturalism. The qualities of monumentality and immobility, which are so admirable in Egyptian statuary (fig. 6-2), are worn somewhat awkwardly by the Greek statues of athletes.

In the early part of the fifth century, the Greeks began a period of extraordinary progress in art and philosophy that was to set them apart from all of the other ancient civilizations bordering the Mediterranean. The aesthetic instinct that endowed the Kouroi of the previous century with a human alertness helped grace later sculptures with a hitherto unknown realism and beauty, exemplified by the 480 B.C. *Kritios Boy* (fig. 6-3). Kenneth Clark, who has made a significant contribution to this subject with his book *The Nude: A Study of Ideal Form*, said of this statue:

> Here for the first time we feel passionate pleasure in the human body . . . for the delicate eagerness with which the sculptor's eye has followed every muscle or watched the skin stretch and relax as it passes over a bone could not have been achieved without a heightened sensuality.

6–3
Kritios Boy,
c. 480 B.C.
Marble,
approx. 34″ high.
Acropolis Museum,
Athens.

6–4
Polykleitos,
Doryphoros (Spear Carrier),
original *c.* 450 B.C.
Roman copy, marble,
6'6" high.
Museo Nazionale,
Naples.

Greek art was progressing rapidly at this time in developing models of male beauty, in bronze and stone, that gave tangible form to the idealistic and humanistic Greek concepts of people.

By mid-century, a scant generation later, Polykleitos had sculpted his famous *Spear Carrier,* known to us today only by a marble copy (fig. 6-4). Looking at this image of an athlete with eyes that have been influenced by photography, movies, television and even realistic statuary in public parks, we may not be too impressed with either its artistic or perceptual contribution. But let us look at the casual stance of the figure. The slight step taken by the *Spear Carrier* was as important to the history of Western art as the step taken by the first astronaut on the moon's surface was to science. The position of the feet and the effect it has on the posture and whole character of the body is a moon's distance away from the stiff stance of earlier statues. The slant of the shoulders (downward slightly to the figure's right), which is countered by an opposite

6–5
Style of Phidias,
Apollo of the Tiber,
original *c.* 470 B.C.
Roman copy,
marble, 7′2⅝″ high.
Museo Nazionale Romano,
Rome.

slant to the hips, is caused by placing the center of the figure's weight on the right foot. This is a convention for representing the human body that can still be found in our own time in every life-drawing class. This swing of the hips, called *déhanchement,* is a very natural way to stand or casually walk. (Nevertheless, it can also be a symbol, almost a cliché in the stance of a woman, for the provocation of sexual desire.) Polykleitos was quite methodical about his art. He developed a code of proportions and movements for the ideal male body, and it is reflected in the copy of his statue. Although it looks natural enough at first glance, the naturalism is actually modified by the artist's concept of perfection. The incisive clarity of shapes in the chest, stomach, groin, and legs is so dominant that it also interrupts a smoothly flowing vision of the whole.

It was the achievement of the most famous of Greek sculptors of that time to project into bronze what many considered the finest image of Apollo. The Apollo statues of Phidias, who sculpted the figures of the Parthenon, survive only in the form of marble copies. Taller and more graceful than the *Spear Carrier*, the *Apollo of the Tiber* (fig. 6-5) accentuates the beauty and sensuality that was underplayed by Polykleitos. The *déhanchement* is there, and so are the conventions of defining muscles and tendons around the chest, pelvis, and knees, but none of these elements are allowed to stop our gaze and obstruct the sensation of supple grace. This statue exemplifies the Greek virtue of balance—between emotion and intellect, naturalism and idealism, and, to a degree, between male and female. This tension between polar opposites was not maintained by succeeding generations of Greek artists. Male images tended more and more to lose the aspect of this controlling intellect, becoming excessively elegant, almost effeminate, as is the case with the *Apollo Belvedere* (fig. 6-6).

The Romans, who were the inheritors and the assimilators of Greek culture, added little to the male nude, being content with reiterations and variations of the themes already invented by the Greeks. Believing that it enhanced their divinity, Roman rulers had their portrait heads placed on top of ideal nude bodies. Despite this decline in its original significance, the practice of sculpting male nudes did survive through Roman times.

After the Roman world was overturned by the new order of Christianity, images of nudes fell into disfavor for around a thousand years. Except for the story of Adam and Eve, Christian theology of the Middle Ages had little interest in nudity, and that only as a way to exemplify the sins of the body rather than its virtues. Many, but not all, pagan statues were destroyed during this period.

The Italian Renaissance

In the fourteenth and fifteenth centuries, the artists of the Renaissance rediscovered Greek and Roman sculpture, and once again the naked body appeared in art. But when applied to the heroic figures of the Old and New Testaments instead of the gods of Mt. Olympus, the male image underwent a transformation.

Michelangelo, perhaps the greatest artist of the time, frequently included male nudes in his sculptures and murals, and probably contributed more to the development of the male image than any artist since Polykleitos. Considering the human body divine, he made images of it that added a new and vital dimension to masculine beauty in art. But beauty alone is only a part of the total content of his sculpture. The eighteen-foot-high statue, David (fig. 6-7), carved for the city of Florence in the early years of the sixteenth century, shows the young man in the moments before battle, his head turned toward the approaching Goliath. We can certainly see something of the Spear Carrier in the stance and proportions of the David, for Michelangelo was an enthusiastic student of the antique statues that could be found everywhere in Italy. But after looking at the defiant head held in place by a column of muscle, our eyes move down across a torso that barely conceals a storm of tensions underneath. We see that although Michelangelo's treatment of the David may have been influenced by the Spear Carrier, its intensity belongs to a world very different from the Classical calm of the older sculpture.

Artists of the Renaissance, including Michelangelo, often dealt with subjects from Greek and Roman mythology as well as from

6–7
Michelangelo,
David,
1501–04.
Marble,
approximately 18' high,
including base.
Galleria dell'Accademia,
Florence.

Christianity. But even when creating images of gods and heroes, they did not attempt to idealize physical beauty so much as to emphasize the strength and energy of these muscular and active figures. To Renaissance artists, the naked male was a powerful and novel subject, one which let them breathe new life into religious and mythological themes and show new masculine ideals.

6-8
Horatio Greenough,
George Washington, 1832–41.
Marble, approx. 11'4" high.
Courtesy National
Collection of Fine Arts,
Smithsonian Institution.

Neoclassicism

After the Renaissance, interest in the male nude declined, although the female nude—as we shall see in the following section—became very popular. Not that the male nude was discontinued; it remained as an established, but not very vital, artistic tradition. And for certain subjects—battle scenes, crucifixions, and episodes from Classical myths—it was still appropriate (though not essential). As an end in itself, whether exemplifying beauty, power, or energy, male nudity no longer captured many artists' imaginations. As a symbol, it usually alluded to the glory of the Classical past; but that glory was becoming more of an empty memory, if not a fantasy, in an increasingly modern age. Still, the late 1700s and early 1800s saw the rise of *Neoclassicism* in the arts, a renewed interest in the simplicity and grandeur that some artists associated with the high point of Classical Greek civilization. The influence of the Neoclassical movement can be seen in a work by the American sculptor Horatio Greenough, who chose to represent George Washington naked from the waist up (fig. 6-8). Washington's wigged head rests upon an idealized body, with broad shoulders and well-defined planes of chest and abdomen that hark back to Polykleitos. But Greenough's attempt to ennoble his subject through the symbolism of the nude did not succeed with the public. Apparently Americans could not accept the idea of a former president looking like a Roman emperor or a Greek god.

The Late Nineteenth Century

The nude male images by the French sculptor Auguste Rodin are among the most successful ones made since the Renaissance. Perhaps this is because Rodin's images rarely referred to the Classical past. His *Age of Bronze* (fig. 6-9) brings to mind Michelangelo's *David*. Both seem to have a reserve of energy waiting to be released; but while the *David*'s firm, aggressive posture announces the violence the young man is about to commit, the tentative posture of the Rodin youth does not clearly indicate what action is called for. The youth seems to be taking a step, clutching his head with one hand and gesturing vaguely with the other. Apparently Rodin himself was vague about the theme, for he originally called the work *The Vanquished*. But despite this lack of clear intention, the sculpture's rising, striving movement is very suggestive. Physically, it expresses the restless energy that seethes beneath the surface of every living thing; psychologically, it expresses the restless emotions of human beings' spiritual longing.

6-9
Auguste Rodin,
The Age of Bronze, c. 1876–77.
Bronze, 5'11" high.
Minneapolis Institute of Arts
(John R. Van Derlip Fund).

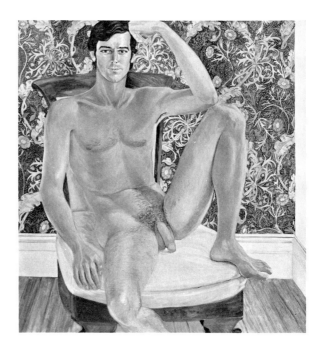

6–10
Sylvia Sleigh,
*Walter Finley
Seated Nude,* 1976.
Oil on canvas,
56″ x 52″.
Collection Dennis Adrian,
Chicago.

Art Today   Although in Rodin's time the idealized figure was still able to convey abstract ideas, it was soon to fall out of favor altogether. The modern art movement was already underway, and by the early 1900s, interest in the nude male, along with other traditional subject matter, was replaced by a preoccupation with abstract forms and color. Only very recently has the male nude begun to reappear as a subject of any importance. And the reasons for this do not seem to have to do entirely with aesthetics, for the artists who paint nude males today are mostly women, and many of them are identified with the growing feminist movement.

Sylvia Sleigh's paintings of naked men are provocative even in an age that thinks of itself as sexually liberated. Not only are her subjects nude, but the view is usually frontal and the pose casual, reflecting a candor about the male body that has been almost nonexistent in art outside of life-drawing classes. Because most people are not used to this sort of thing, a painting like *Walter Finley Seated Nude* (fig. 6-10) seems brash, if not a little shocking. But Sleigh's purpose, like that of the Greek artist who made the *Kritios Boy* (fig. 6-3), was probably to emphasize the beauty of the male subject, which is supplemented by the ornately flowered wallpaper of the background as well as reflected in his relaxed, self-confident pose. Most of Sleigh's models are young men with an abundance of health, good looks, and body hair, which she has called ''natural embroidery.''

Women   Living in a culture in which images of the naked female body constantly appear on the newsstands and in the movies while images of male nudity are still very rare, we may have difficulty understanding attitudes in Greece before the fourth century B.C., where sculptures of young women were usually clothed while those of Apollos and young athletes were likely to be nude.

The Greeks   By the fifth century B.C., when Polykleitos and Phidias were refining their masterpieces of nude males, statues of women were normally clothed in a loose-fitting garment called a *chiton*. We should not, of course, take this to mean that women were not considered sexually attractive; the biological impulse was surely as strong then as it is now. But the desire to make images of a perfected ideal of the feminine body was not nearly as strong as it was to depict the male counterpart. By the fourth century, however, statues of nude women were beginning to be made for the sake of experiencing their ideal nudity. Appropriately, this ideal developed around the cult of Aphrodite, the love goddess, and her Roman equivalent, Venus. Statues of these and other nude figures of women became increasingly popular in the Greek (and Roman) world.

The first significant Aphrodite statue was created by the fourth-century Greek Master Praxiteles for the people on the island of Cnidos (fig. 6-11). By this time the problems of representing the human body had been already worked out by sculpting male nudes. But the posture of *déhanchement*, Polykleitos's legacy, takes on a voluptuous character when applied to the feminine body. The curve of the right hip, as well as the smaller curve underneath the armpit, is much fuller and more pronounced, its smooth line less broken by bone and muscle. The S shape of the female body, which is often called sinuous, becomes a familiar symbol of desire. Praxiteles was well suited to sculpt Aphrodite; even his statues of men have a sinuous quality, and with it a delicate modeling of the surface that almost gives the appearance of flesh. Unfortunately, Praxiteles' Aphrodite is known to us only through Roman copies.

The Middle Ages   The basic formula established by Praxiteles was scarcely varied in any major way through the rest of the Greek and Roman periods. And, just as was the case with nude images of men, the Christian world prior to the Renaissance professed little interest in naked women except in instances where there was a need to symbolize

6–11
After Praxiteles,
Cnidian Aphrodite,
original *c.* 330 B.C.
Roman copy, marble.
Vatican Museum, Rome.

fleshly lusts. In one culture the body had been a focus of religious veneration; in the other it was, at times, considered antireligious. However, in the twelfth and thirteenth centuries, at the height of medieval civilization, women began to play a more important role in courtly life and were celebrated in the arts and letters. The age of chivalry flowered and the cult of the Virgin Mary appeared in the Church. The worship of the Virgin helped to offset the notion of Eve the Temptress that had dominated thinking during the earlier years of the Middle Ages. And Mary had her earthly counterpart in the medieval lady of the court, who achieved a position of honor and even of power in the masculine world of knighthood and the Crusades. Images of women, whether those of the royal courts or the Virgin Mary, were of course depicted fully clothed. Yet their

6-12
The Virgin of Paris,
early fourteenth century.
Cathedral of Notre Dame,
Paris.

femininity was not completely hidden; even a seductive S-curve posture is present in the *Virgin of Paris* as she holds the baby Jesus (fig. 6-12). Furthermore, her clothes and general appearance were probably based on those of the chic ladies of the court. But aside from her indubitable femininity and even the apparently accidental similarity between her pose and that of the *Aphrodite*, the two women are quite different. *Aphrodite* is a goddess of beauty whose nudity implies an acceptance of the human body. *The Virgin of Paris* is a spiritual figure whose beauty refers to a beatitude transcending the earthly body. This beatitude is reflected in the tranquility of her face and the impression of lightness of her body (despite the fact that she is made of stone). Even the way she holds the baby seems to defy gravity.

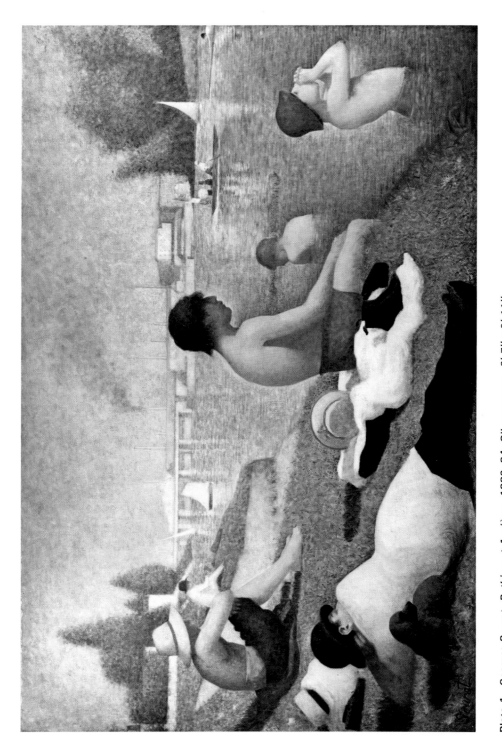

Plate 1 Georges Seurat, *Bathing at Asnières*, 1883–84. Oil on canvas, 6′ 7″ x 9′ 11″. Reproduced by courtesy of the Trustees, The National Gallery, London.

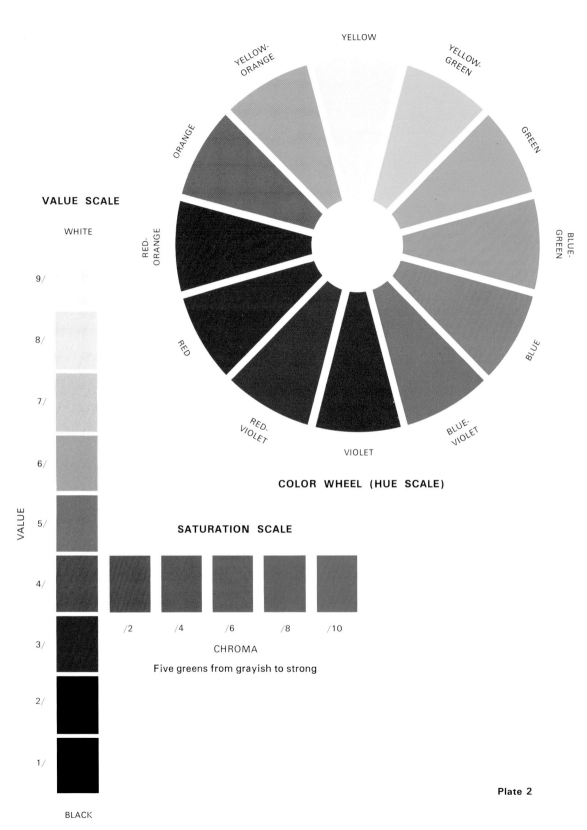

VALUE SCALE

WHITE

9/

8/

7/

VALUE

6/

5/

4/

3/

2/

1/

BLACK

YELLOW

YELLOW-ORANGE

YELLOW-GREEN

ORANGE

GREEN

RED-ORANGE

BLUE-GREEN

RED

BLUE

RED-VIOLET

BLUE-VIOLET

VIOLET

COLOR WHEEL (HUE SCALE)

SATURATION SCALE

/2   /4   /6   /8   /10

CHROMA

Five greens from grayish to strong

Plate 2

Plate 3 Richard Anuskiewicz, *All Things Do Live in the Three,* 1963. Acrylic on masonite, 21⅞″ x 35⅞″. Collection Mrs. Robert M. Benjamin, New York. © Richard Anuskiewicz, 1980.

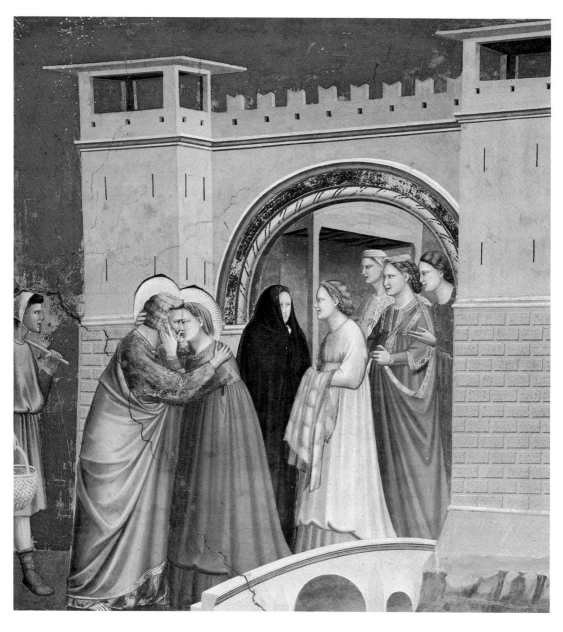

Plate 4 Giotto di Bondone, *Meeting at the Golden Gate,* early fourteenth century. Fresco. Arena Chapel, Padua.

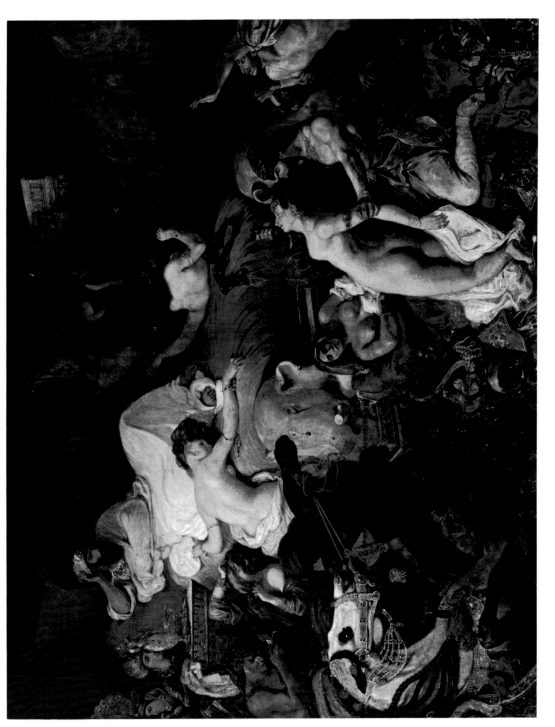

Plate 5   Eugène Delacroix, *The Death of Sardanapoulus*, 1826. Oil on canvas, 12' 1" x 16' 3". Louvre, Paris.

Plate 6 *Wine Merchant,* detail from the *Window of Saint Lubius, c.* 1200–20.
Stained glass, 32″ diameter Chartres Cathedral, France.

Plate 7   Dan Flavin, *Untitled (to Donna) 5A,* 1971. Yellow, blue, and pink fluorescent light, 8' square across a corner. Courtesy Leo Castelli Gallery.

Plate 8 Tung Yuan, *Clear Day in the Valley* (detail), twelfth–thirteenth centuries. Handscroll, ink and slight colors on paper, 14¾" x 59¼". Museum of Fine Arts, Boston (Chinese and Japanese Special Fund, 12.903).

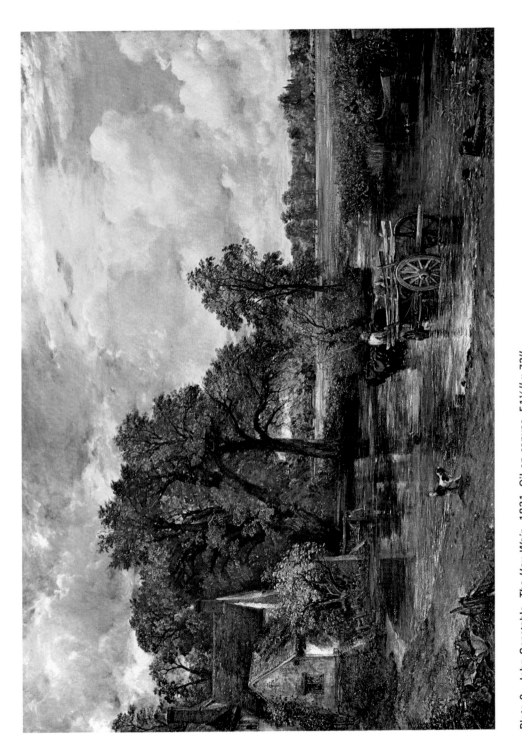

Plate 9   John Constable, *The Hay Wain*, 1821. Oil on canvas, 51¼" x 73".
Reproduced by courtesy of the Trustees, The National Gallery, London.

Plate 10   Sandro Botticelli, *The Birth of Venus, c.* 1480. Tempera on canvas, 5′ 8″ x 9′ 1″. Galleria degli Uffizi, Florence.

Plate 11   Marc Chagall, *Double Portrait with Wineglass,* 1917–18.
Oil on canvas, 7' 7¾'' x 4' 5½''.
Musée National d'Art Moderne, Paris.

Plate 12 Michelangelo, *Creation of the Sun and the Moon*, detail from the Sistine Chapel ceiling, 1508–12. Fresco, approx. 9′ 2″ x 18′ 8″.

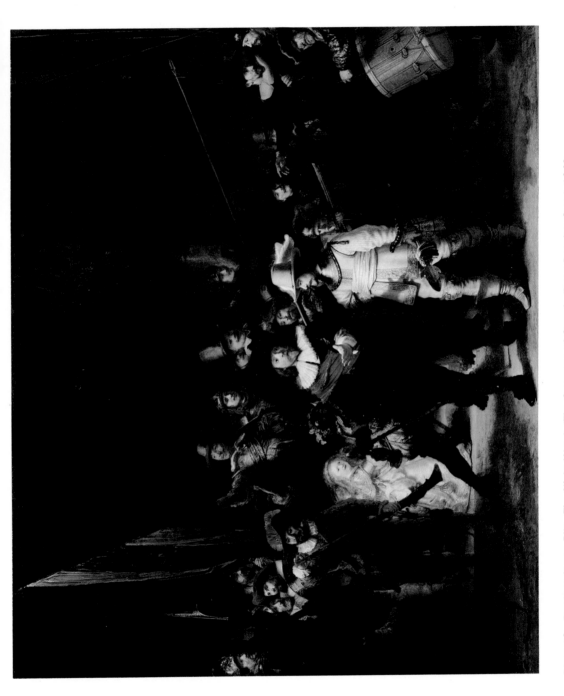

Plate 13 Rembrandt van Rijn, *The Night Watch (The Company of Captain Frans Banning Cocq)*, 1642. Oil on canvas, 12' 2'' x 14' 7''. Rijksmuseum, Amsterdam.

Plate 14 Vincent van Gogh, *The Night Cafe*, 1888. Oil on canvas, 27½″ x 35″. Yale University Art Gallery (bequest of Stephen C. Clark, B.A. 1903).

Plate 15   Jackson Pollock, *One (Number 31)*, 1950. Oil and Duco enamel on canvas, 8' 10" x 17' 5⅝". The Museum of Modern Art, New York (gift of Sidney Janis).

Plate 16　Edward Hopper, *House by the Railroad,* 1925. Oil on canvas, 24″ x 29″.
The Museum of Modern Art, New York.

6–13
Venus de Medici,
early third century B.C.
Roman copy,
marble, 5'½" high.
Galleria degli Uffizi,
Florence.

*The Italian
Renaissance*

As the feudal system of the Middle Ages gave way to another form of society based on city-states, the influence of the Church was weakened, and artists began to work instead for the wealthy noblemen who held political power. Men like Lorenzo de' Medici of Florence cultivated the study of the past, inspiring a new interest in the myths, poetry, and sculpture of the Greeks. And with this, inevitably, came an admiration for the Greek portrayal of the nude. But it was not an easy matter for the artists of the fifteenth century to bridge the gap between the goddess of love and the Christian Virgin. A medieval attitude toward the image of the naked female persisted even when images of naked men had come to be sanctioned as symbols, or even as representations of biblical heroes, like Michelangelo's *David.*

The artists of the first half of the fifteenth century in Italy had begun to apply their knowledge of the art of Classical Greece and Rome to the creation of a new style. Most, however, had concentrated on images of men, for the burgeoning middle-class society of traders was more interested in representations of themselves, or masculine images of knights and pagan heroes that symbolized themselves. Femininity, once again, was out of style; a surprising amount of the art of the period, whether dealing with religious subjects or the nobility, seems to have stressed the attributes of powerful masculinity. With little to go on, therefore, in terms of precedent for painting the female nude within a Classical theme, Sandro Botticelli created one of the most comely versions of Venus Aphrodite in art history (colorplate 10). Initially inspired by an Italian poet, Botticelli's version of the love goddess's birth reaches back over twenty centuries to the original hymn to Aphrodite by the early Greek poet, Homer:

> . . . where the moist breath of Zephyros blowing
> Out of the west bore her over the surge of the loud-roaring deep
> In soft foam. The gold-filleted Hours
> Welcomed her gladly and clothed her in ambrosial garments . . .
> And around her delicate throat and silvery breasts
> Hung necklaces inlaid with gold, . . .*

Venus's pose was probably based on that of the Venus de Medici, a Classical marble statue now in the Uffizi Gallery (fig. 6-13). Botticelli achieved, remarkably for his time, a relatively comfortable version of nudity—and, in addition, an image of a nubile woman who is both desirable and dignified. To this extent his achievement is true to the spirit of Greek female nudity, but it is not very Greek in many other respects. None of the figures, including Venus, is standing solidly on the ground (or the shell). Even allowing for allegorical license and the need to illustrate the fantasy of someone being born out of the sea, Botticelli's Venus is more like the lightweight figures of angels and virgins that populate medieval Christian art than the solidly physical types of the Classical marbles. The ornate delicacies that we can easily appreciate in repeated details like the waves, the leaves, and the sinuous strands of hair are extended by the decorative treatment of the billowing drapery. But for the nudity, the picture could almost be a medieval tapestry.

*Reprinted from *The Homeric Hymns, A Verse Translation* by Thelma Sargent. By permission of W.W. Norton & Company, Inc. Copyright © 1973 by W.W. Norton & Company, Inc.

6-14 Peter Paul Rubens, *The Judgment of Paris, c.* 1636. Oil on canvas, 57" x 75".
National Gallery, London.

The Seventeenth Century Peter Paul Rubens's painting *The Judgment of Paris* (fig. 6-14)—a Greek story of a beauty contest between Athena, Aphrodite, and Hera—presents a view of women that contrasts with Botticelli's *Birth of Venus*. Painted a century and a half after the Italian's canvas by an artist of Flanders (now Belgium), it raises a few interesting questions about the effects of historical versus local influences, on what artists depict. Are Rubens's nudes a reflection of the tastes of a period or an expression of some northern European preference for hearty and healthy farm women? Or, indeed, are these wondrous women an expression of the artist's personal tastes? (The central nude, Aphrodite, is, in fact, a portrait of his wife.) Such questions have often been asked but never satisfactorily answered. So many factors affect the work of any artist that we can only offer a partial answer—that art is always created through a filter of experiences that are both personal and cultural. In this particular case, it would certainly be inaccurate to claim that the artist's preferences were governed by the place he lived in, for Rubens, an aristocrat, was also a successful statesman who held ambassadorial posts and painted in many of the courts of Europe.

More important for our historical examination of the nude in art, Rubens's women seem uninhibited about their nakedness, lacking the medieval reserve that still lingered in Botticelli's Venus. Furthermore, they were intended to be just as desirable as the Italian's slim and (by our standards) appealing goddess.

Neoclassicism   Painted about a century and a half after *The Judgment of Paris*, Marie Guillemine Benoist's *Portrait of a Negress* (fig. 6-15) presents a view of womanhood that is radically different from Rubens's. Benoist stressed simplicity in composition and clarity of line and texture in her treatments of figures and clothing, but her portrait is much more graceful and warm than most Neoclassical art.

According to some observers, paintings of nude females reflect a male point of view. English critic John Berger went so far as to say, "Women are depicted in a quite different way from men—not because the feminine is different from the masculine—but because the 'ideal' spectator is always assumed to be male and the image of the woman is designed to flatter him." If this is the case, Benoist's portrait seems to be an exception. Along with presenting her sitter's sensitive face, long neck, full breasts, and graceful hands, she has emphasized the subject's tenderness and quiet dignity. Benoist captured something of the woman's personality that transcends the anonymity of a sex object.

6–15
Marie Guillemine Benoist,
Portrait of a Negress,
1800. Oil on canvas,
31¾″ x 25¾″.
Louvre, Paris.

149

Victorian Images Nude images continued to appear in art, managing to survive even the nineteenth-century Victorian period, in which antipathy toward the body was at a peak—when the sight of an ankle was considered provocative and the use of the word "leg" was held to be indecent. Oddly enough, the art of the time was full of sexually provocative displays of Turkish harems, Roman slave markets, and decadent orgies. So long as the nudes in a work were sufficiently Classical and the subject matter could be interpreted as intended to teach historical or moral lessons, the most voyeuristic scene was guaranteed public approval. One of the most popular sculptures in the Crystal Palace exhibition in London in 1851 was *The Greek Slave*, by the American Hiram Powers (fig. 6-16). Her body, a denatured version of the traditional Venus, was not nearly as suggestive as the fact that she was in chains.

6–16
Hiram Powers,
The Greek Slave, 1846.
Marble, life-sized.
In the Collection of the
Corcoran Gallery of Art,
Washington, D.C.
Gift of William
Wilson Corcoran.

6-17 Pierre Auguste Renoir, *The Bathers,* 1885–87. Oil on canvas, 3'10" x 5'7".
Philadelphia Museum of Art (Mr. and Mrs. Carroll S. Tyson Collection).

The Late Nineteenth Century The coyness of Powers's marble statue can be contrasted with the warmth of the paintings of nudes by the French artist Pierre Auguste Renoir, whose unaffected young women are even softer and more voluptuous than those of Rubens. Inspired by a seventeenth-century sculpture of nymphs in the Park of Versailles, Renoir positioned the naked figures of *The Bathers* (fig. 6-17) in a manner suggestive of a group sculpture, but without sacrificing any of their vitality. Because these lovely bathers, like the Greek goddesses we have seen in earlier works, are on display, it could be said that this painting also represents a masculine point of view. But if it does, it does so with candor, revealing the artist's unabashed enthusiasm for the female body. Renoir was a member of the late-nineteenth-century Impressionist group of painters who were, for the most part, more interested in developing a fresh approach to painting outdoor scenes than in painting goddesses or nudes. Renoir's healthy and spirited nudes were a significant addition to the Venus tradition and among the most truly vital versions of it.

The Twentieth Century   Because the twentieth century has been a period of extraordinary experimentation, the nude has been relatively ignored. For one thing, subject matter was relegated to a position of less importance, and therefore female nudes, lumped together with landscapes and still lifes, have suffered some pretty rough treatment at times. By the very first years of the century, artists had already begun to seek extreme solutions to the limitations of realism. Picasso's solution was one of willful violence that shattered the rules of composition—and with them the conventions of the nude (fig. 6-18). Matisse's response was to "dry up" the nude by turning it into just another compositional element (fig. 6-19). Later in their lives, both these artists occasionally returned to slightly more traditional methods of representation, often portraying the female nude in ways that demonstrated that they had nothing against the physical appearance of women.

6-18   *(left)* Pablo Picasso, *Dancer,* 1907. Oil on canvas, 4'11" x 3'3¼".
Collection Walter P. Chrysler, Jr., New York.

6-19   *(right)* Henri Matisse, *Le Luxe, II,* 1907–08. Distemper on canvas, 82½" x 54¾".
Statens Museum for Kunst, Copenhagen (Rumps Collection).

6–20 Henry Moore, *Recumbent Figure,* 1938. Stone. 4′4″ long.
The Tate Gallery, London.

After the initial battles with form were fought, many artists began to apply the new techniques to traditional subject matter. The sculptures of the British artist Henry Moore were among the more successful efforts at interpreting the female figure in new ways. While he certainly could not be said to be celebrating the body beautiful, Moore's work was often very sexual in nature, for he used semiabstract shapes that suggested rather than represented parts of the body (fig. 6-20). Moore combined this fascination with the figure with experiments in open sculpture, a direction that had been initiated a few years earlier in France by Julio González (fig. 3-16) and other artists. Frequently, as in the early reclining figure shown here, Moore began with ''natural'' open spaces, such as that formed by the elbow the woman is leaning on or that which exists below her raised knee, and distorted them, making a space larger or smaller than viewers would expect, and sometimes even eliminating parts of the body. Here he seems to have left out part of the torso, perhaps to emphasize the breasts and the physical strength of the arms. Many associations are likely to occur to viewers as they move around the massive form. Some may stem from the body shapes and sexual allusions, others from the landscape-like forms and the surface qualities of the stone, which call to mind mountains and caverns and suggest a reassuring permanence. More than just the body of a woman, this work is an affirmation of life itself.

6–21 Tom Wesselmann, *Great American Nude No. 99,* 1968. Oil on canvas, 60″ x 81″.
Courtesy Sidney Janis Gallery, New York.

By the 1960s, the quest for new images had gone so far that it
had brought many artists all the way back to more realistic representations of the human figure. Using the ''overlooked'' vocabulary of comic strips and advertising, artists such as Andy Warhol
and Tom Wesselmann created satirical versions of the modern
Venus. With cold indifference—and equally cold insight—Warhol
took the ideal woman off her pedestal and put her on the supermarket shelf, as interchangeable as a row of soup cans or any other
marketable commodity (colorplate 28). The judgment implied in
this act, not only about the status of women but about the dehu-
manization that occurs in a mass-media, mass-production world, is
far more devastating than the violence in Picasso's forms. Wesselmann's long series of Great American Nudes, set in assemblage

environments of sexual symbols and products that advertising has made "essential" to life, comments on this from another viewpoint, emphasizing the blandness of a Venus whose only features are sexual (fig. 6-21).

Yet it is largely among the cliché images of popular culture that the traditional concept of Venus survives. Born Aphrodite, arriving naked from the sea, she quickly took the stage-center of artistic nudity from Apollo. And when her role in art became compromised—if not obliterated—by the abstract emphasis of twentieth-century painting, she was reborn from the sea of mass media, arriving naked in the centerfold of *Playboy* magazine and enacting the fantasies of the American male. Although realistic painting and sculpture have lately returned to prominence in the galleries, sexuality is no longer as marked or as one-sided as it once was. Artists, reflecting a new attitude toward women, have abandoned the sex object in favor of the art object; and nudity, when it is portrayed, is often dealt with in a matter-of-fact way, as in the case of John de Andrea's sculptures of women (fig. 3-15) or Sylvia Sleigh's portraits of naked men.

Notions of ideal proportions or appearance are found in many cultures or historical periods, but they can become traps of the imagination and emotions. Mindless rituals like the Miss America or Mr. Universe pageants or demeaning roles such as those of the topless waitress and the football cheerleader are examples of a preoccupation with the idealized body that stunts rather than fosters the development of our perceptions and tastes.

Man and Woman

To merely show how artists have represented men and women separately would be literally incomplete. The union of a man and woman is, after all, the fulfillment of the promise implied by their separateness. The rest of this chapter will complete the theme by surveying a few examples that deal with the relationship between men and women.

Indian Temple Art

One of the most noteworthy—and unusual—depictions of the male-female relationship is to be found in the Khajuraho temples of northwest India, which were constructed in the tenth century A.D. by a people called the Chandels. The major temple of the group is a luxurious beehive of a building, covered with a profusion of detail (fig. 6-22). The visual energy of the walls of the temple suggests that the builders intended it to reflect the primal energy of life, the energy of love and creation. Sculptures of gods and goddesses, saints and mortals, decorate the niches and bands around the turrets, some carved in high relief, others fully round—and nearly all engaged in one form or another of sexual activity. The majority of the figures are *apsaras*, heavenly courtesan-nymphs, who occur either singly or in conjunction with a male figure, and who may in fact be representations of the *devadasis*, women who served as attendants to the temple's deity and as public dancers and musicians. Many of the figures represented actual princes and their wives and courtesans, a fact that calls to mind a parallel with Europe of the same period: the Royal Portals of Chartres Cathedral in France, so called because the Old Testament figures carved alongside the doors represented the kings and queens of France (fig. 6-23). But the comparison only serves to demonstrate the vivid difference in outlook between the two faiths. The stiff, formal figures on the cathedral were clearly intended to de-emphasize the body, whereas the sensuous creatures that populate the temple were sculpted with greatly exaggerated sexual attributes. Their postures and gestures create a sensation of movement, and the jewelry and flimsy scarves that cling to the curves of their bodies accentuate the eroticism of their acts (fig. 6-24).

Unlike most of the artists of the Western tradition, these Indian sculptors did not use live models. Instead, they based their work on earlier sculptures and evolved their conventions for representing the human body by relying more on their religious and sexual views than on their observations of anatomy. Much of the imagery was inspired by literary sources, such as the myth of the creation of woman, in which Twashtri, the Divine Artificer, took the roundness of the moon, the clinging of tendrils, the trembling of grass, the glances of deer, and many other qualities and compounded them to make woman. Accordingly, the young maidens tend to be adorned with breasts that resemble wine-palm fruit. Both men and women seem to have smoothly flowing body envelopes that ignore the relationship of muscle to bone structure. They have volume without seeming to have weight, and their movements deny the sterner mechanics of the real body. Theirs is an emancipated anatomy of supple rhythms that easily evokes the emotion of erotic love.

In the Western world, habits of thinking and conduct in both philosophy and religion have long been guided by the concept of a division between mind and body. Most of the time the body comes out second best, treated as something to be ashamed of—a tradition that reaches back as far as the story of Adam and Eve (fig. 6-25). Only in very recent times has the Western world come to accept the depiction of sexual activity as a possible, if not a proper, subject matter for art. Yet the forthright celebration of human sexuality was completely in keeping with the beliefs of Hinduism, a major theme of which is the life-giving energies: the male-female

6-23
(left) Detail of the Royal Portals, Chartres Cathedral, twelfth century.

6-24
(right) Detail of the Kandarya Mahadeva Temple, tenth–eleventh centuries.

6–25
Jacopo della Quercia,
*The Expulsion from
the Garden of Eden,*
c. 1430.
Istrian stone, 34" x 27".
Main portal,
San Petronio, Bologna.

principle. At times the female aspect, often personified by Shakti, is emphasized; at other times it is the male aspect, Siva, that is stressed. But the principle of wholeness always prevails, necessitating the union of male and female. In certain rites, sexual intercourse itself is considered a divine act whereby the participants become like Siva and Shakti, or god and goddess. Physical sensation and idea are fused, obliterating the divisions between mind and body, heaven and earth.

Chagall   The expression of love between the sexes is as strong in the work of the twentieth-century painter Marc Chagall as it is in the Kandarya sculptures, but it is expressed in a strictly monogamous context. Chagall and his wife Bella first met in their small home town in Russia, when he was about twenty-two. The daughter of a wealthy jeweller, Bella Rosenfeld was an emancipated young woman studying in Moscow. Marc, oldest son in the large family of a laborer, was a sensitive, shy, and somewhat eccentric young man

6–26 Marc Chagall, *To My Wife,* 1933–44. Oil on canvas, 51⅝" x 76⅜".
Musée National d'Art Moderne, Paris.

studying art in St. Petersburg. Though the two were from widely separated social classes, there existed between them such a harmony, or compatible chemistry (Chagall himself frequently uses the metaphor of chemistry to characterize relationships in art or people), that theirs was a truly ideal match.

Bella, perhaps to prove that she was beautiful, posed in the nude for her new boyfriend. Chagall delighted in this enterprise but was so overwhelmed that he did not use the opportunity for making advances. Although Marc and Bella were clearly infatuated with each other, they did not get married at the time, for in 1910 Chagall left for Paris to continue his studies.

The meeting between the young Russian artist and the City of Light had much the same chemistry as that earlier encounter with Bella. Chagall was ecstatic over the world's most cosmopolitan city, which was the undisputed capital of art. As though predestined, the awkward Russian emigrant gravitated toward the work of the best and the most progressive artists, who were at the time revolutionizing the world of art. By 1914 he had already established a reputation, and that year he exhibited in Berlin before returning to Russia.

Despite objections from both families, especially the Rosenfelds, Marc and Bella were married in 1915. Chagall painted several works on the subject of love shortly before and after his marriage. In *Double Portrait with Wineglass* (colorplate II), the fantasy come true is shown with Marc, literally intoxicated with happiness, sitting on the shoulders of his wife, and their newborn child hovering angel-like over both. Logic and the forces of gravity are vanquished by their private happiness. Floating figures are common in Chagall's works; in this one they specifically symbolize the flight of lovers, the buoyancy of the human spirit blessed with marital happiness.

In 1944, while the couple was in America, Bella suddenly died. *To My Wife* (fig. 6-26), a painting that he finished at that time, became a summation of their life together. Into it Chagall brought many elements familiar in much of his work, elements that derive intimately from his fantasies and private experiences. A goat, several musicians, an angel, a clock, and the couple themselves are shown against a background of houses from their native village. There can be little doubt that many of these images echo Chagall's early years as a member of a mystical Jewish sect whose followers lived in communion with God by rejoicing, singing, and dancing as well as praying.

Dominating the picture is the image of Bella, resplendently nude—the dearest memory of all to the sorrowing Chagall. Above her body is a bouquet of lilacs, a motif he had used in earlier works about lovers, but which here has an added connotation of mourning; written on the curtain above the bouquet is the inscription *à ma femme*, to my wife.

Chagall's art is an extension of his private world, a world that freely united the real and the unreal, the present and the past, the sacred and the profane. At times it seems to show a remarkable kinship with the sculptures of Kandarya Mahadeva, but the passion of Chagall's visual poetry was dedicated to the love of a single person, and to the physical and spiritual celebration found in a genuine monogamous union.

Kokoschka   A contemporary of Chagall, Oskar Kokoschka, painted *The Tempest* (fig. 6-27) in 1914, at almost the same time as *Double Portrait with Wineglass*. And like Chagall's painting, it is a young man's artistic response to a personal experience with love. When we look at the painting, several other parallels suggest themselves: for example, the pair of lovers in *The Tempest* also seems to be floating. In fact, the German title is *Die Windsbraut*—literally, ''the bride of the wind''—which would be an apt name for Bella, whose figure floats in so many of Chagall's works. And like the earlier Chagall painting, *The Tempest* is a double portrait of the artist and a particular woman.

Kokoschka's three-year love affair with Alma Mahler—daughter of an artist, widow of a famous composer, and one of the most beautiful women in Vienna—nearly destroyed him. The double trauma of passionate romance and high society was too much for Kokoschka; love, hate, ecstasy, fear, and above all, disillusionment were mingled in the relationship, which was broken up by the First World War. Kokoschka's poetry during the period refers to the turmoil—like the color and forms in his painting—that threatened to engulf his identity and creativity.

6–27   Oskar Kokoschka, *The Tempest,* 1914. Oil on canvas, 71¼" x 87". Kunstmuseum, Basel.

We could speak of both Chagall's *Wineglass* and Kokoschka's *Tempest* as being emotional paintings: the Chagall is intoxicated with joy and the Kokoschka is very agitated. But the kinds of passion presented in the two pictures are quite different. The spirit of *The Tempest* is heavy and turbid, like a gathering storm that has not yet released its fury. Where Chagall's lovers seem as emancipated from the pull of gravity as a kite on a spring day, Kokoschka's couple is neither airborne nor firmly on the ground. The man's face in *The Tempest* reveals neither joy nor satisfaction but the glazed expression of someone who might be deep in thought. In both of the Chagall paintings the love of a man for a woman is without reservations, while Kokoschka's work contains, at best, an ambivalent attitude toward sexual love—more feverish than truly passionate, more desperate than happy, restless rather than satisfied. The theme of Chagall's *To My Wife* has to do with loss, the artist's loss brought about by the physical death of his beloved wife; *The Tempest* also hints at this, but it is more specifically the loss of the relationship itself.

Summary

Of all the subject matter available to the artist, perhaps none has proved more universally and consistently appealing than the human body. Whether as an ideal form or as the portrait of a particular person, it has been viewed and treated differently by the artists of every age. Simply looking at the way in which a naked body was represented can tell us as much about an age as all the objects, clothing, and other things recorded in the work. Style and content tell us whether the people of a given time believed that a man should be athletic or elegant, or whether a woman was considered a piece of decorative property or an object of worship. The relationship between the sexes is often expressed indirectly in these works, but it has much less frequently been the subject matter of art. To be sure, a hidden trove of sexually explicit works produced by artists great and small does exist, but these works are rarely meant to be more than stimulating or amusing. Only in rare cases—such as the Indian temple carvings—has the sexual relationship been treated in a religious way. Western art, needless to say, has had very little of this. Only in the twentieth century has it become possible for artists like Chagall and Kokoschka to come to terms with the sexual as well as the emotional ties between men and women, and to express them with joy or sorrow or whatever emotion they evoke.

7

Four
Artists

The lives of the four artists discussed in this chapter span nearly five centuries of Western history and represent very different artistic, social, and religious points of view. But these artists also had a number of things in common.

For one thing, their names are four of the best known in the history of art, and their works have continued to maintain prominence in the public mind long after their deaths. For another, their artistic careers were marked by a drive to seek new expressive possibilities within the art of their time or, sometimes, a new artistic language altogether. The search was often fueled by a need to express new ideas or meanings that their contemporaries were only dimly aware of. In some cases it led to a significant modification of the artistic traditions they had started with.

All four succeeded in evolving unique artistic statements that stood out sharply from those of their fellow artists. And, in different ways, all four suffered for their rebellion and uniqueness. In every case, the problems related to their artistic careers were compounded by serious personal problems.

These similarities help to make the vast differences between them meaningful. These differences have to do with not only their art but their relationship with the public, the various intellectual, religious and political issues that involved them, and the challenges they faced when rebelling against established ways of thinking.

Michelangelo (1475–1564)

Michelangelo Buonarroti's early life was spent in Florence, Italy, at a time when that city was at the peak of its glory as the principal artistic and intellectual center of Renaissance Europe. It was there that the famous circle of gifted writers and artists gathered around Lorenzo "The Magnificent," the greatest patron of all the Medicis and the ruler of Florence at the time.

Michelangelo discovered at an early age that he preferred sculpture. His earliest training in that medium was under a sculptor named Bertoldo, who conducted his classes in the splendid Medici Gardens. There the fifteen-year-old Michelangelo not only learned something about his craft and explored the many classical sculptures of the Gardens but also had the opportunity to talk with some of the humanist scholars and poets of Lorenzo's circle. It was because of their influence that he himself became a scholar of classical and early Renaissance writings. He also became an enthusiastic follower of *Neoplatonism*, a synthesis of Greek and Christian beliefs and a major intellectual movement in Renaissance Italy. Indeed, Michelangelo's artistic development was in many ways more influenced by the ideas he gained from his contact with Lorenzo's scholars than by the training he received from Bertoldo.

The Early Pietà

When he was about twenty-five years old, Michelangelo was commissioned to sculpt a Pietà—an image of the Virgin Mary holding the dead Jesus—for a chapel in St. Peter's Basilica (fig. 7-1). In spite of its sorrowful subject matter, the Pietà's beauty and technical mastery are stronger than its suggestion of pathos. The limp body of Christ, slumped in the heavy folds of the Virgin's skirt, has the graceful proportions of a slender Apollo. The heroic figure of Mary is too large—perhaps larger than the figure of Christ—and too youthful to be the mother of a thirty-three-year-old man. The artist's goal, however, was not objective realism but the harmonious relationship of the two figures—which meant that Mary had to be larger than usual—and the expression of an ideal, a Neoplatonic Mother of God who is as beautiful as she is tender.

The qualities of idealization, monumentality, and harmony found in the *Pietà* were beginning to be reflected in the works of other leading Italian artists of the time, particularly Leonardo da

7-1
Michelangelo, *Pietà*,
1498–1500.
Marble, 5'9" high.
Saint Peter's, Rome.

Vinci, who was a generation older than Michelangelo. In the famous *Mona Lisa* (fig. 5-9), Leonardo's aim was to make an idealized portrait in which the foreground figure harmonized with its landscape background. But a sketch of a group of figures, *The Virgin and Child with Saint Anne and the Infant Saint John* (fig. 7-2), serves as a better example to compare with the *Pietà*. Da Vinci endowed each of the women and children with the handsome proportions and noble bearing of Greek statues, and, by giving careful attention to the postition and movement of each figure, saw to it that they all related to one another as a group—united by a single flow of rhythmic movement.

But the beautiful *Pietà*, which established Michelangelo's reputation as the leading sculptor in Italy, is not typical of his later work. Although the later pieces often consist of idealized figures, they also contain elements that tend to contradict the sense of harmony characteristic of the *Pietà* and other art of the period. These elements were already present in his statue of David (fig. 6-7), which was commissioned by the city fathers of Florence in 1501, the same year the *Pietà* was finished. This work's intensity and defi-

7–2
Leonardo da Vinci,
cartoon for *The Virgin and Child
with St. Anne and the Infant St. John,*
c. 1498. Charcoal heightened with white
on brown paper, approx. 54" x 39".
Reproduced by courtesy
of the Trustees of the National Gallery,
London.

ance symbolize the civic virtues and the force and anger needed to arouse the courage of the citizens in their struggle for liberty. But these qualities are also signs of the artist's own ferocity of spirit (his contemporaries referred to it as *terribilitá*), which was to show up more and more in his art as time went on.

There has been a great deal of speculation about the links between the events of Michelangelo's life, his personality, and his work. He was certainly a man of paradoxes: a servant of the Medicis and a follower of Savonarola, the fiery monk who denounced the Medicis and their culture; a passionate admirer of physical beauty who was ashamed of his own body; a devout Catholic who was enthusiastic about pagan art and ideas; and a celebrated artist who was withdrawn and alienated from those around him. Some scholars allude to events of his early childhood to explain these paradoxes; others believe that he suffered from repressed homosexuality. But all agree that his life was torn with neurotic conflict and that this generated an enormous amount of creative energy as well as being the source of some of the restless and disturbing qualities that make his work so fascinating.

7–4
Michelangelo,
ceiling of the Sistine Chapel,
1508–12.

The Sistine Ceiling

In 1505, Michelangelo was summoned to Rome by the ambitious and powerful Pope Julius II to build a grandiose tomb. But soon after the artist started work on the project, the Pope lost interest in it and began instead to pressure him to paint a fresco on the immense ceiling of the Sistine Chapel (fig. 7-3). Michelangelo, after protesting that he was a sculptor and not a painter, reluctantly accepted the commission in 1508 and started what was to be his greatest enterprise.

The work required four years. Lying on his back atop a scaffold some sixty-five feet above the floor, Michelangelo painted a fresco of more than seven hundred square yards (fig. 7-4). Just the painting itself was an awesome technical feat, but the concept and the scope of the ideas are equally awesome. Using the story of Genesis as his basic source and the human figure as his principal means of expression, he constructed a complex interpretation of the Judeo-Christian Creation liberally infused with Greek ideas.

The episodes of Genesis are chronicled in a series of nine rectangular panels running down the center—the crown of the ceiling—beginning with scenes of the Creation and ending with the drama of the Flood. God, who appears in each of the Creation panels, is represented by two figures in the *Creation of the Sun and*

7–3
Interior of the
Sistine Chapel,
Vatican, Rome.

Moon (colorplate 12). Both of the figures have the pagan body of Zeus, chief of all the Greek gods, but the face of the figure on the right does not have the distant stare of a Greek statue, the classical calm that we expect of a Greek god. Instead it has the fierce look—full of holiness and wrath—that we often associate with the Old Testament God.

Occupying the narrow spaces between the central panels are naked youths, whose roles in this work are something like those of angels. Flanking the panels on all four sides of the ceiling is a series of large figures—the biblical prophets and pagan sibyls who predicted the coming of Christ—each seated within a shallow niche. Between the prophets and sibyls are lunettes (triangular spaces directly above the chapel's arched windows) containing the kings and queens of Judah, the ancestors of Christ. The larger lunettes at the corners contain events from the Old Testament that are believed to have foreshadowed Christ's crucifixion.

Perhaps the most impressive thing about the Sistine Chapel ceiling is the sense of order that Michelangelo managed to impose on it. No work in the history of art can compare with it for scope, conception, or sheer expressive power. Over three hundred figures populate the space, drawn to several different scales. Worlds are being created and destroyed. Christian, Jewish, and Neoplatonic themes intermingle. Yet the artist has managed to contain it all, using every bit of the inconveniently parceled space to further his ends, dividing it up into an architectonic arrangement of rectangular and triangular spaces that lend order to the complex narrative and symbolic components as well.

The Last Judgment

Twenty years later, Michelangelo was prevailed upon by one of Julius's successors, Paul III, to paint an interpretation of the Last Judgment on the altar wall of the same chapel. By now the artist was nearly sixty, and, in addition to the trials of aging, he was depressed by the deterioration of the world around him. The foundations of the Catholic Church were being threatened by the Protestant Reformation; Rome, the home of the Church, had been sacked and laid waste seven years earlier by Spanish and German soldiers; and the Medicis had been forced to leave Florence, only to return as tyrants who eradicated its freedoms. Meanwhile, Michelangelo had involved himself in too many projects. He was harrassed from all sides by those who commissioned him, including the executors for Pope Julius, who were still trying to get him to

7-5 Michelangelo, *The Last Judgment,* altar wall of the Sistine Chapel, 1534–41. Fresco, approx. 43′ high.

7-6
Michelangelo,
detail of fig. 7-5
with "self-portrait."

7-7
Michelangelo,
Pietà Rondanini, c. 1555–64.
Marble, 77½" high.
Castello Sforzesco, Milan.

finish the tomb. It would appear that Michelangelo's mounting frustrations were released in all their fury in his painting of *The Last Judgment* (fig. 7-5).

Rather than Christ the Redeemer, Michelangelo's *Last Judgment* portrays Christ the Avenger—whose image discourages any interpretation other than one of fear and despair. And rather than a vision of human beings as a divine creation, there is a dark and pessimistic view of them as being virtually incapable of achieving grace. The saved are not easily distinguished from the damned, for neither group looks happy or possesses the physical beauty that characterizes the creatures on the ceiling. Once again the human body is naked—and even larger and more muscular than before—but this time it is brutish rather than heroic, base rather than glorious. The scene is a thunderous vision of doom, an unrestrained *terribilitá*. Clumps of twisting flesh whirl around the angry Christ as souls are wrenched from the earth (in the lower left) to be lofted before Christ, who decides which are to remain with him and which are to be dragged struggling into hell (in the lower right) where devils and figures from Greek mythology await them. Finally, there is a sign of Michelangelo's own sense of guilt—as well as of his perverse sense of humor—to be seen in his self-portrait, the flayed skin held by the martyred St. Bartholomew (fig. 7-6).

The structure of the *Last Judgment*, like its content, is a turmoil of unevenly distributed clusters of figures arching around the central figure of Christ. When we compare this with the ceiling—with its balance of figures and spaces and its rectangular, ordered composition—we become aware not only of the vast difference between the two works but of the extent to which Michelangelo had gone in breaking with the values of his earlier art.

The achievements of Michelangelo were legendary throughout Europe even during his lifetime—which lasted for another twenty-five years after the completion of *The Last Judgment*. But rather than simply bask in his celebrity he continued his prodigious work (including, in addition to murals and sculptures, several significant architectural projects).

The Last Pietà   Michelangelo's last sculpture was, once again, a Pietà (fig. 7-7). These two sculptures offer interesting contrasts as landmarks at either end of a difficult artistic and spiritual journey. Whereas the first was a celebration of beauty, the last is an expression of death—a requiem in stone made by an artist who was personally close to death. Its unpolished surfaces and unfinished figures are, of course, partly the result of a faltering hand and an aging spirit, but they are also the result of a religious beatitude at the end of a long and very troubled life. Michelangelo's struggle was finally over.

Between the two Pietàs, Michelangelo's substantial reputation had come about more because of his painting than because of his sculpture—although sculpture was his preferred medium. The

7–8
Peter Paul Rubens,
*St. Ignatius Exorcising
Demons from the Church,*
1619.
Oil on canvas, 17′6½″ x 12′11½″.
Kunsthistorisches Museum,
Vienna.

Sistine ceiling enlarged the concept of the heroic in art and showed how the human figure could convey energy and drama. *The Last Judgment* demonstrated that great art did not have to be beautiful and that the figure could convey terror. Michelangelo dealt with the most august themes of Western culture, and gave them visual forms that left a lasting impression.

Rembrandt (1606–1669)

The Dutch Republic of the early seventeenth century—a union of cities in the northern Netherlands—had recently achieved independence from Spain. Among other things, self-determination had meant economic opportunity and religious freedom for the mainly Protestant population of the tiny nation. Taking advantage of the Netherlands' ports and seafaring history, the hard-working Calvinist traders proceeded to dominate the oceans and establish commercial relations in all parts of the world—including the Far East and America. Amsterdam, which was an insignificant fishing village in the fifteenth century, became in many ways the Florence of the seventeenth century. By the time Rembrandt van Rijn was born (in Leiden, the second city of the Netherlands at the time), Amsterdam was the richest and most powerful city in the Dutch Republic and the commercial metropolis of the world.

Dutch art at the time that Rembrandt came of age was almost completely outside the seventeenth-century mainstream. There were, basically, two schools of art in Holland at the time. One, called the Italian school because the artists studied in Italy, was partial to historical or religious subjects filled with posturing, idealized bodies and impressive settings. Its roots went back to the High Renaissance (and the works of Michelangelo) and its principal counterpart internationally was the Baroque art of the Catholic countries, a style magnificently exemplified by the Flemish painter Rubens (fig. 7-8). The other was the emerging Dutch school, which favored the portrayal of everyday life in the form of household objects, down-to-earth people, and landscapes—subject matter that is commonly referred to as *genre*.

The patrons of Protestant Holland were not the Dutch Reformed Church—which refused to harbor art in its buildings—but individual people, particularly well-to-do burghers who found comfort in the images of genre painting and therefore created a demand for it. Yet there were also many patrons and artists in Holland who still admired the Italian school, among them Rembrandt's teacher Pieter Lastman. Rembrandt, of course, was influenced by elements of both schools, but his own work lacked the exaggeration and idealization of the Baroque style and the trivial content of genre. He was, in a sense, out of step with both of the principal alternatives of the art of his day. Unlike most genre painters, he persisted in making religious pictures; unlike Baroque painters, he endowed his religious pictures with a simplicity and realism characteristic of genre art.

Some believe Rembrandt's interest in the Bible was inspired by his mother. If so, it was strengthened and given some artistic direction by Lastman, who liked to do biblical subjects. Whatever the reasons, Rembrandt created a great many paintings, prints, and drawings that could be thought of as biblical illustrations. Unlike Michelangelo's religious interpretations, Rembrandt's did not depict larger-than-life beings inhabiting an abstract world but ordinary-looking people living in a concrete, personal world familiar to all of us—a Protestant conception that emphasizes the personal relationship between God and the lives of human beings.

7-9   Rembrandt van Rijn, *The Blinding of Samson,* 1636. Oil on canvas, 93" x 119".
Staedelisches Kunstinstitut, Frankfurt.

The Blinding   In some of his early biblical paintings, Rembrandt displayed an
of Samson   affinity for heightened effects that was reminiscent of Baroque art.
But the theatrical elements of Rembrandt's religious dramas were
derived from realism, lighting, and a vivid imagination rather than
from superhuman figures and grandiose gesturing. The ten-foot-
long *Blinding of Samson* (fig. 7-9) is alleged to have been made to
please one of Rembrandt's patrons, Constantyn Huygens, who had
a taste for violence and horror. Huygens was probably not disap-
pointed, for Rembrandt portrayed the savagery of the attack with a
forcefulness and terror that few of his contemporaries would have
dared to match. The scene is in the tent of Delilah, who is fleeing
with Samson's hair as soldiers wrestle him to the ground and
commit the atrocity. The terrible agony of the stabbing is seen not
only in Samson's face but his entire body, arching and kicking—
even the toes are clenched with pain.

Violence, moreover, is expressed by the picture's strong diago-
nals: the figure of the soldier on the left, his spear, the flaps of the

tent, the figure of Delilah, Samson's right leg, and the alignment of the metal-clad soldiers, almost all of which point to Samson's face. The major means of creating dramatic effect and focusing attention is the contrast of light and dark. The greatest area of this contrast is around Samson's body and face, as if the ugly act were starkly exposed by the glare of a spotlight shining through the tent opening. In addition to highlighting the victim, the glare silhouettes the soldier with the spear. The fleeing Delilah, on the edge of the light, appears somewhat spectral while the soldiers, defined chiefly by the highlights on their armor, are partially concealed in the murky shadows.

The Night Watch   Rembrandt's greatest period of personal happiness and professional success was the decade of the 1630s. After moving his studio from Leiden to Amsterdam he obtained several important commissions, enjoyed the esteem of the social world of the latter city, and married Saskia van Ulenburgh, the daughter of a wealthy burgomaster. By the end of the decade he was the most celebrated painter in Holland, and was wealthy enough to make a down payment on a spacious house in Amsterdam. But the year 1642 proved to be a turning point in his career and for his family.

In that year, Rembrandt completed a major work, a group portrait of the civic guard under Captain Cocq that came to be known as *The Night Watch* (colorplate 13). Not content merely to use the traditional solution of portraying the company of men sitting in rows around a banquet table, Rembrandt decided to show them at the moment of being called to parade formation. Caught in the act of hasty preparation, each figure is doing something different—cleaning a musket, hoisting a banner, grabbing a halberd, or scurrying to position. Each also seems to be wearing something different; their "uniforms" are a conglomeration of colors, lace collars, embroidery, chain mail, sashes, plumed hats, and metal helmets. To add to the tumult, Rembrandt included a few strays: a boy dashing off to the left, a girl bathed in an eerie light (and carrying a chicken and a dagger on her belt) in the middle left, and a barking dog on the right. Yet in spite of the confusion, each man's face is at least partly visible—and, supposedly, a faithful likeness.

The Night Watch surpassed its simple portrait function and came to be regarded as the most exciting work of Rembrandt's middle period and one of the greatest paintings in the history of art. It is a truly heroic piece—not in the sense associated with Michelangelo of superhuman theme and scale but in a swashbuckling sense—full of pomp, fanfare, and martial splendor. One can almost hear the shuffle of boots and the clang of metal. It is also full of movement, demonstrating the artist's remarkable inventiveness and his ability to record a variety of gestures. At the same time, it is full of enough contradiction—the chaos of actions, the oddities of dress, the presence of the girl—to endow it with a certain amount of mystery and poetry and to make it something more than a picture of a military company.

Augmenting the drama, movement, and even the sense of mystery is Rembrandt's employment of light and dark, which serves here, as in the Samson painting, to structure the whole composition. The hour of the scene is probably late afternoon rather than night (the nocturnal appearance is due to the darkening of the layers of varnish), but the lighting does not conform to the rays of the sun. It conforms instead to the pictorial needs of emphasis and balance and the expressive needs of mood and excitement. The eye, guided by the distribution of light and dark, focuses on the two officers in the foreground and scans the fascinating throng of men behind them.

The painting, for all its virtues, was not well received by everyone. Apparently some of the men in the company, who had paid a hundred guilders apiece for it, were dissatisfied with their lack of visibility. Others were critical of the painting's unconventional characteristics. While Rembrandt's reputation did not plummet because of *The Night Watch*, it was undoubtedly hurt by the public reaction.

A Self-Portrait Still, Rembrandt never compromised his frank realism and his self-proclaimed right to paint a subject with the full freedom of his considerable imagination—no matter how idiosyncratic that imagination might be at times. This obstinacy—especially his refusal to flatter his portrait subjects—contributed to his continuing decline in popularity. The fact that he also refused to flatter himself was probably of little comfort to his public. A 1652 self-portrait (fig. 7-10), in which the artist appears at once defiant and vulnerable, is unsparing in its disclosure of the effects of aging and stress. It also reflects changes that had taken place in Rembrandt's art. The composition is simpler, the details and textures of the things represented are less emphatic, and the texture of the paint itself—

7–10
Rembrandt van Rijn,
Self-Portrait,
1652.
Oil on canvas,
45" x 32".
Kunsthistorisches Museum,
Vienna.

because of looser and broader brushwork—is more in evidence. Light is still the chief means of emphasizing objects and of focusing attention, but Rembrandt has used it differently. Instead of a spotlight for creating excitement, it is a tool for probing the subtler aspects of a subject's inner life and emotions as they are revealed in the face and body.

Commitment to his own artistic values, together with changes in taste on the part of the public, eventually led to Rembrandt's financial ruin. Seventeenth-century Holland was the first society to develop a system of patronage based on the middle class rather than the church or the courts. Arnold Hauser, a social historian of art, has explained that such a system helped Rembrandt's powers to grow because it gave him freedom to experiment. On the other hand, it did not provide the security of the former system, thereby causing him to lose everything when his popularity dropped.

Rembrandt's professional problems were further aggravated by the death of Saskia and then by the public disapproval of his living with Hendrickje Stoffels, a young servant girl with whom he fell in love about seven years after Saskia's death (and whom he could not marry, because he would have lost his former wife's estate). Surprisingly, none of his many problems affected the quantity of his production; he continued to paint in spite of deaths, lawsuits, and bankruptcy proceedings. His problems, however, seemed to have had the effect of making his work even more subdued and profound.

The Return of the Prodigal Son

Hendrickje died in 1662. Rembrandt himself was to live for only seven more years, during which time the prices of his works were absurdly low and he became financially destitute. In one of his last paintings, *The Return of the Prodigal Son* (fig. 7-11), there is a softness and an apparent tendency to de-materialize reality that is reminiscent of Michelangelo's later Pietà (fig. 7-7). The simplicity of the scene, without any distracting movement in the sacred stillness and halflight, allows the miracle of reunion to take place. Although leaving much unsaid, this painting effectively suggests the meaning of the parable and the significance of family bonds in general. The son surrendering himself to the tender embrace of his father summarizes the healing message of Christian pardon. The depth of feeling can be related to Rembrandt's own life, which saw the old artist outlive almost his entire family.

Rembrandt did not leave behind a family of artists, either. None of his students produced a significant body of work in his style and other artists of his time ignored it. By contrast, Rubens's grand style was extended and modified in the next century by a host of artistic heirs. Indeed, Rembrandt's work went relatively unnoticed until the nineteenth century, when its distinctive qualities were finally recognized and appreciated by the Romantics. But although Rubens's art is still respected today, it is not honored nearly as much as Rembrandt's, which has grown steadily in stature—and which now is appreciated more for its insights into human character than for its romantic qualities.

7-11 Rembrandt van Rijn, *The Return of the Prodigal Son, c.* 1665. Oil on canvas, 8'8" x 6'8¾". Hermitage Museum, Leningrad.

The artists of seventeenth-century Holland, discouraged by their Calvinistic religion from glorifying God or the church through art, turned to representing the world around them. So did Rembrandt, but unlike his countrymen, he also applied his remarkable gifts to the task of making gospel stories real and vivid. In his earlier work—both religious and secular—he aimed at dramatic effects that often required elaborate compositions. In his later work, he stressed the psychological aspects of his subjects in simpler, more restrained compositions. Perhaps because of the problems he faced in his own life, his later art was extremely penetrating in its portrayal of human feelings. When using a story from the Bible, Rembrandt was able to express its religious content in a very human way. His later work constitutes a rare—perhaps the greatest—collection of artistic interpretations of the Scriptures from the Protestant perspective.

7–12 Vincent van Gogh, *The Potato Eaters,* 1885. Oil on canvas,
32¼″ x 44⅞″. Vincent van Gogh Collection, Stedelijk Museum, Amsterdam.

Van Gogh
(1853–1890)

In the eighteenth century, Holland's influence among the nations
of Europe began to decline sharply. By the middle of the nineteenth century, after a series of disastrous struggles with England
on the seas and France on land—including French control from
1795 to 1813—Holland's importance as an international power
and Amsterdam's influence as a major city were severly reduced.
In art, especially, Holland was a provincial country.

Vincent van Gogh, the son of a Protestant minister from the
North Brabant province of Holland, decided to become an artist at
the relatively late age of twenty-seven. He had already failed as an
art dealer (in a business owned by his relatives), a theological
student, and an evangelist. His failures were not due to incompe-
tence but to a chronic inability to relate to people and to periodic
outbursts of emotion followed by self-recrimination. Theories about
his mental disorders vary from epilepsy to cerebral tumor and from

schizophrenia to turpentine poisoning, but regardless of the explanation, his life consisted of alternating, almost unbearable, extremes of feeling that were barely concealed by his outer behavior and dealings with others. Immersing himself in something—first religion, then art—was a way of overcoming his loneliness and avoiding complete mental chaos.

As both artist and former evangelist, Vincent often looked to the works of Rembrandt for inspiration, feeling "there is something of Rembrandt in the Gospel, or something of the Gospel in Rembrandt." To Van Gogh, the seventeenth-century master, more than anyone else, had blended art and religion, making them virtually synonomous; and, like Rembrandt, he sought to express his feelings of compassion and tenderness through depictions of common people.

The Potato Eaters   Van Gogh's first important work, *The Potato Eaters* (fig. 7-12), painted in 1885 when he was thirty-two, summarizes his thinking and artistic direction at the time. There is a significant difference in approach between Van Gogh and Rembrandt—indeed between Van Gogh and almost all other artists up to that time. Rembrandt conveyed emotion through realistic depictions that were based on his profound understanding of human nature. Van Gogh expressed emotion primarily through line, color, the texture of the paint, and the distortions of some of the shapes. In *The Potato Eaters*, the emotional focus is not just on the humble peasants and their existence as it is depicted, but also on the earthy, lumpy qualities of their forms. The painting itself, as Van Gogh explained, is "like the color of a very dusty potato."

Even after finding his vocation in art, Van Gogh's behavior did not change enough to keep him from having periodic emotional crises or getting in trouble with the people around him. He moved often, living with this relative or visiting that one, and spending some time studying art in both Holland and Belgium. Through it all he received financial support from his brother Theo, who had become an art dealer in Paris. In 1886, deciding that the environment of the Netherlands was physically, intellectually, and emotionally stifling, he went to Paris to join Theo and to gain what he could from what was then the world's most progressive center of art.

At first that city was a tonic for Van Gogh's spirits. In the gallery where Theo worked and in Fernand Cormon's studio, where Vin-

7–13
Hokusai,
The Great Wave,
from *Thirty-Six Views
of Mt. Fuji,*
Tokugawa period.
Woodcut, 10″ x 14¾″.
Museum of Fine Arts,
Boston.

cent studied, he met many of the younger and more advanced artists. His style was influenced by the lighter, brighter colors favored by Impressionists like Monet (colorplate 19) and the flat and precise designs of Japanese prints (fig. 7-13), with which nearly everyone in the Paris art world was fascinated. For a while his temperament improved, perhaps because his feelings of being an outcast were overcome by his being a part of the lively crowd of artistic rebels (including such people as Gauguin and Toulouse-Lautrec). But he soon wearied of Paris as tensions grew between him and Theo and his bouts of melancholy returned. In February of 1888—perhaps on the suggestion of Toulouse-Lautrec, who wanted to get rid of him—Van Gogh left for Arles, a small city in the south of France.

View of Arles

The two-year period that Van Gogh spent in southern France was the most brilliant in his short life as an artist. Like the Paris episode, that of Arles started out happily—even more so. The fresh air and warmth of that first spring had a good effect on his art and, at least for a time, his feelings about life. Each painting of orchards, fields, drawbridges, and the like tended to suggest optimism rather than pessimism. *View of Arles with Irises in the Foreground* (fig. 7-14), painted in May, is a celebration of spring and an affirmation of life in general. The strong colors and bold shapes that are woven together by thick, lively brushstrokes not only convey the radiance of spring but reveal the artistic self-confidence Vincent had acquired in only eight years. Every form—iris, buttercup, tree, building—is brilliantly delineated from inside to outside, with each brushstroke doing the job of drawing as well as painting. *View of Arles*, like so many paintings that he made in his first months there, demonstrates that Van Gogh, in spite of his tendency to become depressed, could make very positive paintings. Southern France in the spring had brought out his enthusiasm for life; according to one art historian, "the painting of Arles was a return to Eden."

The Night Cafe   *The Night Cafe* (colorplate 14), painted in September of the same year, characterizes another side of this region as well as Van Gogh's changing feelings about it. The city of Arles, according to many witnesses of the time, was a miserable working-class town full of taverns, brothels, and people who were prone to violence. Van Gogh's painting is of the inside of one of the taverns that stayed open all night as a refuge for night-prowlers, the Cafe de l'Alcazar. It is a taut, unreal environment, a nighttime scene

7–14   Vincent van Gogh, *View of Arles with Irises,* 1888.
Oil on canvas, 21¼" x 25½". Vincent van Gogh Collection, Stedelijk Museum, Amsterdam.

flooded with an unearthly light that suggests frustrations and tensions. The acrid colors—citron yellow in the lamps and floor, chartreuse in the pool table, bar, and ceiling, and blood red in the walls—clash with one another, and their violence, along with that of the exaggerated perspective, contradicts the sullen, eerie stillness. Van Gogh wrote, ''I have tried to express the idea that the cafe is a place where one can ruin oneself, go mad, commit a crime.''

In that same month, Vincent also made a self-portrait (fig. 7-15). Like the *View of Arles*, it has a tapestrylike system of brush-strokes that define the structure of head, face, neck, and clothing. The same lively paint texture animates the background by forming a whorl around the subject's head. At the same time, this consistent textural treatment tends to reinforce the face's staring expression as well as the severity of the facial features and closely shaved head. Like *The Night Cafe*, Van Gogh's self-portrait has a tautness that suggests the barely controlled tensions of a man who could ''ruin himself, go mad, commit a crime.''

That fall, Paul Gauguin had arrived in Arles at the invitation of Van Gogh, who hoped that the two would form the nucleus of a brotherhood of artists—a dream Van Gogh had had since Paris. He admired, even worshiped, Gauguin, who was a mystic, adventurer,

7–15
Vincent van Gogh,
Self-Portrait, 1888.
Oil on Canvas,
24½" x 20½".
The Fogg Art Museum,
Harvard University
(bequest—collection
Maurice Wertheim,
Class of 1906).

7–16   Vincent van Gogh, *The Starry Night,* 1889. Oil on canvas, 29" x 36¼".
The Museum of Modern Art, New York (acquired through the Lillie P. Bliss Bequest).

and notorious debauchee as well as a potentially important painter in the modern movement. Unfortunately, Gauguin either could not or would not return Van Gogh's admiration, and his instinct for sarcasm and provocation found an easy target in the sensitive younger artist. The circumstances of their association led to a series of nervous breakdowns for Van Gogh, including the now-legendary story of his cutting off an earlobe and presenting it to a prostitute on Christmas Eve of 1888. From this time on, he was in and out of hospitals until he commited suicide in the summer of 1890.

The Starry Night   During this time, however, he never ceased to paint and draw. Much of his work from this period, not surprisingly, is even more subjective and charged with even greater energy than his earlier pieces. *The Starry Night* (fig. 7-16), painted from the window of his room in the hospital at St. Rémy-de-Provence, is overflowing with excited forms. At the lower right is a village sheltered by the mountains and dominated by a church spire reminiscent of those in Holland. Commanding the left side is the flamelike shape of a huge cypress tree, an ancient symbol of death, which extends from bottom to top, overlapping the dramatic sky, the main feature of the picture. The town is painted with short, measured strokes, and is relatively quiet; the tree is painted with long, thick, serpentine strokes and is much more restless; the sky, a phantasmagoria of celestial activity depicted with sweeps and spirals of thickly applied paint, represents the furthest stage of frenzy.

Like the late works of Michelangelo and Rembrandt, *The Starry Night* seems to reflect the thoughts and feelings of a man anticipating his own death. But here, reality has yielded to the artist's inner vision far more than it did in the late Pietà or *The Prodigal Son*. The painting stands on the edge of a period in which emotional content would be generated less through subject matter and symbols and more through the visual qualities of spontaneously created abstract forms.

Except for one favorable article appearing in a French magazine six months before his death, Vincent received very little recognition during his lifetime. Yet not many years after his death, he became a hero among the artists of the modern movement, many of whom were greatly inspired by his work. Although Van Gogh's style and approach influenced much of the art of the twentieth century, the spirit of his art is definitely a part of the same religious-humanistic tradition as that of Michelangelo and Rembrandt. His intense concern for life can be equated with the theological doctrine of immanence—God's love and presence in all things—which he expressed in a subjective style that transformed every person and object he included in his pictures.

Pollock (1912–1956)

During the early years of the Great Depression, Jackson Pollock studied art at the Art Students League in New York. Each summer he hitchhiked, rode freight trains, or drove an old jalopy across the country to his family's home in California. On the way he would do some sketching, but mostly he would observe the life of America, especially that of people whose lives had been broken by the Depression. His travels provided the opportunity to see the impressive murals then being painted by Mexican artists like José Clemente Orozco and to discover Indian sand painting—two things that undoubtedly influenced his later art.

7–17
Jackson Pollock,
Seascape, 1934.
Oil on canvas,
12″ x 16″.
Collection of
Lee Krasner Pollock,
New York.

Seascape   In 1934, Pollock painted *Seascape* (fig. 7-17), in which a tiny sailboat is nearly engulfed by a stormy sea that symbolizes the overwhelming forces of nature. Its content, along with its curvilinear forms and dark, brooding colors, is reminiscent of *Starry Night,* except that the Van Gogh work, for all its halucinatory energy, is much more disciplined. Although *Seascape* reflects some influence of the teachers at the Art Students League, it also has the robust brushwork and rhythms that were to characterize Pollock's mature paintings. His early works, like those of Van Gogh, did not attract very much attention outside of the artist's immediate circle of friends and relatives.

In 1935, Pollock signed on with the newly created Federal Arts Project—part of a relief program set up by the government for the purpose of creating jobs—as a member of a division that was supposed to create art for schools, post offices, and other public buildings. He remained with the project, with few interruptions, until 1943.

One of those interruptions had to do with a four-month hospital stay, for treatment of acute alcoholism, in 1938. No one is sure just when Pollock's drinking problem started, but by his mid-twenties he was an alcoholic. Moreover, he tended to become violent when drunk and was often involved in barroom fights, reckless driving, arrests, and generally agressive behavior. Like Van Gogh, he seemed to be on an emotional roller coaster with good

7–18 Joan Miró, *The Harlequin's Carnival*, 1924–25. Oil on canvas, 26" x 36⅝".
Albright-Knox Art Gallery, Buffalo, New York (Room of Contemporary Art Fund, 1940).

times followed by crashing lows; and when he was low, he drank. Otherwise, his personality was not like Van Gogh's; he did not have that artist's chronic inability to relate to people. When he was not drunk he was warm and likeable, even charming, and maintained several enduring friendships with both men and woman, among them the painter Lee Krasner, who later married him.

The late thirties and early forties were difficult and challenging times for young American artists. The social crises of the Depression and World War II were, of course, bad enough, but the real problem for artists was a kind of identity crisis. The relationships between American art and the nation and between American art and the international art world were inconsistent if not contradictory. *Regionalism* was the leading American movement of the time, but its old-fashioned realism, rural subject matter, and homespun values were inappropriate for a nation that was becoming increasingly involved in international affairs. European art, particularly that of Paris, seemed equally inappropriate. It was looked upon by some as effete, and American efforts to emulate it did not sell well or receive much critical attention. However, several important European artists had fled to America at the onset of World War II and had settled in New York. Pollock, among others, was stimulated by their presence and their ideas. But the direction of Ameri-

7-19   Jackson Pollock, *Pasiphae,* 1943. Oil on canvas, 56⅛" x 96".
Collection of Lee Krasner Pollock, New York.

can art—not only its form and content, but its potential role in American and world culture—was very much of an enigma at that time.

By 1940, Pollock had dropped what Regionalist tendencies he ever had, retaining at most the taste for vigorous curvilinear forms and interlocking compositions that he had inherited from Benton. He was becoming increasingly interested in the ideas and methods of European modernism—especially the work of such artists as Joan Miró (fig. 7-18)—and was being influenced by those European artists in New York who emphasized the function of the subconscious in making art. Another important influence was a series of sessions with a Jungian psychiatrist, who stimulated Pollock's interest in archetypes—basic images and ideas that are supposedly present in everyone's subconscious—and how these might be used and expressed in art.

Pasiphae *Pasiphae* (fig. 7-19) was painted when Pollock was thirty-one, about the same age as Van Gogh was when he painted *The Potato Eaters.* Pollock's painting represents his attempts up to this point to bring together the many themes of his life and artistic influences into a new artistic expression. The figurative images of earlier work had by this time been replaced by abstract signs and symbols,

7–20
Jackson Pollock,
Cathedral, 1947.
Oil, 75" x 35".
Dallas Museum of Fine Arts
(gift of Mr. and Mrs. Bernard J. Reis).

which can be related to ancient myths—as the title *Pasiphae* implies—or the Jungian subconscious. In addition, the opulence of its rhythms and colors contains an echo of the Mexican murals Pollock had seen in his earlier travels, while the calligraphic character of the lines reflects American Indian art. But this painting's most unique quality, a curious and compelling mixture of awkwardness and force—a sort of an American *terribilitá*—was what caught the attention of the New York art world.

The abstract signs and symbols of *Pasiphae* and other works of that period began to disappear in some of the paintings Pollock made in 1946. Consisting of freely painted, primarily circular brushstrokes, they implied an approach to painting that could be thought of as "automatic writing." In other words, the forms were produced spontaneously, rather than by conscious use of images or symbols.

Cathedral The following year, Pollock developed a new way of working that made the 1946 paintings appear restrained and inhibited by comparison. No one knows for sure how it came about—whether it was the influence of the Surrealist painter Roberto Matta, an accident, the result of a fit of frustration, or just one of those revelations that surface quietly, although unexpectedly. Pollock's revolutionary method? Not brushing the paint onto the canvas.

Cathedral (fig. 7-20), made with liquid Duco and aluminum paint, was one of the first made this way. The canvas was not fixed to a wooden frame and hung on an easel, but spread on the floor so that Pollock could walk around and across it and apply paint by dripping, spilling, splashing, and scraping. Not only had he dispensed with signs and symbols—indeed with form itself as it had been known up to this point—but also with the traditional techniques of painting. What remained was the art of pure freedom that he had been looking for. Beginning a painting with very little premeditation, he would develop it intuitively as he went along (fig. 7-21). According to Pollock:

> When I am *in* my painting, I'm not aware of what I'm doing. It is only after a sort of "get acquainted" period that I see what I have been about. I have no fears about making changes, destroying the image, etc., because the painting has a life of its own. I try to let it come through. It is only when I lose contact with the painting that the result is a mess. Otherwise there is pure harmony, an easy give and take, and the painting comes out well.

His new work was met with both praise and antagonism, but there was no question that Pollock was the artist that everyone was talking about—and "everyone" this time was more than just the tiny New York art world. In the fall of 1948, *Life* magazine devoted twenty-four pages to a "Round Table on Modern Art" in which, among other works, Pollock's *Cathedral* was discussed (and roundly defended by critic Clement Greenberg). A year later, *Life*

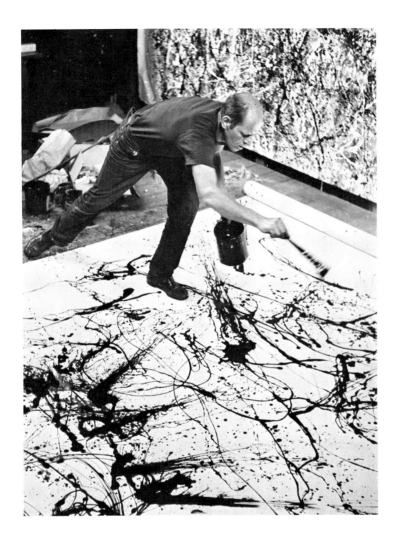

7-21
Jackson Pollock painting,
1950.

devoted an article just to him—"Jackson Pollock: Is He the Greatest Living Painter in the United States?"—with photos of him
working in his barn-studio. In the days before the omnipresence of
television, an article in *Life* was the ultimate in mass-media cover-
age. How did Americans respond to Jackson Pollock? Having very
little knowledge of modern art, they were startled by his radical
paintings and working methods and also—as Pollock's biographer,
B.H. Friedman, points out—impressed with his image as "a new,
non-arty American-style painter."

One   Some people denounced paintings like the enormous *One* (colorplate 15) as chaotic and unintelligible, but many others recognized
what Pollock called "pure harmony." They were also moved by the

scale of such works, which filled the viewers' visual space and made them feel a part of the work—as Pollock himself did when he made *One*. At the same time, the colors and tones reminded viewers of the natural environment, although without reference to a specific landscape. Because Pollock's work was unfamiliar, it allowed people from different backgrounds to read into it almost anything they wished. Marxists saw the gestural lines as radical signs of social protest; Existentialists related them to Pollock's search for a personal form of expression; others connected them with the artist's western origins and the mythology of cowboys. But they all recognized in the painting's dancing lines and rhythms a radical new art of total spontaneity.

In spite of his fame, Pollock did not prosper financially or emotionally. The work of the ''shining new phenomenon in American art,'' as *Life* referred to him, did not sell very well. The actual market for abstract art—especially in his day—has always been small in America, and after expenses and dealers' commissions the Pollocks had very little left over. In addition to a serious lack of money, Pollock experienced a certain amount of critical backlash along with the inevitable pressures of being in the spotlight. *Time*, for example, referred to him as ''Jack the Dripper,'' and even Greenberg, who had been a strong supporter, cooled toward his later work. In the last two years of Pollock's life, his drinking problem became more acute than ever and his artistic production almost stopped completely. He died at the age of forty-four when the car he was driving crashed into some trees not far from his home.

Pollock was an important force in bringing American art out of its cultural isolation and into a position of world leadership, where it has been ever since. Regarding this achievement, a fellow painter once said that Pollock had ''broken the ice'' for other American abstract artists. Indeed, some believe that Pollock's success inspired and influenced other aspects of the progressive culture of the 1950s—the Beat Generation's poetry, cool jazz, and other forms of fine and popular art—whose emphasis on the artist's personal freedom and improvisation was similar to that of Abstract Expressionism. Pollock's work reflects the modern obsession with the person's own inner life. By a leap of insight, he developed the idea of painting as a pure psychological event, supposedly eliminating the gap between the subjective world of the artist's thinking and feeling and the objective world of paint and canvas.

Summary   From Michelangelo to Pollock, we have seen a trend away from religious content or, at least, a progressive modification of that content. Almost all of Michelangelo's subjects were religious; Rembrandt's were both secular and religious; Van Gogh's were nearly all secular—although most had some religious significance. Pollock's art was not religious at all, at least not in the traditional sense.

We have also seen a progressively stronger emphasis on the individual personality. Although Michelangelo's art was intensely emotional—and to that extent reflective of his personality—its content had to do with major theological issues, and its emotional qualities were intended to relate to those issues and not to the artist's or anyone else's personality. By the time of Pollock, however, the emotional qualities of the work were not simply reflective of the artist's personality but supposedly a direct result of his subjective state at the time the painting was made.

Considered within their own time periods, the four artists have some things in common. Like all other artists, they started their careers within the available art styles and themes of their time, but unlike most others, they challenged tradition. In each case they were successful, but the measure of their success was not always immediately apparent. Both Michelangelo and Pollock lived to see the impact of their ideas on the art of others. Rembrandt experienced success early in his career only to see his work actually decline in value—its rebirth in popularity coming long after his death. Van Gogh never received recognition from more than a small group during his lifetime.

Finally, all four experienced various crises in their artistic careers and personal lives. Was this an important factor in their art? According to scholar of mythology Joseph Campbell, suffering is revered in nearly all the world's myths and religions as a positive experience leading to significant revelation. He quotes, as an example, this statement by an Eskimo shaman: "Privation and suffering alone can open the mind to all that is hidden in others." In many ways, the creative artists are the shamans of our own culture, for the sentiment expressed in the line above echoes those of a poem by Michelangelo:

> Not without fire can any workman mold
> The iron to his preconceived design,
> Nor can the artist without fire refine
> And purify from all its dross the gold.

8

Images of America

It has often been said that art is a reflection of the society that produces it, affected by a particular geography, climate, historical background, set of attitudes, and other factors. To sum it all up, art reflects a place and a people. This chapter is about a relatively young art that has expressed an acute awareness of place and people. Perhaps because most Americans, at one time or another in their family histories, came from someplace else, they seem to have been uniquely conscious about where they are and who they are in America. And much of their art has focused on the American continent as a specific place on this planet and the American people as a particular species in the history of human civilization.

Like the American people, American art was an immigrant, and its ambivalent relationship to the art traditions of Europe was a dominant theme in its history up to recent times. The search for a specific artistic identity, both in form and content, was a major preoccupation. Images of America, therefore, were related to discovering not only what America was but what American art was. The following examples, spread over approximately a century, reflect a many-sided interpretation of the American experience.

Before the Civil War: Painters of the Land

Throughout the greater part of its history, the growth of American civilization was virtually synonymous with the settlement of its land. The American countryside, therefore, played a central role in establishing the American mentality. Its spaciousness was seen not only as a physical challenge to the ambitions of the settlers, but also as a symbol of the scale of American dreams. Both the land and the state of mind conducive to a tradition of landscape art were present almost since the first days of independence. But in the late 1700s and early 1800s—when Constable was painting the English midlands—no significant landscape painting had yet appeared in America.

Cole

Thomas Cole was the first artist to point out the epic qualities of the American landscape. When he started painting, fashionable art consisted of portraits and historical subjects. But Cole preferred to depict landscapes and satisfied this desire by hiking through the Catskill Mountains in New York with a sketchbook. His work soon began to attract the attention of artists and patrons, and by the time he was twenty-eight he had achieved sufficient popularity to get financial backing for the first of two trips abroad to study European art.

In *The Oxbow* (fig. 8-1), a gnarled tree on a wedge of hill in the left foreground sets off a spacious view on the right, in which we see a great bend in the Connecticut River. The leading edge of the storm coming in from the left tends to continue the line of the hillside in an arc that goes off the canvas, further dividing the picture between the left and right—and between dark and light. It is a dramatic re-creation of the lighting that accompanies a summer storm, when some parts of the land are darkened while others remain bathed in light—an alternation that Cole repeated in the highlights on the tree and the cloud shadows of the distant hills. The drama unfolding in the atmosphere adds to the quality of wildness that Cole admired, and that he further emphasized in the unruly underbrush on the hill and the sense of unencumbered distance beyond. European landscape paintings of the time were more "civilized," depicting more serene vegetation and including many more reassuring reference points to counteract the impression of openness.

This kind of landscape, appropriate to the American sensibility, captured the people's imagination and fostered the American version of Romanticism. Cole expressed in paint what certain writers of New England expressed in words. One of these, the philosopher Ralph Waldo Emerson, believed that a profound encounter with nature was also a profound religious experience: ''Standing on the bare ground—my head bathed by the blithe air . . . the currents of the Universal Being circulate through me; I am part and parcel of God.''

Cole had a major following of east-coast artists who came to be known as the *Hudson River School*. Like Cole, they were European trained and applied their skills mostly to making heroic images of the wooded hills of New York. But not all good landscape painting was by the Hudson River artists, nor was that part of the country the only area being painted.

8–1   Thomas Cole, *The Oxbow,* 1846. Oil on canvas, 51½" x 76". Metropolitan Museum of Art, New York (Gift of Mrs. Russell Sage, 1908).

8–2 Robert S. Duncanson, *Blue Hole, Flood Waters, Little Miami River,* 1851.
Oil on canvas, 29¼″ x 42¼″. The Cincinnati Art Museum (Gift of Norbert Heermann).

Duncanson Robert S. Duncanson, a black artist who spent most of his life in Ohio, was largely self-taught, but his work reflected the influence of the Hudson River School and expressed a deep reverence for nature. His *Blue Hole, Flood Waters, Little Miami River* (fig. 8-2) is a quiet paradise that emphasizes nature's peace and equilibrium rather than its power and drama. The painting is evidence of Duncanson's interest in the minute details of rocks, foliage, and clouds, and of his ability to re-create them. But because of his careful organization of the shapes and the lights and darks, the variety of texture and detail does not overwhelm the picture's unity. The basic compositional scheme is that of four triangular shapes—the sky, the lagoon, and the right and left tree masses—all pointing toward the center, which is at the far side of the lagoon. On the near side stand a few shaded figures, who establish the scale of the scene and set off the brightly illuminated water behind them—the main focus of the painting.

8-3 George Caleb Bingham, *Watching the Cargo,* 1849. Oil on canvas, 26" x 36". State Historical Society of Missouri, Columbia, Missouri.

Bingham   George Caleb Bingham grew up in the frontier state of Missouri, where, as a boy, he decided to take up art when he met a frontier portrait painter. He studied briefly in the East, where he learned how to make monumental figures. But rather than stay there to learn more about painting in the grand manner, he returned to Missouri and adapted the concept of heroically proportioned figures to the representation of the scruffy trappers and raftsmen who were his favorite subjects. The Mississippi River, the setting for many of those subjects, was the dividing line between the East and West and has become a significant part of the myth and legend of America. And Bingham's interpretation of river life had a bit to do with creating the legend.

   Watching the Cargo (fig. 8-3) shows three rivermen relaxing on a mudbank of the Mississippi while their barge is stranded on a sandbar in the shadows behind them; a sunlit piece of driftwood, to the right of the men, brings our attention back to the foreground and provides some visual balance. The lazy, late-afternoon atmosphere, accented by long shadows, expresses a peacefulness more like Duncanson's painting than Cole's. But because of the emphasis on the earthy people, together with their work-a-day belongings and a faint suggestion of humor, this painting is not nearly as lofty in sentiment as either Duncanson's or Cole's.

Watching the Cargo is a good example of American genre art. In Bingham's era, genre artists were well known for recording America's village and country life in terms of the anecdote—that is, some event considered amusing or sentimental—and Bingham showed a definite preference for the anecdotal. But some of his paintings, like *Watching the Cargo*, transcend mere recording and remind Americans of the majestic and timeless qualities of their land.

The Hudson River School and genre art flourished in the decades preceding the Civil War, a time of robust optimism when the adventures of industrialization and westward expansion were just getting underway. America was moving away from being the simple, non-manufacturing utopia of small farmers that Thomas Jefferson had dreamed of. In many ways, the spirit of that change is reflected in the works of Cole, Duncanson, and Bingham, which, for all their emphasis on the outdoors, do not celebrate American agriculture but the American wilderness, as a symbol of freedom and of the potential for economic and social growth.

After the Civil War

In the period after the Civil War, the industrial and territorial expansion that had been set in motion earlier became more pronounced than ever. And in the process, immense fortunes were made, as tycoons fought for control of the railroads and the new industries like petroleum and meat-packing. Although the late nineteenth century in America was an age of rampant materialism, the new wealth also demanded culture—or at least the outer display of it. And culture to the new-rich Americans meant Europe. It was axiomatic that quality was to be sought overseas rather than at home, and American millionaires vied with one another to acquire European art and associate themselves with the art of the old world. Needless to say, it was a depressing period for America's artists, many of whom gave up on their own country and settled in Europe themselves.

Sargent   One American artist, John Singer Sargent, enjoyed the best of both the Old and the New worlds. Like so many nineteenth-century American artists, he studied in Europe. He acquired a broad, fluid-line painting style in a Parisian studio at the age of eighteen, and a few years later traveled to Spain to learn about shadows and luminosity from the work of Velázquez. Equally at home in Europe or America, his reputation was international and ''European'' enough to make him popular in his own land. A good eye, a deft brush, and a taste for elegance were the ideal requirements for a portrait painter of the time, and he was in demand by fashionable people during the period that Mark Twain called the Gilded Age.

8–4   John Singer Sargent, *The Daughters of Edward D. Boit,* 1882. Oil on canvas, 87⅝" x 87⅝". Museum of Fine Arts, Boston.

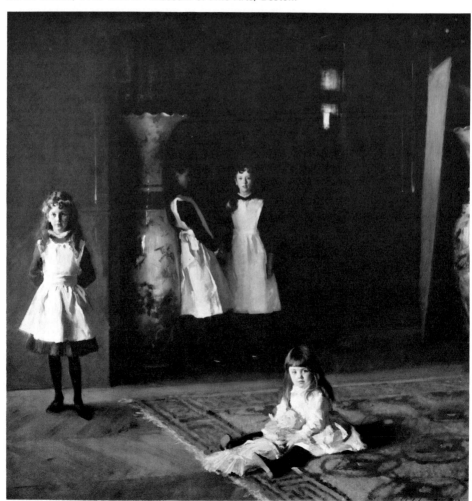

One of Sargent's best paintings, *The Daughters of Edward D. Boit* (fig. 8-4), is of four girls who appear to have momentarily stopped playing. The signs of nineteenth-century gentility are seen everywhere: in their scrubbed faces, their crisp clothes, the spacious interior, and the furnishings of the room—especially the pair of large oriental vases. Sargent made the scene seem quite casual, not only by his facile painting style and unerring sense of draftsmanship but also by boldly placing one girl way off on the left. But if we look again, we see that he offset her weight in the composition by the pull of several things on the right, including the edge of the vase and the light coming from the deep space of the room behind the girls. The shadowy atmosphere that flows around every figure softens their forms and makes the light seem all the more luminous. It is a scene of refinement and grace that makes use of some of the stylistic advances of European art without taking the risks; it is also a domesticated art that reflects the values of a particular class of Americans.

Homer   Winslow Homer's art reflects the life style of a different class of citizens. Homer began his artistic career as a free-lance illustrator for picture magazines, an experience that probably developed his ability to observe contemporary subjects and re-create their mood as well as their essential appearances. Although he had spent some months in Paris and may have seen the work of the young Impressionists, whose directness of approach and emotional detachment were very compatible with his own tendencies, Homer was largely self-taught.

Compare the plain, well-lighted interior of the *The Country School* (fig. 8-5) with the softly-shadowed interior of the Boit mansion. The walls display little more than the patina of wear, their plainness accentuated by the expanse of unvarnished floorboards in the foreground. About the only similarity between Homer's schoolchildren and the Boit children is the naturalness of their appearance and actions. Otherwise the people and setting of *The Country School* are as ordinary and humble as a school lunch.

If we sense any nostalgia in Homer's work, it is not because of the artist's treatment of the subject, which lacks any trace of sentimentality, but because of our own conceptions (or misconceptions) about an America that existed a century ago. In its day, the apparent lack of charm in this and others of Homer's paintings troubled his critics. Henry James, who was familiar with European art, once commented that Homer "cares not a jot for such fantastic

8–5 Winslow Homer, *The Country School,* 1871. Oil on canvas, 21⅜" x 38⅜". The St. Louis Art Museum.

hair-splitting as the distinction between beauty and ugliness'' and complained about ''his barren plank fences . . . freckled, straight-haired Yankee urchins . . . flat-breasted maidens . . . .'' Yet to the general public, it was the simple factualism and the lack of high-flown subjects that made Homer's pictures appealing. Apparently, the American people sensed that he portrayed them honestly from *their* point of view.

The Ash Can Artists

The story of the great westward movement tends to dominate people's thinking about America in the late 1800s, crowding out another story that is even more important—the growth of American cities and the steady migration of people from rural to urban areas. By 1890, five urban areas had populations of one million or more, and thirty percent of all Americans were city-dwellers. The modern city, furthermore, was responsible for a new social phenomenon—the inner-city slum. In a preindustrial city, the elite lived in the center while the poor lived on the unprotected fringes; in a postindustrial city, the elite fled to the relative cleanliness of the edges, leaving the center to the poor.

Sloan   It was not until the first decades of the twentieth century that artists like John Sloan began to observe and depict the life of the inner city. The shadowy atmosphere of *McSorley's Bar* (fig. 8-6) is something like that of Sargent's picture, but here the interior is a smoke-filled tavern—a murky refuge from the noisy street rather than a spacious Victorian parlor. Sloan was a member of a group that specialized in the portrayal of the heretofore ignored urban lower classes. But this group's work was so offensive to gallery-goers that it came to be known as the *Ash Can School*.

In terms of style, however, the Ash Can School's rebellion was mild, for these artists painted in ways that the more advanced painters in Europe had already rejected. Sloan's broad brushwork, although earthier and blunter, is not essentially different from Sargent's. His simplified but accurate observation of human anatomy was influenced by an earlier career of illustrating for a newspaper—a fact that may also have accounted for his interest in working-class themes. When he settled in New York in 1904, he was impressed by the throbbing street life of the city. His portrayals of beach scenes, grubby buildings, broken fences, and clotheslines were extremely provocative in the years before the First World War, but the city and its slums have become such a commonplace experience that these subjects no longer shock.

Bellows   George Bellows, although not a member of the original group, was closely associated with the Ash Can School. Also a former newspaper illustrator, Bellows's style was even more exaggerated than Sloan's. In *Stag at Sharkey's* (fig. 8-7), he used long, fluid strokes to render the bodies and lively movements of the boxers. And, somewhat in the manner of both Sargent and Sloan, he emphasized the central figures by making them very light against a shadowy background. The overstated postures of the fighters approach caricature, and the ugly audience of cigar-chomping fans surrounding the ring would probably make the spectators at a contest of Roman gladiators seem genial by comparison.

The people in Sloan's and Bellows's paintings are in many ways the same working-class Americans celebrated by Bingham and Homer a few decades earlier—the principal difference being that they live in the city instead of the country.

8–6
John Sloan,
McSorley's Bar,
1912.
Oil on canvas,
26″ x 32″.
Detroit Institute
of the Arts (gift of
he Founders Society).

8–7
George Bellows,
Stag at Sharkey's,
1907.
Oil on canvas,
36¼″ x 48¼″.
Cleveland Museum
of Art
(Hinman B. Hurlbut
Collection).

	After the First World War, some American painters moved in the

Early Modernists   After the First World War, some American painters moved in the direction of abstraction. This was partly due to the influence of styles that had begun to develop in Europe, for a large colony of expatriate American painters and writers had sprung up in Paris, and there was a great deal of communication between the artists of that city and New York. Other forms of abstraction developed independently, in large part inspired, it appears, by a strong desire to find a fresh way to approach American subject matter.

O'Keeffe   The work of Georgia O'Keeffe is one example of the new approaches. The highly personal form of abstraction she developed was derived more from an interpretation of nature than from any particular twentieth-century school of abstract art. Her work aimed at simplification, a tendency that can also be seen in the paintings of Sloan and Bellows. But O'Keeffe's brushwork is much more refined, and her forms are far less detailed. These factors made it possible for her to create powerful and evocative paintings out of subjects as banal as flowers. By taking a single blossom and enlarging it until the shapes filled an entire canvas, she turned the sensual curves and colors into an almost erotic display. O'Keeffe liked living and working in the American Southwest because the clean, austere forms of the landscape lent themselves to her style. In *Black Cross, New Mexico* (fig. 8-8), we see the cool, clear, economical approach that characterizes all her work. Combining abstraction with realism, she reduced the sand dunes in the background to almost geometric forms, yet modeled them to appear three-dimensional. The fragment of black cross in the foreground is so smooth that it looks like it might be carved from a very hard stone. Much of the excitement of O'Keeffe's work lies in these tensions between the real and the abstract, nature and the spirit. The abstract element is due not so much to actual distortion as to a stark revelation of the latent harmony in nature—an art that strongly implies a form of nature worship. In this sense, artists like O'Keeffe belong to the American tradition that began with Cole.

Stella   Joseph Stella found lyricism in the city rather than in nature. He had come under the influence of the Italian Futurists, whose principal stylistic device was to break up their subjects and rebuild them into an overall harmony of planes and surfaces. Their objective was to express the dynamism of the modern world. Stella found their approach well suited to his enthusiasm for the subject matter of

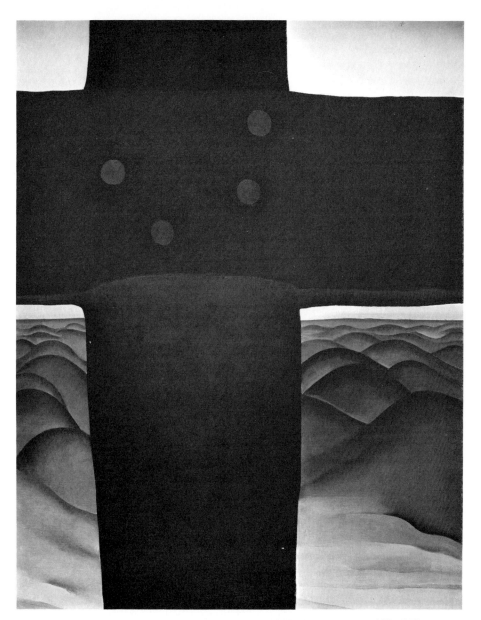

8-8 Georgia O'Keeffe, *Black Cross, New Mexico,* 1929. Oil on canvas, 36" x 30". The Art Institute of Chicago (Special Picture Fund). Copyright Georgia O'Keeffe.

New York. Unlike the Ash Can artists, Stella was interested in portraying the city's technological aspects rather than its sociological aspects—that is, the new architecture, engineering, and methods of travel and communication that were becoming part of modern urban existence.

In *Skyscrapers* (fig. 8-9), the planes of city forms have a geometric precision similar to that of the shaded volumes of O'Keeffe's natural forms. Despite the abstraction, we can still make out familiar features of the city—skyscraper towers, bridges, cables, and smokestacks. Other features, though less specific, are very suggestive of the city, such as the radiating lines that could be searchlight beams and the numerous hollows that might represent the city's many cavernous alleyways and subway tunnels. We can almost hear the noise of buses and cabs and the wails of sirens. To many people, these things spell confusion and chaos; the very thought of the city inspires indigestion and frayed nerves. But to Stella, it was all poetry—a kaleidoscopic harmony of exciting impressions. His extravagant statements reflected the vision of his paintings: ''The steel had leaped to hyperbolic altitudes and expanded to vast latitudes. . . .'' His faith in the man-made world was comparable to the Romantic's faith in the natural world; he intended his art to ''affirm and exalt the joyful daring endeavor of the American civilization.''

Critical Views

Not all the artists who worked in the period between the two world wars shared the Modernists' enthusiasm for abstraction. During the twenties and thirties many artists began to stress American subject matter in more traditional styles. Some turned to an idealized version of rural America that praised the virtues of the simple life. Others focused instead on the problems of urban life, such as unemployment, the decay of neighborhoods, and the growing demoralization of the average citizen.

Hopper

Edward Hopper had more than a casual knowledge of the work of the Ash Can School, having studied with Robert Henri, a leading teacher of the time who was to become one of the more important members of that group. Hopper also had some knowledge of the newer trends, since he had spent some time in Europe at the beginning of the century, but he remained an original artist who rejected both the excesses of the Parisian avant-garde and the New Yorkers' tendency to sentimentalize their subjects. Hopper's America, epitomized in *House by the Railroad* (colorplate 16), was immobile and remote rather than vital and lusty.

Hopper was a skillful pictorial composer, not because he mastered fixed principles of design, but because he precisely arranged

8–9
Joseph Stella,
Skyscrapers,
1920–22.
Oil on canvas, 54″ x 99¾″.
Collection of the Newark Museum
(Purchase 1937,
Felix Fuld Bequest).

a limited selection of details to evoke a great amount of content. In *House by the Railroad*, just enough detail is used to depict an old house in a forlorn environment. The reflected light and its complementary shadows reveal the house's volumes but also help to emphasize its starkness. The railroad track and its roadbed brutally cut off the bottom of the house, while the empty sky completes the feeling of isolation and loneliness. Hopper seems to suggest that the alienation of neighborhoods (and the people in them) is brought about by railroads, empty lots, thoroughfares, or any number of things to which declining areas of the city are susceptible. In this forbidding context, human occupation is suggested only by the randomness of the window shades. As Hopper's biographer Lloyd Goodrich pointed out, "Seldom has an inanimate object expressed such penetrating melancholy as *House by the Railroad.*"

8–10 Edward Hopper, *Nighthawks,* 1942. Oil on canvas, 33⅛" x 60⅛".
The Art Institute of Chicago (Friends of American Art Collection).

The general content of *Nighthawks* (fig. 8-10) is more immediately apparent: a few people in a lonely cafe on a street isolated by the night. But because of Hopper's economy of means and studied arrangement, every detail—a triangle of reflected light in an upstairs window, a cash register in the window below, a snap-brim hat, a row of bar stools, a door to the kitchen—seems to have its own mysterious private meaning, just as these lonely people seem to be separated by their private worlds.

Lawrence *Tombstones* by Jacob Lawrence, painted in the same year as Hopper's *Nighthawks,* makes a much more explicit criticism of America (fig. 8-11). If we were to regard Hopper as a painter of the dream that failed, Lawrence would have to be the painter of the dream than never began. His social comments were made all the sharper by his hard-edged, caricature-like images and brightly colored shapes. *Tombstones* records a group of people in front of an apartment building that houses a tombstone shop on its ground floor. The people are of all ages, from an infant in a mother's arms to an old man slowly climbing the steps. The collection of tombstones, like a small cemetery, not only suggests the end of a life cycle (implied in this range of ages) but also the eventual death of the neighborhood.

The simplified, schematic character of Lawrence's forms led art historian David Driskell to identify his work as "neo-primitive." But this does not mean that Lawrence, who studied art in New York and worked in the Federal Arts Project, was not a sophisticated artist. On the contrary, he intentionally adopted some of the characteristics of folk art and comic strips in order to endow his own art with a greater power and directness. Other critics have related Lawrence's bold patterns and intense, flat colors to similar tendencies in African art and modern European art. But Lawrence's images and compositions are very individual, and his work has a very definite message, making statements about the life of a particular group of people. It is realistic art, not in the optical sense of being true to outward appearances, but in the sense of seizing, by means of exaggeration and caricature, the essence of what life is like under dehumanizing circumstances. As Driskell said of Lawrence, "His work is tough, urbane, unsentimental."

8–11
Jacob Lawrence,
Tombstones, 1942.
Gouache on paper,
28¾" x 20½".
Collection of the
Whitney Museum
of American Art,
New York.

Contemporary Viewpoints

By the 1950s, the avant-garde of New York had become deeply involved in abstract painting, but this was not the only important movement in America at the time. A number of artists in the San Francisco Bay Area had experimented with totally abstract styles and then returned to basing their paintings on the human figure.

Diebenkorn

Richard Diebenkorn was one of the members of this group, and perhaps the most successful in applying the dynamic brushwork and bold forms of the prevailing abstract style to the subject matter of everyday life. In *Man and Woman in a Large Room* (fig. 8-12), we can easily recognize the forms of two people and detect a crude perspective in the shape that appears to be a carpet and in the lines of the wall and door on the right. The static qualities of the scene are reminiscent of the world that Edward Hopper painted, and indeed Diebenkorn's man and woman seem every bit as isolated

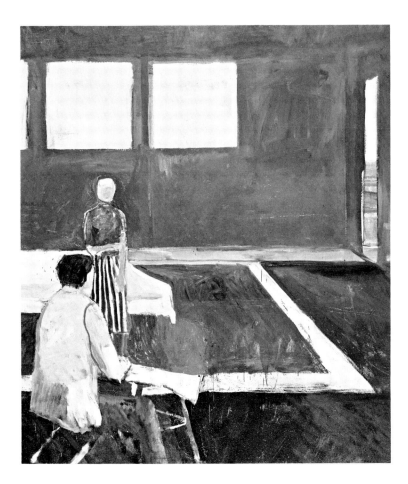

8–12
Richard Diebenkorn,
*Man and Woman
in a Large Room,*
1957.
Oil on canvas, 71″ x 63″.
The Hirshhorn Museum
and Sculpture Garden,
Smithsonian Institution,
Washington, D.C.

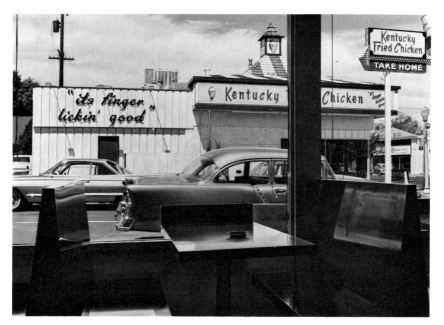

8-13   Ralph Goings, *Kentucky Fried Chicken,* 1973. Oil on canvas, 48" x 68".
Private collection.

and pathetic as the nighthawks. Yet the sense of tragedy is offset
by the emotional qualities of the color and the broadly conceived
composition—carry-overs from his earlier abstract style. Beyond
the open door, which is a mere crack in the right-hand wall, we see
a few daubs of warm, glowing color, like a glimpse of the California
countryside. Ironically, the sliver of the California dream only
serves to emphasize the element of disenchantment that dominates
the room.

Goings   A generation later, the art of northern California had changed
radically. Not only was the rebellion against abstraction complete,
it had been carried a step beyond: the Bay Area school of the
seventies was one of photographically precise realism. The emotional subjectivity of works like Diebenkorn's had been replaced
with the scrupulous objectivity of artists like Ralph Goings.

   Kentucky Fried Chicken (fig. 8-13) shares certain elements with
the Diebenkorn painting and, for that matter, with those of Hopper,

but it does not share the spirit of any of them. Goings was concerned entirely with painting problems—the reflections of light on surfaces, the varying degrees of color on a wall seen through one, three, or five windows—and made no judgments on his subject matter. No meaning was attributed to the Colonel's roost or the snack bar other than that which is visible to the eye. They are not presented to us as friendly gathering places or tragic refuges but as simple facts of the California landscape. But it is easy to read things into those simple facts. Even though Goings was concerned with painting problems, his consistent choice of such subject matter implied an interpretation. Just as Cole and the Hudson River painters recorded the epic qualities of the American landscape, Goings and other realists like him recorded the spirit-numbing banality that had spread across the continent.

Conclusions

One of the most interesting things about American art is that it has so often been torn between polar alternatives. In the nineteenth and early twentieth centuries, there was constant disagreement about whether the emphasis in our native art should be on the word *native* or the word *art*. Nearly everyone tried to reconcile the two, but the Europeans were so much more advanced that it was impossible for Americans to be innovative in anything other than subject matter. Only after the Second World War did they catch up with the masters of European art—and, a short time later, surpass them. By the early 1960s their position was so secure that the next important movement, Pop Art, carried an unmistakably American stamp in style as well as subject matter.

Scholder But America's art has also been subject to other divisions, both those that are typical of all art—the lyrical versus the dramatic, a love of nature set against a preference for the diversions of the city, the subjectivity of the emotions contrasting with the belief that art should be an objective record—and a few others all its own. The paintings of Fritz Scholder often capture some of this distinctly American mood, for he is both a successful contemporary American artist and an Indian. And though he was originally determined not to become known as an ethnic painter, he eventually began to incorporate Indian elements into his work and now uses Indian themes and content almost exclusively, believing that a ''merging of traditional subject matter with the contemporary idiom will give us a truer statement of the Indian.'' The figure in Scholder's *Super Indian #2 (with ice-cream cone)* is assertively large and set in the middle of the canvas, painted in a dark, brooding brown, and surrounded by rich colors (colorplate 17). He stares out at us from deep inside this image of himself. Like the people in the Diebenkorn, the Hopper, and even the Lawrence pictures, he too is a tragic figure, but for different reasons. He is dressed in a ceremonial costume that identifies him with the folkways of an all-but-obliterated culture, yet he holds an ice-cream cone, a folk object of the culture that overwhelmed his. Like the often-contradictory art and history of America, the painting mingles the past and present, pathos and humor, and radically different ways of life.

8–14   Fritz Scholder, *Indian #16*, 1967. Oil on canvas, 71″ x 71″. Collection Mr. and Mrs. Robert E. Herzstein, Washington, D.C.

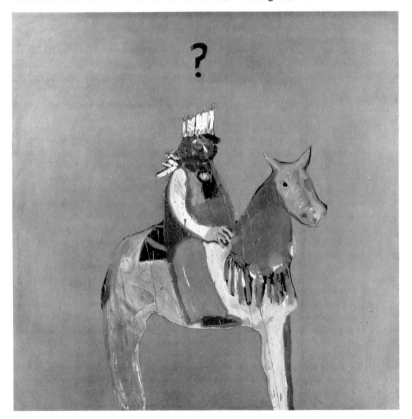

HISTORICAL CONTEXT

The first two parts of this book considered art's relationship to perception and to the expression of important themes, but Part III will examine art as a phenomenon in itself, concentrating on the ways it exists in history. By looking at some of the major works of art of the past in the order in which they appeared, we can begin to discern a very definite pattern—almost as if we were watching a time-lapse movie of a blossoming flower. This overall pattern is sometimes more revealing than the individual works themselves. Yet because art is a product of human behavior, the process of change and the directions it takes are neither foreordained nor inevitable. Art is subject to the will and actions of individual artists as well as to the circumstances of history. In this section we will first see how art-historical change relates to major styles and to individual artists. Then we will examine a specific period of art history in detail.

The period to be examined is the modern one—that is to say, the long sequence of images and ideas that has developed in the past hundred years or so. Modern art did not begin with a sudden change; it had complex roots that went back centuries. Behind it were not only the attitudes and technical discoveries of many artists, but also such things as the invention of photography, scientific discoveries about the nature of light, and the great social upheaval that grew out of the rise of democratic forms of government. Conditions have changed greatly since then, and so, of course, has art. It is by studying these changes in their historical context that we can be able to understand something of the how and why of the art of our own period.

9
Art
and
Change

A painting or sculpture can be thought of as existing in time as well as space—not the "real" time of music or poetry, but the "abstract" time of history. That is to say, each object of art can be thought of as an event that marks a specific point in time and offers some clue to understanding the character of that time. As you will recall from Chapter Seven, Michelangelo's *Last Judgment* (fig. 7-5) communicates something of the agony of the Reformation and Counter-Reformation struggles without making any direct reference to the politics of the period. Or, again, Edward Hopper's *House by the Railroad* (colorplate 16) expresses something of the melancholy and social isolation of twentieth-century life without showing a single human being.

Another effect of time on an object, art or otherwise, is that of physical wear and aging. In this sense every object is a continual event, undergoing constant but not necessarily visible change. And finally, in a dynamic society like our own, the art object also undergoes a change in people's perceptions. What seemed to be stylish only a few years ago now seems old-fashioned, or what seemed outlandish now seems pleasing. New designs are created that

9-1 The 1934 Chrysler Airflow.

surpass others, and new ideas come to replace the old—a new context evolves that is sometimes alien to an old object, or sometimes helps to make it more acceptable. Every new and different object forces us to see other things in a slightly different way, so that, we might say, it changes the appearance of those objects that came before.

Prime Objects

In 1934, a revolutionary car called the Chrysler Airflow (fig. 9-1) was shown for the first time. A critic wrote that it looked strange at first but that after a while ''. . . you are quite likely to come around to the viewpoint that these cars look right and that conventional cars look wrong.''

The Chrysler Airflow

As it turned out, the Airflow sold very badly, and after three years of production, it was discontinued. The Airflow was not a bad car in the engineering sense; it had demonstrated remarkable capabilities in road tests. But apparently the buying public rejected it on the basis of its looks.

9-2 The 1934 Plymouth.

9-3 (*above*) The 1939 Plymouth.
(*left*) The 1936 Plymouth.

Before we discount the critic's prediction, we should look at the history of automotive design during and just following the appearance of the Airflow. A sister car, the Chrysler Plymouth (fig. 9-2), was typical of the year 1934. The rear seat was directly over the rear wheels and the engine was situated behind the front axle. Although showing some evidence of modern ''sculptured'' styling, its basic contours were still square, and the fenders, body panels, headlamps, and spare tire were separately attached. In the Airflow, on the other hand, the rear seat had been moved ahead and the engine was placed over the front axle. An ''aerodynamic'' frame gave the car a much different shape, while the continuous body sheath gave it the appearance of a single organic unit. Now, if we look at the automotive industry *after* 1934, we find that the Airflow's radical styling was gradually incorporated into the design of other cars throughout the rest of the decade. Again, the Plymouth is typical (fig. 9-3): in the 1936 version, the rear seat and engine were moved forward, and the slanted windshield and the more aerodynamic body line resemble the 1934 Airflow more than they do the 1934 Plymouth; in the 1939 model, the headlamps and grill were finally blended into the body shape. Plymouth, along with other American cars, did maintain the long, straight hood and vertical front end—an accent that probably symbolized power to the American buyer. Despite this and a few other minor modifications, the entire automobile industry turned out products that were essentially descendants of the 1934 Airflow. One direct descendant was still around many years later: the German Volkswagen, whose basic lines were almost identical to those of the two-door Airflow, even preserved the sloped front end and round fenders (fig. 9-4).

The Shape of Time

Relative time and formal change are the subject of art historian George Kubler's book *The Shape of Time*, which provides a useful scheme for considering artworks and artifacts in their historical context. His system not only gives us some insight into why some works are accorded more recognition than others but also explains the mechanisms of stylistic evolution.

The basic ingredient of Kubler's theory of change is a concept of relative time as opposed to absolute (or calendar) time. In other words, saying that the Airflow came out in 1934 A.D. tells us very little by itself. What we need to know is when this car made its appearance in relation to other models of passenger cars. This leads us to his concept of *formal sequences*: "Every important work of art can be regarded both as a historical event and as a hard-won solution to some problem." A radical change in the

9–4
The 1963 Volkswagen
and the
1934 Chrysler Airflow.

9–5 Temple of Hera, Paestum, Italy, *c.* 460 B.C.

9–7
Changes in
Doric-order
proportions

shape of a significant art object (or an artifact such as a car) is usually a purposeful solution within a sequence of designs. The solution is related to those that came before and, if it is successful, will be connected with solutions that follow. Within a sequence of linked solutions there are *prime objects* and *replications*. Prime objects are successful major inventions; they affect certain traits of all the objects that follow them in such a way that these cannot be traced directly to any of the objects that came before them. Replications, on the other hand, are merely simple variations on the theme created by the previous prime objects. (In the case of mass-produced objects, a model may have thousands of identical "editions," but this is not what is meant by replications in this usage.) In Kubler's scheme, the Airflow deserves the label *prime object*, while the Plymouths of the late 1930s were its replications. If we were to look at a large enough span of automobile history to discover the next prime object (or the one just prior to the Airflow), we might see an example of a formal sequence or series of design solutions that significantly modified the shape of the car.

The series of Greek sculptures of nude youths in Chapter Six gave us a fair idea of the steps taken by the Greeks over nearly two

9-6   The Parthenon, Acropolis, Athens, 448–432 B.C.

hundred years in modifying the sculptural treatment of the human figure. Their architecture paralleled this process during the same period with the steady refinement of the Doric order, a system of architectural proportions that governed the building of temples. By comparing the Temple of Hera (fig. 9-5), built by Greek colonists at Paestum, Italy, with the famous Parthenon of Athens (fig. 9-6), we can follow the evolution of a formal sequence.

The overall sensation of the Parthenon compared to that of the older temple is one of slenderness and lighter weight, even though it is larger. This is chiefly due to the narrower columns, the greater width between the columns, and the fact that the part supported by the columns is relatively lower. The diagram (fig. 9-7) shows the stages of evolution in the silhouette of the column and the entablature (the part of the building between column and roof), and it is a simple matter to perceive the changes that took place in the proportions of each part and between related parts.

Unlike the development of the Airflow, the impulse to change the Doric order was not largely caused by the need for engineering improvements. Nor was it caused, as in Greek sculpture, by new discoveries about the subject. The motivation seems to have been

9-8 Thomas Couture, *Romans of the Decadence*, 1847. Oil on canvas, 15′1″ x 25′4″. Louvre, Paris.

almost entirely aesthetic. One thing should be noted: the 460 B.C. Temple of Hera is not really a prime object; the Archaic temple, which was the first to show these traits, is no longer standing. Therefore, a replica has to represent this phase for our purposes.

In recent art history, the problem is not that of prime objects disappearing but of being able to recognize them at all in the profusion of artistic developments. The old adage of not being able to see the forest for the trees applies here; it is difficult for us to discern the broad outline of an artistic sequence in our own time simply because there are so many different objects and ideas.

The Modern Movement

Over a century ago, a series of major changes began to take place in Western art. Many historians feel that the series began with a single work of art—one of those prime objects of which Kubler spoke—and that the revolution it started is still going on in our own day.

The early stages of the revolution were directed against the art of the French Academy, of which Thomas Couture's *Romans of the Decadence* (fig. 9-8) is a good example. A jaded style of realistic painting that illustrated lofty moral themes in imaginary historical settings was surely out of touch with life and therefore ripe to be overthrown. But in the long run, the modern movement did much more than overturn the French Academy; it virtually annulled one of the most fundamental premises of Western art since the Renaissance—that a picture was supposed to imitate visual reality. This was not the only issue of the modern movement. New possibilities for content and media were also investigated. But in the last part of the nineteenth century and the early part of the twentieth, the more advanced painters began to move away from the realistic treatment of subject matter toward an art in which the major focus was on structure—lines, shapes, and colors—and its capacity for conveying an aesthetic meaning independent of a recognizable scene.

Manet   Thirty-one-year-old Édouard Manet, a Parisian painter (and former student of Thomas Couture), submitted his *Luncheon on the Grass* (colorplate 18) for exhibition in the Paris Salon of 1863. Held annually, these Salons were the principal artistic events of nineteenth-century France; more than just a marketplace for art works, they were the arena for establishing reputations and careers. (In this respect they resembled the American institution of the Academy Awards.) To show in one was a necessity; to receive a prize or favorable public recognition was very advantageous. Manet's painting was turned down. But the Salon turned down so many works that year that the government was prevailed on to open up another section for a parallel exhibition of rejected works—called, appropriately, the "*Salon des Refusés.*" There, Manet's work was at least in a position to be noticed by the public, and it was—it received more attention than most of the paintings in both shows. *Luncheon on the Grass* was thought to be uncompromisingly scandalous by both the critics and the public.

Today it is a little difficult to see why *Luncheon on the Grass* caused such a furor. After all, nudes in art were obviously quite acceptable to Couture's public. Moreover, the painting is very reminiscent of, and indirectly based on, a distinguished sixteenth-century painting in the Louvre, *Pastoral Concert* by Giorgione, which also shows two naked women in the company of two clothed men in an outdoor setting. However, the figures in Manet's painting are not Greek goddesses romping about a pictorial, fairytale scene with Venetian troubadours, but two young women—one clothed, wading in a pond, and the other completely naked—in a

9-9 Édouard Manet, *Olympia,* 1863. Oil on canvas, 51¼" x 74¾". Louvre, Paris.

contemporary picnic setting, with two young men dressed in contemporary clothing. Such behavior was considered extremely indecent, and therefore the painting itself was looked upon as indecent. But perhaps what shocked the public most was that the naked woman shamelessly stared (or worse, smiled) directly at the viewer.

Manet's painting also upset people because it ignored the basic rules of composition to which they were accustomed. Great art meant the kind of grouping seen in *Romans of the Decadence,* where the artist took pains to pose each character, to set off the central group, and to arrange everything so that a viewer would not miss the point. The scenery, the costumes, and the props are all in place (one vase has been tipped over to indicate rowdiness). MGM in the thirties could not have done any better. Manet, on the other hand, presented a casual scene without heroic gestures or a contrived composition.

But equally outrageous, and ultimately more important to the future of art, were Manet's methods of painting. *Luncheon on the Grass* does not strike us today as unusually colorful, but for a painting of 1863 it was an extravaganza of color. Ordinarily, bright hues—such as we see in the clump of clothing and basket of fruit—were not placed side by side without gradations or intermediate hues. Manet also took liberties with the lighting and virtually ignored the time-honored formula of chiaroscuro, flattening out forms that people were used to seeing as soft and sculptural.

Olympia (fig. 9-9) demonstrates Manet's radicalism even more vividly. Although it was also based on an established theme used in many classic paintings—in this case, specifically Titian's *Venus of Urbino* (fig. 9-10)—Manet's variation was a clearly provocative one because of its modern setting, which suggests that the reclining woman is a prostitute and not the goddess of love. Here again, Manet discarded the subtle gradations of light and dark that indicate the roundness of forms, and flattened out the figures. He also reduced the amount of detail, suggesting the forms of bedsheets and flowers with a minimum number of brushstrokes. Another artist, commenting on this reduction, complained that Manet's paintings looked like playing cards; a critic compared the

9-10 Titian, *Venus of Urbino, c.* 1538. Oil on canvas, 47¼" x 65". Galleria degli Uffizi, Florence.

9-11 Mary Cassatt, *The Cup of Tea,* 1879. Oil on canvas, 36⅜″ x 25¾″. **The Metropolitan Museum of Art (anonymous gift).**

woman's body to a corpse. Again, the protest probably stemmed more from the picture's excessive realism than from the purported lack of realism. The indifferent expression on the woman's face and the naturalness of her pose convey an unmistakable quality of real life, as if one had momentarily distracted the naked woman by accidentally walking into her room. And the lack of shading and detail enhances rather than detracts from this feeling of reality. Manet was clearly aware that light does not always enhance and reveal form, but sometimes flattens it out with a cold glare.

Monet and the Impressionists Another young Parisian artist, Claude Monet, carried Manet's insights about the nature of vision much further. In *La Grenouillère* (colorplate 19), the appearance of rippling water is startlingly real; a closer look reveals that he constructed the picture out of nothing more than bright daubs of paint—not a single ripple or object has been ''drawn'' in the conventional sense.

In the 1870s Monet became the central figure of a small band of artists who eventually adopted the name *Impressionism* for their style, a term invented by a journalist who wished to deride their work. Other members of this loosely organized group included Edgar Degas, Berthe Morisot, Camille Pissarro, Auguste Renoir, and the American expatriate Mary Cassatt. Like Monet, they had been influenced by the colors and forms of Manet's paintings and shared a taste for contemporary subject matter. Their work often reflected the life of wealthier middle-class Parisians who possessed the leisure and the means to enjoy horseraces, regattas, and weekend outings. All the signs of membership in this class are present in *The Cup of Tea,* a painting of the artist's sister wearing a handsome pink costume and sitting in a silk-covered armchair in front of white hyacinths (fig. 9-11). The affluence and tastefulness of the setting are reflected in the casual pose of the young woman and in the relaxed way in which she holds the saucer and cup in her gloved hands. These qualities are also reflected in the confident manner with which Cassatt painted *The Cup of Tea.* The loose and spontaneous brushwork not only helps us to savor the paint itself, but also flawlessly captures the appearance and mood of the subject.

The Impressionists preferred outdoor subjects in and around the city of Paris, and typically painted a scene at the site in order to capture its freshness. To the Impressionists, the whole world was a radiant garden. Yet their works are often impersonal—as indifferent as the looks on the faces of Manet's and Cassatt's women—and notably lacking in romanticism (in that they do not emphasize the heroic and stately qualities of their subjects). If there is a romantic note at all, it is to be found in the daylight that was the glory of their paintings.

The Impressionists' methods of applying paint—often with short strokes and bits of color—were indirectly influenced by the broken color and flickering effects found in the landscapes of Constable (colorplate 9). Their preference for flat, simplified planes, high points of view, and abrupt cropping of foreground objects owed a great deal to their fascination with Japanese prints, which were very popular in the Paris art world of the late nineteenth century (fig. 7-13). But their overriding obsession was with the phenomena of the world of vision—the raw materials of light and color—and the search for their equivalents in oil paint. Sometimes this led to an almost total neglect of the underlying physical structure of things. Monet, more systematically than any of the others,

9–12 Claude Monet, *Rouen Cathedral, Sunset,* 1894. Oil on canvas, 39½″ x 25¾″.
Museum of Fine Arts, Boston (Juliana Cheney Edwards Collection.
Bequest of Hannah Marcy Edwards in memory of her mother).

pursued a study of the effects of light by selecting a particular subject—it did not matter whether it was a haystack or a Gothic cathedral (fig. 9-12)—and painting it numerous times under differing light conditions. Carried to this extreme, color in his paintings became detached from the objects represented and came to have a life of its own, and to suggest the possibility of an abstract art of colors, textures, and shapes that did not necessarily resemble those of the everyday world. Ironically, the Impressionists' contributions to realistic painting actually helped to lead art away from realism.

The Birth of the Avant-Garde

There was still another legacy that Manet passed on to later generations. The furor over *Luncheon on the Grass*, rather than repelling other artists, attracted many to Manet's way of thinking. The scandal itself helped to bring about Manet's leadership among the more advanced young painters whose works were also attacked because of their unorthodox styles. If it did anything, ostracism served to encourage them, and, beginning in 1874, the Impressionists had the audacity to sponsor their own series of public exhibitions.

By the 1890s, the Impressionists had obtained the acceptance and acclaim of the official art world that had spurned their work earlier. But the lag in recognition and the temporary hostility between the artists and their public was a predicament that has continued to exist in the art world right up to the present day. Since the late nineteenth century, there has always been an *avant-garde*—a small number of artists whose understanding of art is more advanced than that of their contemporaries, and who are therefore at odds with the public.

Rodin

One artist who especially exemplified the independent spirit of the times was Auguste Rodin, a sculptor the same age as Monet. Rodin received enthusiastic support from the avant-garde painters, but he also succeeded in gaining recognition from the general public. At the time, academic sculpture was, if anything, in a lower state than academic painting, and the artistic and spiritual vacuum being filled by the bold works of young Rodin was appreciated even by some members of the regular art establishment.

Rodin's unusual ideas and style were not always greeted with wholehearted acceptance. His first major public monument—begun in 1884 for the city of Calais—engulfed him in a decade of controversy. The purpose of the monument was to honor the

9–13 Auguste Rodin, *The Burghers of Calais,* 1884–86.
Bronze, approx. 82″ x 94″ x 75″. Musée Rodin, Paris.

fourteenth-century heroes of Calais who offered to sacrifice their
lives to the English army to save the entire city from destruction.
Rodin elected to depict all six men at the moment each made the
decision to sacrifice himself. The sponsors, however, objected to
his plans, preferring a more traditional monument, with a statue of
a single heroic figure to symbolize all six. But Rodin refused to
compromise, and for a while the sponsors went along. However,
when they saw the preparatory models for the six figures they
objected once again, this time to the style. Rodin's roughly finished, extremely emotionalized figures had none of the marks of
conventional sculpture—which at that time were noble gestures,
carefully planned proportions, and highly polished surfaces. Yet,
despite the objections and other problems that arose, Rodin stuck
to his original idea, and *The Burghers of Calais* (fig. 9-13) was
finally installed in the city in 1895.

The complex textures of Rodin's bronze are reminiscent of
Monet's broken colors and reflect Rodin's interest in the Impres-

sionists' methods. The rough surfaces affect the play of light, sometimes giving the figures the appearance of movement. When Rodin's sculptures first received notice, critics had accused him of casting from life, so suspicious were they of the vibrant modelling of the surfaces. The right kind of lighting could imbue a Rodin sculpture with an uncanny degree of life; on the other hand, the busy texture, like the many daubs in Monet's painting, could dissolve the form to such an extent that one becomes conscious only of its glittering abstract surface.

But the gravity of the subject matter and the heavy drama of Rodin's *Burghers* have little in common with the emotional detachment of most Impressionist painting. The heroic sacrifice of these historical figures is a world away from the sun-filled, passive landscapes of Impressionism. It was to be the emotionalism of Rodin's works rather than their Impressionistic tendencies that had the greatest influence on early twentieth-century sculpture.

Cézanne   By the late 1880s, when Impressionism was on the verge of its popular triumph, the avant-garde had already passed into the hands of new artists, three of whom—Cézanne, Van Gogh, and Gauguin—deserve special attention. While all three had been associated to a greater or lesser degree with the Impressionist movement, each broke away to pursue his own separate artistic goals. In different ways all three began to renounce pictorial reality. Collectively these three are often referred to as *Post-Impressionists* because their individual styles crystallized later than Impressionism's and their work was a more advanced phase of the modern movement. But these men and their work were so different from one another that Post-Impressionism, unlike Impressionism, never really amounted to a single movement.

Paul Cézanne—whose art was among the most influential in the modern movement—hardly resembled the self-assertive hero-artist of the avant-garde. Unlike Manet or Rodin, he was, during his most productive years as an artist, a conservative and serious provincial, a recluse who went to early mass and spent the rest of the day at work on his paintings. But even though he was isolated from the activities of Paris, Cézanne almost rewrote the rules of painting.

The key to these rules had to do with a new translation of reality. Artists before Cézanne, including the Impressionists, generally attempted in one way or another to imitate the appearances

9–14   Paul Cézanne, *Mont Sainte-Victoire Seen from Bibemus Quarry, c.* 1898.
Oil on canvas, 25½" x 32". Baltimore Museum of Art (The Cone Collection).

of nature. Though Cézanne did not disregard appearances entirely, he substantially altered them in the process of painting—which to him was a difficult, methodical labor of penetrating to the essence of a subject. Above all he wanted to capture the subject's inherent solidity. He did this for each apple in *Still Life with Basket of Apples* (colorplate 20) by juxtaposing distinct hues rather than shading with intermediate values. This de-emphasis of chiaroscuro had, of course, been started by Manet and continued by the Impressionists, but they had de-emphasized the solidity of objects in order to capture fleeting effects of reflected sunlight. This would not do for Cézanne, who methodically applied slablike strokes of red, orange, and yellow as he built each apple. This method of constructing forms is found throughout the painting.

Cézanne's translation of reality also took liberties with the traditional rules of perspective and foreshortening. *Still Life with Basket of Apples* intermingles a number of contradictory viewpoints: the cookies stacked on the plate do not all lie on parallel planes, the bottle is tilted, and the surface of the table is distinctly higher on the right than on the left. These liberties are even more pronounced in his landscape painting *Mont Sainte-Victoire Seen from the Bibémus Quarry* (fig. 9-14). Rather than use a traditional one- or two-point perspective system, Cézanne combined the rock surfaces, trees, and bits of sky into a multiperspective system of many focal points. Such a system may in fact represent the conditions of normal vision more truthfully than traditional perspective. (Our field of vision is broad, but we can only focus on one small area at a time. Therefore when we scan a scene, we focus on several different points while not being conscious of all of them.) But the overall effect in a Cézanne painting is not that of visual reality but of visual energy. Although the competing viewpoints produce a certain amount of tension, they have been played off against one another to create a vital stability. Cézanne was a master at balancing opposing forces.

We can see from these works that another important element of Cézanne's approach to painting was an emphasis on composition. Every canvas was a problem to solve, not in transcribing nature but in translating the energy and order of nature into painted surface. Every color, every arrangement of objects had its purpose in the harmony of the whole. The many distortions and dislocations, far from being arbitrary, were absolutely necessary to this harmony.

Because of a substantial family inheritance Cézanne did not have to paint for money. (Up to the last decade of his life he scarcely sold a painting.) He did not paint for the public either. No works of his were ever accepted by the official Salon, and when they were shown in the Impressionist exhibits of the 1870s, they were the object of ridicule. He eventually left Paris and returned to his family's home in Provence, where he spent the rest of his years pursuing his demanding art to satisfy himself. He lived long enough, however, to see that art receive moderate recognition and come into vogue as a model for emulation by a new and much younger avant-garde.

Van Gogh   Vincent van Gogh, whose story was told in Chapter Seven, was, like Cézanne, an outsider. Both were unknown to the public and ignored by all but a small portion of the art world of their generation. Van Gogh was able to survive with his brother's help, and

Cézanne inherited a fortune. Both were very aware of the work of the Impressionists, but came to reject the Impressionist philosophy and methods, sharing only Impressionism's brighter palette and emphasis on color. But there was also a fundamental difference between Van Gogh and Cézanne in their approach to art. Cézanne's interest lay in discovering and transforming the essential structure of material reality in art; Van Gogh's was that of possessing the most intense human meanings of everything around him.

Gauguin   Paul Gauguin, the third major Post-Impressionist painter, aggressively pioneered the same basic principle as Cézanne and Van Gogh—that the elements of form have artistic power in their own right. A profound colorist, his paintings often display an exotic palette of purples, pinks, yellow greens, and bright oranges, yet their effect is usually ingratiating and never as disconcerting as Van Gogh's vivid colors can be. Instead of Cézanne's multiple planes and viewpoints, Gauguin's forms are generally flat and endowed with an ornamental vigor suggestive of tropical plants and reflective of Japanese prints. And instead of Van Gogh's thick texture of brushstrokes, Gauguin's painting surface is also flat. In *Vision After the Sermon, Jacob Wrestling with the Angel* (colorplate 21), the artist simplified and stylized the bonnets of the peasant women to stress their abstract shapes and lines. The field where the struggle takes place has been tilted upward to provide a vertical backdrop for the foreground shapes, and painted red orange to contrast with the white of the bonnets and the greens and blues in the rest of the picture. But despite his emphasis on abstract form, Gauguin did not disregard the importance of subject matter and religious content. His mysticism and love of myth are reflected in *Vision After the Sermon* as well as are his decorative tendencies. Indeed, the simplicity of the images lends the picture a naive flavor that heightens the sense of piety and mystery. Gauguin chose freely from primitive religions as well as Christianity for his themes. In fact, his enthusiasm for primitive culture, together with a distaste for ''civilization,'' eventually led him to settle in Tahiti.

While still in France, Gauguin was a prominent figure in the avant-garde movement of the late 1880s. Gregarious and verbal, he was given to expounding on art—especially his theories about the ''autonomy'' of color, shape, and line. In this respect he differed markedly from his friend Van Gogh, who manifested these theories in his art but was too backward socially to circulate his

ideas beyond writing letters to Theo. Gaugin had a striking personality, and young artists were naturally drawn to him. He kept them
spellbound talking about his theories at informal gatherings in
Pont-Aven, a small fishing village on the coast of Brittany. His
influence extended beyond artists. The Symbolists, an intellectual
movement mostly of poets, saw an embodiment of their own ideas
in his intensification of color and simplification of form as a means
of expressing a mystical reality. An experimental avant-garde of the
literary world, the Symbolists were also obsessed with the dilem-
mas of conveying the invisible realities of the inner life through
outer visible forms.

Because of his following of young artists and his contacts with
the Symbolists, Gauguin had a more immediate impact on art than
either Cézanne or Van Gogh. And this impact was instrumental in
creating a climate for a new art to develop and for the work of all
three of these artists to achieve recognition and acceptance.

Summary   Using the gist of George Kubler's theory of relative time, this
chapter has examined the relationship between time and art, and
provided a framework for explaining the evolution of artistic forms
and the sensibilities behind those forms. Kubler's theoretical construct can be used to identify prime objects, that is, innovative
artworks that have affected the appearance of works that followed
them. Implicitly, it is also a system for attributing aesthetic value or
artistic worth. If a painting or sculpture has played a key role in art
history, it achieves art-historical status, regardless of its aesthetic
appeal.

The modern period, in which change appears almost to have
become a permanent condition, has seen the most rapid evolution
of art forms in the entire history of art. We have reviewed the
beginning of that period, starting with Manet and the Impressionists and ending with the Post-Impressionists—by whose time the
aesthetic revolution was well underway.

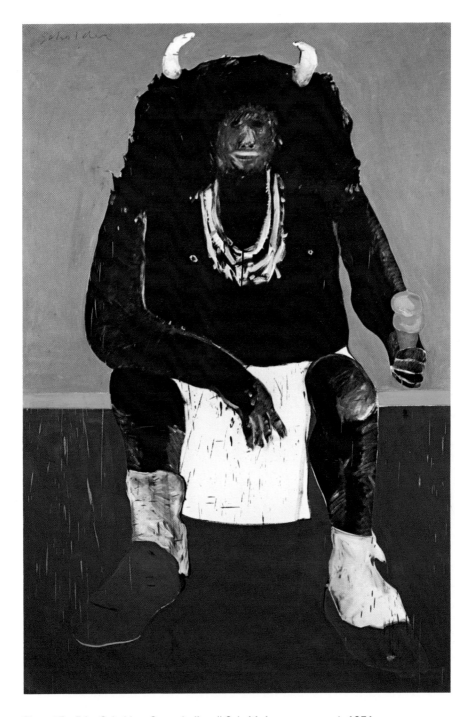

Plate 17   Fritz Scholder, *Super Indian #2 (with ice cream cone),* 1971.
Oil on canvas, 7' 6'' x 5'.
Collection Solomon Schechter Day School of Nassau County, New York.

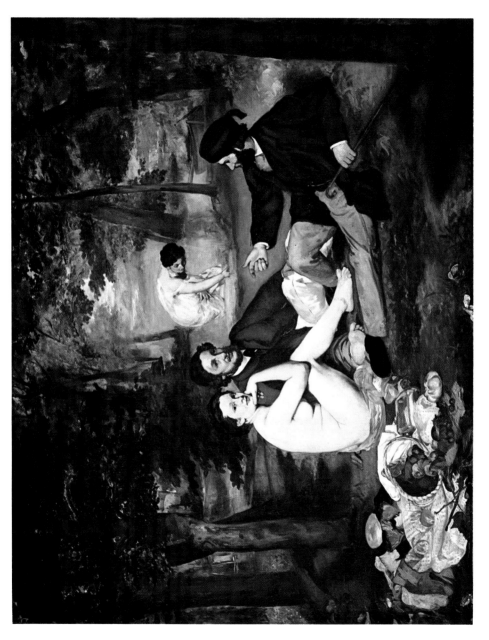

Plate 18   Édouard Manet, *Luncheon on the Grass*, 1863. Oil on canvas, 7' x 8' 10''. Galerie du Jeu de Paume, Paris.

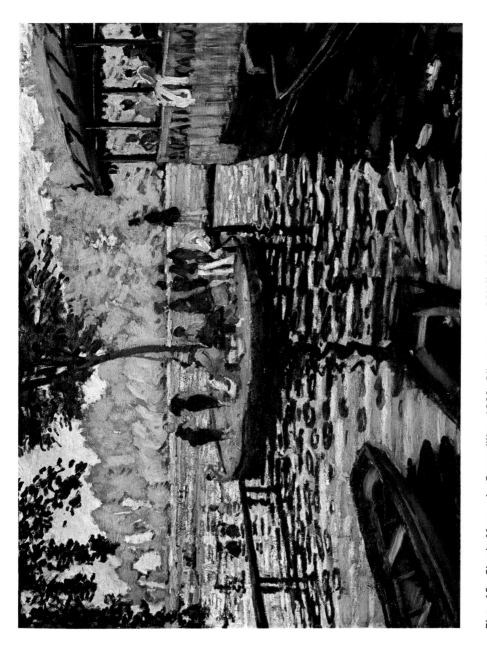

Plate 19   Claude Monet, *La Grenouillère*, 1869. Oil on canvas, 29½'' x 39¼''. Metropolitan Museum of Art, New York (bequest of Mrs. H. O. Havemeyer, 1929, The H. O. Havemeyer Collection).

Plate 20   Paul Cézanne, *Still Life with Basket of Apples*, 1890–94. Oil on canvas, 25¾″ x 32″.
The Art Institute of Chicago (Helen Birch Bartlett Memorial Collection).

Plate 21 Paul Gauguin, *The Vision After the Sermon (Jacob Wrestling with the Angel)*, 1888. Oil on canvas, 28¾″ x 36¼″. National Gallery of Scotland, Edinburgh.

Plate 22   Henri Matisse, *Window at Collioure,* 1905. Oil on canvas, 21¾'' x 18⅛''. Private collection.

Plate 23   Max Beckmann, *Departure*, 1932–33. Triptych, oil on canvas, center panel 84¾″ x 45⅜″, side panels each 84¾″ x 39¼″. The Museum of Modern Art, New York.

Plate 24   Piet Mondrian, *Composition,* 1929. Oil on canvas, 17¾″ x 17¾″.
The Solomon R. Guggenheim Museum, New York (gift of Katherine S. Dreier Estate).

Plate 25 Mark Rothko, *Untitled,* 1956. Oil on canvas, 79⅜" x 69".
Collection Mr. and Mrs. Lee V. Eastman.

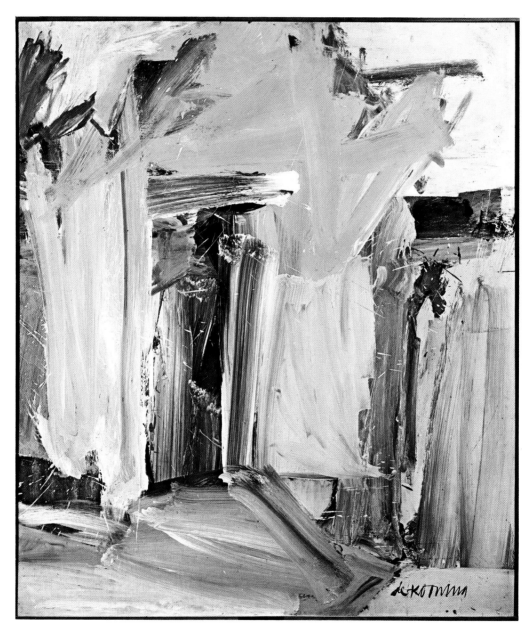

Plate 26   Willem de Kooning, *Door to the River,* 1960. Oil on canvas, 6′ 8″ x 5′ 10″.
Whitney Museum of American Art, New York (gift of the Friends
of the Whitney Museum of American Art [and purchase]).

Plate 27　Roy Lichtenstein, *Little Big Painting,* 1965. Oil on canvas, 5′ 8′′ x 6′ 8′′.
Whitney Museum of American Art (gift of the Friends
of the Whitney Museum of American Art).

Plate 28 Andy Warhol, *Marilyn Monroe Diptych,* 1962. Oil on canvas, 6' 10'' x 9' 6''. Collection Mr. and Mrs. Burton Tremaine, Meriden, Connecticut.

Plate 29   Helen Frankenthaler, *Cravat,* 1973. Acrylic on canvas,
5' 2½" x 4' 10¾". Collection Mr. and Mrs. Gilbert H. Kinney.

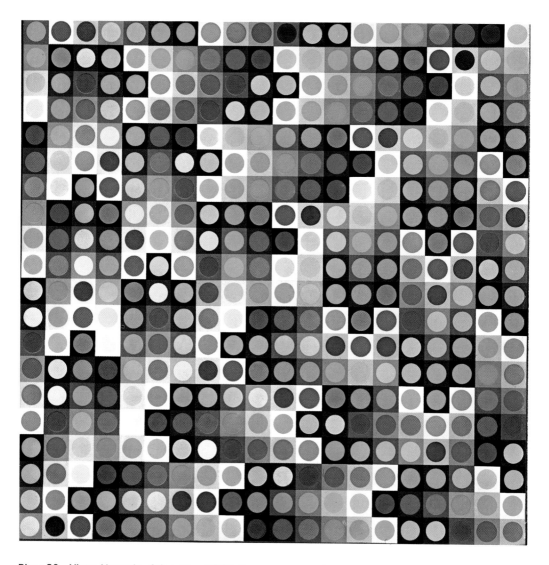

Plate 30   Victor Vasarely, *Orion Bleu,* 1965. Tempera on wood,
          32½″ x 32⅝″. Private collection. Courtesy Gallerie Denise René.

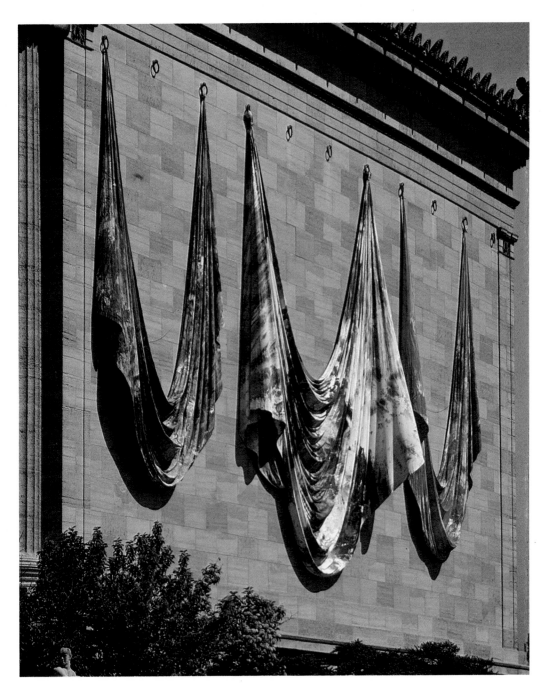

Plate 31   Sam Gilliam, *Seahorses*, 1975. Acrylic on canvas, largest piece 30′ x 90′.
As exhibited at the Philadelphia Museum of Art.

Plate 32   Chuck Close, *Kent,* 1970–71. Acrylic on linen, 8′ 4″ x 7′ 6″.
Art Gallery of Ontario, Toronto. Photo courtesy Bykert Gallery.

10

The
Early
Twentieth
Century

As we saw in the last chapter, the modern movement, launched in 1863 with Manet's *Luncheon on the Grass*, continued to evolve throughout the rest of the nineteenth century. The Impressionists developed ideas that Manet had introduced, and the Post-Impressionists carried those ideas another step or two. But the development of the movement was not narrow, for it also influenced other artists whose work was not directly concerned with those ideas.

Fin de Siècle   The 1890s, known as the *fin de siècle*, or end of the century, were a period of great artistic activity but few real advances. The ideas implied in the works of the three principal Post-Impressionists were particularly influential at this time, even though the artists themselves were no longer part of the Parisian art world. Van Gogh was dead, Cézanne was working in seclusion in Provence, and Gauguin was in self-imposed exile in the South Pacific. Gauguin's ideas, especially, were receiving quite a bit of attention. His popularity with the Symbolists—who wrote about him in their magazine— helped to give him an audience. The Nabis, a group of young

10–1
Henri de Toulouse-Lautrec,
At the Moulin Rouge,
1892.
Oil on canvas,
47½" x 55¼".
Courtesy of the
Art Institute
of Chicago
(Helen Birch Bartlett
Memorial Collection).

artists which was an outgrowth of his Pont-Aven following, spread his theories still further. Moreover, his tendencies toward stylized images and decorative patterns were starting to be reflected in the popular arts of the time—particularly posters and newspaper caricatures.

Georges Seurat, who died in 1891, was another artist whose ideas continued to receive a great deal of attention in avant-garde circles. Although more closely related to Impressionism, Seurat's work carried an aspect of that style to an extreme that had not been anticipated by the Impressionists themselves. He invented *Pointillism,* a system of painting based on scientific theories of color. He formed his images with separate strokes or dots of bright color that were intended to blend in the viewer's eye (colorplate 1). Seurat was a very methodical artist who took great care in composing his paintings and worked in a studio from studies he had made outdoors. As a result, his works were not as spontaneous as those of the Impressionists (most of which were painted outdoors), and the luminosity produced by the Pointillist dots implied a greater degree of abstraction.

Another major artist of the period was Henri de Toulouse-Lautrec, whose paintings represent still another variation on Impressionism. Using an artistic vocabulary of flickering color, flat-

10-2
Edvard Munch,
The Scream,
1893.
Oil on canvas,
36" x 29".
Munch-museet, Oslo.

ness, and bold design, Toulouse-Lautrec celebrated the artificial lights and shadows of the night. An aristocrat, and also a cripple with a man's body on a child's legs, he showed a perverse empathy for the "society" of the Parisian brothels and cabarets (fig. 10-1). His paintings, which combined sympathy and keen observation with a tinge of satire, reflect something of the cynicism that was symptomatic of the *fin de siècle.*

The intellectual climate of the time also contained a profoundly defeatist attitude about modern life. Anxieties stemming from the unresolved social problems of a new industrial-urban society had a spiritual counterpart in the disturbing questions and self-doubts that surfaced in the writings of poets and philosophers. The art of the generation wallowed in mysticism and eroticism. The most poignant expression of this general climate can be found in the art

10–3
Aubrey Beardsley,
The Climax, **1894.**
Drawing.
Originally published in
Oscar Wilde's *Salome,*
A Tragedy in One Act.

of Edvard Munch, whose painting *The Scream* (fig. 10-2) both
signifies and protests against the spiritual crises of the day. A
Norwegian, Munch spent the most creative part of his life in the
cities of Berlin and Paris, and, like Van Gogh, another Northerner,
showed sensitivity and a talent for expressing intense psychological
experiences.

Art Nouveau, a decorative movement that flourished all over
Europe, was the equivalent of Symbolist aesthetics in the realm of
applied arts. Its practitioners, rejecting traditional ornamental
styles, sought to base Art Nouveau on natural motifs taken from
the world of plants (fig. 10-3). The graphics of this style were
known for striking patterns reminiscent of Japanese prints, and
lurid, serpentine lines that were almost a caricature of the lyrical
forms in the paintings of artists like Gauguin or Van Gogh.

10–4   Henri Matisse, *Joy of Life,* 1905–06. Oil on canvas, 68½" x 93¾".
Copyright 1980 by The Barnes Foundation, Merion, Pennsylvania.

Matisse and the Fauves

The first of the major twentieth-century artists was Henri Matisse, who had begun to paint after completing law studies. He first tried to work in the style of Impressionism, then became acquainted with the work of Cézanne, whose discipline suited his own logical mind. He was also attracted for a time to Seurat's work, but found that Seurat's tedious technique did not appeal to him—though it did improve his understanding of color. He discovered Van Gogh's work at a retrospective exhibit, where he also met other artists who were under the spell of this emotional use of color. Through his association with them, Matisse also came under the same spell, adding the audacity of bold color to his analytical temperament.

The public of Paris was given a taste of this explosive mixture at an exhibition in the fall of 1905. The outbreak of color in works like the jarring seascape in *Window at Collioure* (colorplate 22) so exasperated one critic that, as legend has it, he called the group of painters *fauves* (wild beasts). To critics, this orgy of color, most of it completely unrelated to its subject, was an insult to both art and life. Nevertheless, the colors in *Window at Collioure* do reflect a sense of purpose. The relatively solid areas of pink and blue-green within the room correspond to an exaggerated interpretation of light and shadow, while the sky and water outside are indicated with smaller, isolated strokes that suggest the brightness and the reflections. Thus the overall effect of this image of a summer day by the Mediterranean shore is all the more expressive because of the vivacious color.

Almost as soon as Matisse had achieved his controversial success with Fauvism, he felt compelled to consolidate his gains as the leading innovative artist of the time. He examined the work of his predecessors—the Impressionists, Cézanne, Seurat, Van Gogh, and even the other Fauves—and developed a style that incorporated their advances while remaining completely his own. The first painting in this new manner was *Joy of Life* (fig. 10-4), a large canvas of rather conventional subject matter—a pastoral setting of naked nymphs and lovers—but treated in a highly unconventional way. Though flat and colorful like Gauguin's, Matisse's figures and forms go far beyond Gauguin's in simplicity and distortion; nature for the first time is openly subordinated to the spirit of the picture. The joy in *Joy of Life* is not conveyed by the figures of the dancing nymphs but by the rhythmic line and the ordering of color contained in flat shapes—hallmarks of a style that Matisse pursued for the rest of his life.

German Expressionism

Such was the strength of the new spirit in art that the Fauves had counterparts in other European countries, particularly Germany, where a band of young artists calling themselves *Die Brücke* (The Bridge) developed a related style at about the same time that the Fauves made their splash in Paris. A few years later, another group called *Der Blaue Reiter* (The Blue Rider), consisting of Germans and expatriates such as the Russian Wassily Kandinsky, formed a loosely knit brotherhood dedicated to similar artistic ideals. The work of these groups and other artists in Germany around the First World War has come to be known collectively as German Expressionism.

The brief Fauvist movement was a stimulus to the early German Expressionists. Its image-provoking label symbolized their own sense of rebellion, and the liberation of color and shape from the rules of conventional realism corresponded to their own artistic strivings. But there was a crucial difference in approach between the Germans and the French. The themes and subject matter used

10–5
Paula Modersohn-Becker,
Old Peasant Woman Praying,
1906.
Oil on canvas,
29¾" x 22¾".
The Detroit Institute of Arts
(gift of Robert H. Tannahill).

by the French were essentially unprovocative. Color was used for color's sake; Matisse served up a delectable and challenging concoction of color and form as food for the viewer's mind and senses. On the other hand, the Germans' themes were usually provocative, and the German artists used color and distorted form not for their own sake but for the sake of expressing the artists' deeply felt personal reactions to life. Thus these artists were the true spiritual heirs of the late-nineteenth-century artists Van Gogh and Munch.

Paula Modersohn-Becker, who was not affiliated with Die Brücke or Der Blaue Reiter, is generally regarded as the earliest of the German Expressionists. She was the first German artist to respond to Post-Impressionism and make use of it in an original way, much as the Fauves were doing around the same time. The robust shapes in *Old Peasant Woman Praying* (fig. 10-5) are reminiscent of the vigorous patterns of Gauguin and the Nabis; the strong planes of the face, indicating the structure of the head, reflect the work of Cézanne; and the sympathetic approach to the subject recalls Van Gogh's *Potato Eaters*. Modersohn-Becker em-

phasized the dignity of the woman by the simplicity and monumentality of the figure, which fills most of the composition. The
directness, primitive tendencies, and human concern of her art
were much admired by the German Expressionists, and she would
no doubt have been a leader in their movement had it not been for
her untimely death at the age of thirty-one.

Of all the early Expressionists in Germany, only Kandinsky
occupied himself more with the abstract elements of form and color
than with human emotions. He was fond of equating the elements
of painting with those of music, feeling that they could be treated
in much the same way. Abstract painting can be said to have been
born in 1910, when Kandinsky painted his first completely abstract
work. In order to counteract the temptation to seek ''real'' images
in his work and to emphasize the intention of providing a perception of pure form, he often titled his paintings as if they were
musical compositions. His earliest experiments, consisting of floating colors and lines, were somewhat amorphous (fig. 10-6); his

10–6   Wassily Kandinsky, *Improvisation,* 1914.
Oil on canvas, 30¾″ x 39⅞″. Philadelphia Museum of Art
(Louise and Walter Arensberg Collection).

10–7
Wilhelm Lehmbruck,
Standing Youth, 1913.
Cast stone,
approx. 7'8" high.
The Museum of Modern Art,
New York (gift of
Abby Aldrich Rockefeller).

later works were often organized around geometric figures floating in rainbow-colored space.

Max Beckmann, who did not become involved in the Expressionist movement until after the First World War, passed through successive phases before arriving at the boldly conceived and disjunctive imagery that can be seen in *Departure* (colorplate 23). The painting is in the form of a triptych, a three-section work of the type once used for religious subjects and placed over altars. But instead of the holy acts of saints, this triptych seems to chronicle the depravity, violence, and fear that were increasingly common in Germany in the years before the Second World War. In the two side panels, people are being tortured and mutilated; in the center, a group of people in classical costume stands in a fishing boat, perhaps departing, as the title suggests, perhaps even going into exile (as Beckmann himself was soon to do).

German Expressionism included sculpture as well as painting. The rough finish and emotionalism of Rodin's sculptures (fig. 9-13) were the primary inspiration to Wilhelm Lehmbruck, who introduced these qualities into his own work. But the elongation and distortion of his *Standing Youth* (fig. 10-7)—a typical Expressionist method of intensifying emotion—represent a tampering with proportions that even the bold Rodin would not have dared. Lehmbruck's sculptures convey a depth of concern about human life that was characteristic of German Expressionism in general.

Picasso and Cubism

The Fauves were not the only ones in Paris who responded to the spirit of the new century. Indeed, the excitement they stirred up may have been a direct stimulus for the experimental turn that took place in the work of the Spanish artist Pablo Picasso. There is reason to believe that after he had seen Matisse's *Joy of Life*,

10-8
Pablo Picasso,
Self-Portrait, 1906.
Oil on canvas,
36¼" x 28¾".
Philadelphia Museum of Art
(A.E. Gallatin Collection).

10-9   Pablo Picasso, *Les Demoiselles d'Avignon,* 1907.
Oil on canvas, 8' x 7'8". The Museum of Modern Art, New York
(acquired through the Lillie P. Bliss Bequest).

Picasso felt the challenge to produce an innovative painting of his
own. Up to this time, his work was based on a progressive form of
Post-Impressionism (fig. 10-8)—some of it similar to the work of
Modersohn-Becker. At any rate, after working for several months,

Picasso produced his own landmark painting—*Les Demoiselles d'Avignon* (fig. 10-9). (Ironically, Matisse himself was indignant about the work, calling it an outrage and a mockery of the modern movement.) The paintings of Cézanne and the influence of African sculpture were also important elements in Picasso's breakthrough work. The breaking up of the forms into planes had been learned from Cézanne; the severity of some of these planes—especially those of the faces—was influenced by African art (fig. 1-7). Picasso was the first, but not the only, twentieth-century artist to adapt primitive art in his painting. Ignored for centuries by Europeans who could appreciate only realistic art in the Greek tradition, primitive art objects were finally being recognized for their aesthetic values. At the same time, their abstract forms and directness of communication provided inspiration for modern artists in search of new artistic solutions. The Fauves rummaged in junk shops for African masks, and members of Die Brücke were attracted to Melanesian art.

Les Demoiselles was the first in a long series of bold experiments with structure in painting. Together with Georges Braque, Picasso launched a major new artistic style called *Cubism*. While the Expressionists and the Fauves rushed headlong into color, the Cubists retreated to an art of values alone, painting in grays and browns in order to concentrate on structure. And while Matisse attempted to stress the physical flatness of the painting surface, Picasso and Braque resorted to techniques that created the impression of shallow, three-dimensional space.

Braque's *Violin and Palette* (fig. 10-10) is a representative work from the early phase of this style, which is known as *Analytic Cubism*. The entire picture is a medley of fractured objects transformed into angular, interlocking, semi-transparent planes—recalling the brushwork and the multiple planes in a painting by Cézanne (colorplate 20). But this structure goes far beyond Cézanne's by completely ignoring the original shapes of the objects—such as the violin—and remaking them so that one can see their surfaces from several angles simultaneously. The space around the objects becomes part of them, so that the whole composition is suggestive of a multifaceted and very complicated gem. The color, more subdued and conservative than any seen since before Manet's breakthrough nearly half a century earlier, does not detract from the shallow but complicated spatial relationships. Thus, while this art roughly paralleled Matisse's in its increased

10–10
Georges Braque,
Violin and Palette,
1910.
Oil on canvas, 36¼″ x 16⅞″.
The Solomon R. Guggenheim Museum,
New York.

abstraction, it disfigured reality with different means and for differ-ent reasons. Matisse looked to nature for lyrical harmonies of color and pattern; Picasso and Braque systematically broke nature down into abstract volumes and rhythms.

By 1912 the original ideas of the Cubists had been fully devel-oped and had inspired many other movements. Chief among these was, not surprisingly, a style that Picasso and Braque developed as a variation on their earlier ideas. *Synthetic Cubism* tended toward flatness rather than dimension, and depended less on real objects as a starting point. According to the painter Juan Gris, who be-came one of the outstanding figures of this movement, ''I compose with abstractions (colors) and make my adjustments when these colors have assumed the form of objects." Gris carried the new style to its purest expression, translating the world into a vision of smooth forms and precise edges (fig. 10-11).

Elsewhere, the Cubist impulse took other forms. In Italy, a particularly dynamic version was produced, under the name of *Futurism*, that directly influenced the work of the American Joseph Stella (fig. 8-9). In France, it launched a multitude of styles and affected a great many artists, even those who, like Marc Chagall, were involved in very different pursuits (colorplate II). And in Russia, where a generation of avant-garde artists had appeared on the eve of the Revolution, it was influential in the drive of the *Con-*

10–11
Juan Gris,
The Violin,
1916.
Oil on wood,
45½" x 29".
Kunstmuseum, Basel.

structivists toward a nearly pure geometry that reached its ultimate expression in the landmark painting by Kasimir Malevich, *White on White* (fig. 10-12).

Cubism was also responsible for the geometrical abstraction of Piet Mondrian, a Dutchman. Beginning with a variation on Analytic Cubism, Mondrian's work became progressively simpler until he arrived at a very basic geometric style that he called *Neoplasticism*. In *Composition* (colorplate 24), the carefully planned, off-center arrangement of horizontals, verticals, and primary colors lays bare his basic principle of composition. As Mondrian once stated: "Plastic art affirms that equilibrium can be established through the balance of unequal but equivalent oppositions." He raised the issue of balance almost to that of a religion—"rising above all suffering and joy is balance"—and hoped that his art would satisfy the spiritual need that people have to discover the universal harmony that is within them.

Cubist painting naturally had its equivalents in the art of sculpture. The breaking up of the image into exaggerated and fragmented planes which tried to re-create the appearance of volume had to lead inevitably to experiments with real space. Picasso and Braque had developed collage (described in Chapter Three), which they expanded into three-dimensional forms. Constructions of wood or metal (fig. 10-13), however, appear to have served Picasso largely as studies for his painting. The most impressive

10–12
Kasimir Malevich,
Suprematist Composition: White on White,
1918.
Oil on canvas,
31¼" x 31¼".
The Museum of Modern Art,
New York.

10-13
Pablo Picasso,
Musical Instruments,
1914.
Wood construction,
23⅝" high.
Collection the artist.

10-14
Umberto Boccioni,
Development of a Bottle in Space,
1912.
Silvered Bronze,
15" x 12⅞" x 23¾".
The Museum of Modern Art,
New York
(Aristide Maillol Fund).

sculpture of this type came from Italy, where several of the Futurist painters essayed occasional works. Umberto Boccioni's *Development of a Bottle in Space* (fig. 10-14) is far more dynamic than the works that were done in Paris, for in addition to breaking up the forms in order to reveal their structure, he imposed a swirling instability on the composition. Where Picasso's ''instruments'' are destined to hang against a wall, Boccioni's bottle insists on in-the-round viewing. With its clashing planes and varied perspectives, it seems like a more direct descendant of Cézanne's still lifes than any Cubist painting.

Duchamp and Dada

The battles of the aesthetic revolution had been fought and won, up to this time, mostly on French soil. America had felt a few of the shock waves coming from the European continent, but no city in America had as yet enjoyed a bombshell comparable to those of Manet's *Luncheon on the Grass* or the Fauves exhibit; at least not until the International Exhibition of Modern Art of 1913. This exhibition, now known as the Armory Show, contained more American works than others, but it was the European collection, especially the recent French works, that created all the stir.

The painting that inspired the most comment of all was Marcel Duchamp's *Nude Descending a Staircase* (fig. 10-15). One wag called it ''an explosion in a shingle factory,'' and Theodore Roosevelt said that it reminded him of a Navajo blanket. Ironically,

10–15
Marcel Duchamp,
Nude Descending a Staircase, No. 2,
1912.
Oil on canvas, 58" x 35".
Philadelphia Museum of Art
(Louise and Walter Arensberg Collection).

10–16
Marcel Duchamp
(signed R. Mutt),
Fountain,
1917.
Porcelain,
24⅝″ high.
Arturo Schwarz Collection,
Milan, Italy.

Americans ridiculed the right artist for the wrong reasons. *Nude Descending a Staircase* was a comparatively tame version of Cubism with a touch of Futurist motion, having neither the raw shock of *Les Demoiselles* nor the novelty of the latest collage inventions.

But many of the artworks created by Duchamp in the years following the *Nude* were very radical even by today's standards: for example, a sculpture of 1917 that consisted of a urinal turned on its side and entitled *Fountain* (fig. 10-16). Christened *readymades* by Duchamp, these radical artistic gestures added a confounding feature to an already changing and bewildering art scene. The assumption that the artist controlled the form in some personal manner had never before been challenged. Duchamp seemed to be demonstrating by these acts that the premise of the uniqueness of form did not really matter; that a randomly selected object—even a banal one—could also be thought of as art; that a mass-produced urinal could rest in a museum alongside a Cézanne.

The works of Duchamp have come to be associated with *Dada*, an intellectual movement characterized by cynicism and buffoonery that was launched in Zurich in 1916. During the First World War, that city had become a haven for refugees of all kinds, including writers and artists who felt pessimistic about the state of European civilization—an outlook they expressed in actions and works that were considered preposterous at the time. Poetry was created by drawing words out of a hat; pictures by randomly arranging cut-out shapes. Even the name Dada (French babytalk for "rocking horse") was selected by opening a dictionary and taking the first word that appeared. Implied in these kinds of actions was an attack on the meaning of any cultural endeavor, including art. Although Dada artists were sympathetic to the avant-garde because of its own reputation for recklessness, their contemporaries were not spared their sarcasm. Yet, in spite of the impudence and madness, the stunts of the Dadaists did serve to reassess cultural values and also to discover new approaches to meaning—especially meaning that had to do with unconscious associations. "Automatic drawing," a sort of spontaneous doodling, was one of the experiments Dada artists pursued to promote the notion of releasing subconscious forces in the creation of art.

Surrealism

The Dada movement faded away in the early 1920s, but its influence on writing and painting continued. The Dada artists, for all their perversities, made a serious case for the subconscious. They were instrumental in generating the twentieth-century preoccupation with the ironic, the magical, and the unconscious—which became the foundation of *Surrealism*. A prominent Dadaist, André Breton, personally bridged the gap by leaving the Dada movement shortly before its demise to seek to establish a new brotherhood of poets and artists. His first Surrealist manifesto, expounded in 1924, describes the purpose of the new movement as "to resolve the previously contradictory conditions of dream and reality into an absolute reality, a super-reality."

10–17
Giorgio de Chirico,
The Mystery and Melancholy of a Street, 1914.
Oil on canvas,
34¼" x 28⅛".
Private collection.

10–18 Salvador Dalí, *The Persistence of Memory*, 1931.
Oil on canvas, 9½" x 13". The Museum of Modern Art, New York.

The super-reality of Surrealism had been anticipated by Giorgio de Chirico (fig. 10-17), who began painting pictures of disturbingly deserted plazas as early as 1913. The exaggerated open spaces, painted in a tense and contradictory perspective, the long shadows, and the ambiguous architecture conspire to create the kind of ominous and mysterious sensation that we often experience in our dreams; but they also suggest the magical life of lifeless things—a carry-over from childhood, when we might have projected fantasy identities onto inanimate objects. His style, called *Metaphysical painting*, opened up possibilities for dealing with subjective experiences. As de Chirico himself explained: ''The terrible void that has been discovered is the unchanging, inanimate and calm beauty of matter.''

The impulse to paint dream phenomena led some artists in a direction that seemed, in one way, contrary to that of the modern movement. Salvador Dalí (fig. 10-18) dusted off the old methods of chiaroscuro and perspective in order to represent the irrational world of dreams as vividly as possible; hence hallucinatory images and the inhabitants of the dark world of the unconscious assume in his paintings the authority of photographs. Intrigued by the theories of Freud, Dalí was incredibly resourceful in inventing all sorts of dream fantasies. René Magritte also painted in a more or less realistic style, but did not choose to dramatize either the style or content of his work. His paintings are evocative rather than provocative. Typically, they pose compact puzzles about what we perceive or think with simple images that are reminiscent of de Chirico's. For example, we can see *The Empire of Light, II* (fig. 10-19) as a nighttime scene and wonder why the sky is blue and the clouds are white, or visualize it as a daytime scene and puzzle over the fact that the street is dark and the windows and street lamp are illuminated. Logic is being mocked to create a new experience out of two opposing realities.

Another branch of Surrealism pursued visions of the unconscious through automatic painting and drawing, a practice that led some of its adherents into forms of abstraction. This frontier had already been pioneered by the Swiss artist Paul Klee, who developed a method he called *psychic improvisation*. Klee would begin a picture in an intuitive, poetic way, without an image or theme in mind, manipulating pictorial elements at random until some distant memory or association began to influence the process. The result was sometimes like a child's drawing, but there was nothing child-like about Klee's talent (fig. 10-20). An influential teacher at the

10–19 René Magritte, *The Empire of Light, II,* 1950. Oil on canvas, 31" x 39". The Museum of Modern Art, New York (gift of D. and J. de Menil).

10-20   Paul Klee, *Tropical Gardening*, 1923. Watercolor and oil
on paper, 7⅞" x 19¼". The Solomon R. Guggenheim Museum, New York.

Bauhaus (a famous German art school during the 1920s) who was
respected for his intellect, Klee was very sophisticated and clever in
conjuring up the mysterious life of the subconscious. The principal
Surrealist in the abstract vein was Joan Miró (fig. 7-18). He too
was playful and humorous and unusually inventive in creating
pictorial signs for the same mysterious world.

Summary   Most of the innovations—the prime objects—of early twentieth
century modernism were made before the First World War. These
included the breakthrough works of the Fauves, the German Expressionists, the Cubists, the first completely abstract paintings of
Kandinsky, and even the metaphysical pictures of de Chirico.

   The brief Dada movement started during the war, and Surrealism emerged during the 1920s. Other than the liberation of the
subconscious produced by these two movements, no significant
breakthroughs took place between the two world wars. The aesthetic revolution had not come to a stop, but it seemed to have
slowed down, concentrating more on consolidating the advances
made earlier than on making new ones.

11

The
Late
Twentieth
Century

The next important stage of the modern movement occurred in the United States with major breakthroughs coming just after the Second World War. Even though these new breakthroughs took place on American soil, they were very much an outgrowth of ideas and approaches initiated in Europe. But before looking at this phase of the aesthetic revolution, it would be helpful to review the situation of American art prior to the end of the war and to note some of the factors that would be influential in these developments.

Prelude   Even before the 1913 Armory Show, the work of such artists as Matisse and Picasso had been exhibited in New York in the gallery of photographer-art dealer Alfred Stieglitz. In addition to dealing in modern art, Stieglitz published an avant-garde magazine that printed articles by American artists and writers who were followers of the new developments in Europe. But the growth of an indigenous modern movement was very meager, with relatively few American artists experimenting with newer approaches. Their work had little influence outside this country and was not popular in this country—not even among American collectors interested in modern art, most of whom bypassed their work to collect that of Matisse and Picasso.

In the 1930s the development of modern art in America almost stopped. The mood of the time did not favor either experimentation or European influences. American artists concentrated instead on American themes and worked in rather conservative styles. The dominant movement of the time was Regionalism, typified by the works of Thomas Hart Benton, who romanticized the figure of the rural American—or, at least, his particular concept of the rural American (fig. 11-1). Most of the Regionalists were inspired to create populist myths about life in the small towns and farms in their own part of the country. Not surprisingly, this more traditional art was popular with the home audience, but it did not receive much recognition internationally.

Europeans still thought of American culture, especially its painting, as provincial—an opinion that was shared by the American artists and intellectuals themselves, especially the

11-1 Thomas Hart Benton, *Arts of the West,* 1932. Tempera, 8' x 13'.
New Britain Museum of American Art, New Britain, Connecticut
(Harriet Russell Stanley Fund).

younger ones. But in New York, various forces were already at work to counteract this provincialism. Modernist painting and sculpture by Europeans was showing up in greater and greater quantity in that city's collections, especially that of the Museum of Modern Art. At the same time, European artists were fleeing to the United States because of the political crisis on their own continent. These artists—including Chagall, Dalí, Duchamp, Gabo, Masson, and Mondrian—settled mostly in New York. Among the various groups, it was the Surrealists who made the biggest impression on young American artists.

During the forties, a new form of abstract painting began to emerge in New York. It was based in large part on the Surrealists' idea of automatic drawing (or psychic automatism), but at the same time it broke with their tendency to base forms on images—even the vaguely recognizable images reminiscent of children's art. The new painting was also influenced by other intellectual currents. The war had contributed to a somber vision of human existence, and the writings of Jean-Paul Sartre—a leader in the Existentialist movement—were very influential during the postwar period. Sartre and other Existential thinkers argued that existence came before essence; that life was not necessarily a part of a greater scheme of things under the protection and guidance of a supreme being. On the positive side, this meant that people were free to choose and shape their own destinies. But such freedom came with a high price: according to the Existentialists, humankind was physically and spiritually abandoned on earth and ultimately vulnerable. At the same time, Existentialism attributed a great deal of importance to the subjective aspects of the individual personality. The abstract painters, who had reached similar conclusions on their own, were already searching deeply within themselves to liberate this source of expression. But many, influenced by the theories of the psychologist Carl Gustav Jung, also believed that there was a universal dimension to this source. According to Jung, everyone shares certain experiences, part of a collective unconscious that is inherited as a part of the brain. Although the contents of this experience are not consciously remembered, they show up in dreams and myths of all cultures all around the world. The artists who subscribed to this view felt, therefore, that they could find abstract symbols that would be both intensely personal and universal. And from these efforts, the first major American art movement was born—*Abstract Expressionism.*

Abstract Painting

The painters of one branch of the new art, often called *Chromatic Abstraction*, emphasized color in a new way. Typically, these painters filled huge canvases with large areas of color that would tend to monopolize the visual space of anyone standing within the normal viewing distance. Like Pollock, these painters eliminated all intentional images, but many also severely limited the number of details of any kind that might distract the viewer's perception of a huge, engulfing field of color. Mark Rothko made a specialty of luminous, blurred rectangles that seem to float in space (colorplate 25). The delicate color transitions around the edges of each shape provide a hazy, almost spectral, effect similar to that of mist-shrouded landscapes. Rothko's paintings seem intended to provide a sensation of boundless space and encourage a feeling of revery. Barnett Newman's canvases were usually divided vertically by one or more stripes set in an expansive sea of flat, unmodulated color. In *First Station* (fig. 11-2), Newman has embedded a thin, sharp-edged stripe in a narrow field of loosely-brushed color which in turn is surrounded by the color of the background, an ambiguous treatment that confuses the usual relationship between figure and ground. Some of Newman's canvases are so enormous that the effect of the bright color is almost overwhelming. One critic said of this color that it was used to ''shock the mind,'' but Newman held that his works were meant to inspire religious feelings. The paintings of both Rothko and Newman appeal to the viewer's visual sense in a most direct way, but both are ultimately intended to move us to contemplation.

The other branch of Abstract Expressionism—usually known as *Action Painting*—consisted largely of what Pollock called ''energized marks of paint.'' It was believed that these paintings were created out of some inner necessity on the part of the artist, and were capable of conveying the artist's inner feelings without the aid of symbols. Action painters seemed to revel in surface variety; their paintings are covered with bold, freely shaped forms, agitated textures, and rapid shifts of color and value. Within this style a variety of approaches emerged. Franz Kline's muscular, broad slashes of black on white (fig. 11-3) contrast with Pollock's thin, nervous lines (colorplate 15). The pronounced figure-ground relationship of black/white in Kline's canvases seems to symbolize a fundamental principle of antithesis—male/female, life/death, and so on. But his crisscrossing bars could also be a kind of reference to the urban landscape, alluding to bridges and buildings under

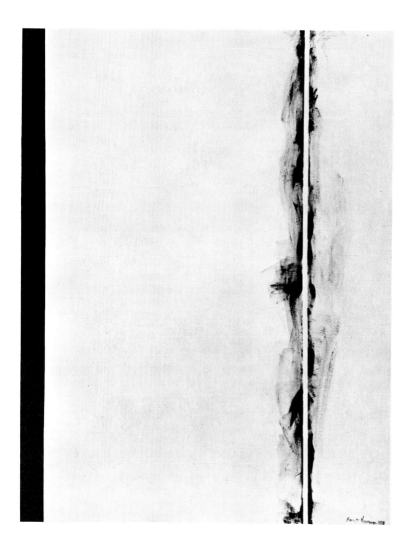

11-2
Barnett Newman,
First Station, 1958.
Magna on raw canvas,
78" x 60".
From the series
*The Stations of the Cross:
Lema Sabachthani.*
Collection Annalee Newman.

construction. Willem de Kooning's highly agitated paintings represent yet another approach to Action Painting (colorplate 26). The violence of de Kooning's brushwork is all the more disturbing because of his tendency to use soft colors—warm yellows, fleshy pinks, and so on. Yet this combination of elements often lends itself to figurative and sexual interpretations. His paintings, in which broad brushstrokes go in all directions, best epitomized the gestural style.

The year 1947, in which Pollock began "drip painting," was an important year in Europe, too. There, a number of gallery showings revealed that several artists—many working separately—had similar goals. Under a number of different labels, such as *Art Informel, Abstraction Lyrique,* and *Tachisme*—this painting featured freely brushed abstract forms, usually thick with paint. What is all the more interesting about this phenomenon is the fact that the art world in Europe was largely unaware of the Abstract Expressionists until 1950, when these painters' works were shown there rather extensively. A major exhibition held in Paris that year featured representatives of both the European and American avant-garde. In general, the American abstract art was bolder and more dramatic, and the European more lyrical, stressing a greater sensitivity to the subtle possibilities of the new style. One European branch emphasized texture above all else, relying on the evocative power of the material itself. The French artist Jean Dubuffet (fig. 2-19) sometimes created working surfaces out of cut-up pieces of canvas, thick glue, and asphalt, which he would knead, trowel, and scrape, allowing the material itself to suggest the way in which

11-3   Franz Kline, *Mahoning*, 1956. Oil on canvas, 80" x 100". Whitney Museum of American Art, New York (gift of the Friends of the Whitney Museum of American Art).

11–4   Antoni Tàpies, *Gray with Two Black Stains,* 1959. Mixed media on canvas,
38½″ x 51¼″. Albright-Knox Art Gallery, Buffalo, N.Y., The Martha Jackson Collection, 1974.

it should be manipulated. The work of the Spaniard Antonio Tàpies
also focused on textures, but in combination with strong, often
almost geometric structures. *Gray with Two Black Stains* resembles
an American Chromatic Abstraction in that it features delicate
transitions of hue and value as well as texture (fig. 11-4). And, like
a painting by Rothko, its subtle relationships of abstract form are
capable of inspiring contemplation.

In retrospect, the most important consequences of Abstract
Expressionism appear to have been more cultural than aesthetic.
For one thing, the relationship between European and American art
had changed; for the first time in history the latter was looked upon
as a vital force in the art world. Now European artists had to run to
keep up with a vigorous new American competition. And, ironically, even as American art broke out of provincialism, its new
avant-garde began to acquire a strong (and sometimes arrogant)

sense of national identity. Abstract Expressionism had a romantic quality and a distinctly American accent. Its raw style and defiance of conventions fit the image Americans had of themselves as being boldly individualistic.

Abstract Sculpture

During the fifties, developments in sculpture were generally overshadowed by the exuberant world of abstract painting. Although the aesthetic advances immediately after the Second World War were pioneered by painters, sculptors were attuned to the new thinking and managed to express it in their own way.

In the late forties, a number of sculptors developed ways of working with metal that corresponded roughly to the spontaneous methods of Abstract Expressionist painters. Their dramatic works often equalled those of Kline or de Kooning in boldness. Some, following the lead of Julio González (fig. 3-16), shaped their works by welding successive layers of metal, capitalizing on the naturally rough residues and the oxides left over by the welding process. However, unlike most Abstract Expressionists, these sculptors were addicted to biological forms, and their works often resembled such things as animal skeletons, spiny plants, seed pods, and thorns. Many were influenced by the work of Henry Moore in England (fig. 6-20) and were reacting against what they considered to be the arid impersonality of geometrical abstraction in sculpture (represented by Naum Gabo, fig. 3-17).

The closest tie between the abstract sculpture and the abstract painting of the 1950s is to be found in the work of David Smith. Trained as a painter, he first came under the influence of the work of such people as Kandinksy, Miró, and Mondrian. But a summer job in a car factory, where he learned to cut and weld metal, together with his discovery of the welded sculptures of Picasso and González, stimulated him to pursue the art of steel sculpture. Throughout his career, he saw the aims of sculpture and painting as being essentially the same, saying that they were separated by only one dimension. He was not averse to painting on his sculptures, sometimes covering a piece with layers of epoxy, zinc, or auto enamel. But the most basic relationship between a painting and Smith's early sculpture, such as *Hudson River Landscape*, was the sculpture's frontality (fig. 11-5). Rather than being intended for in-the-round viewing, most of his works were designed to be seen from only one angle.

11–5
David Smith,
*Hudson River
Landscape,*
1951.
Welded steel,
75″ x 49½″ x 16¾″.
Whitney Museum
of American Art,
New York.

11–6
David Smith,
Cubi XVII,
1963.
Stainless steel,
107¾″ high.
Dallas Museum of Fine Arts
(The Eugene and Margaret
McDermott Fund).

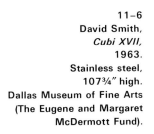

In his later work, Smith concentrated on simpler shapes, like those of the *Cubi* series—compositions of stainless steel geometric forms that look as though they are about to fall apart (fig. 11-6). Most of these are also relatively frontal works, and their novel construction and precarious balance are mindful of the impromptu nature of an Abstract Expressionist painting. Even the random buffing swirls on the surfaces have the character of brushstrokes. However, the most influential things about the *Cubi* sculptures for later art were the reduction of their forms to a simple, straightforward geometry and their similarity—both in form and manufacture—to industrial objects.

Assemblage The technique of assemblage became relatively popular in the late 1950s. Pollock had already experimented with the addition of pebbles and other small objects to the painting surface, much as Dubuffet and Tàpies had done. To the younger American artists this direction seemed particularly promising. If personal expression could be accomplished by the spontaneous spreading of paint or other materials, it could also be accomplished—with even richer possibilities—by the spontaneous assembling of objects.

Robert Rauschenberg and Jasper Johns—the two artists who experimented most radically and most successfully with assemblage in the fifties—were experienced painters who grew out of Abstract Expressionism. Rauschenberg would attach objects such as torn photographs, neckties, broken umbrellas, clocks, old trousers, or pillows to a vigorously painted surface. Although he called these works "combine-paintings," some of them developed into rather substantial three-dimensional objects (fig. 11-7). Rauschenberg's use of objects ran counter to the basic methods of Abstract Expressionism, but his bravura use of paint revealed a profound understanding of those methods. The rich coating of drips and smears that permeates and surrounds everything in a Rauschenberg work surprisingly creates unity out of what would otherwise perhaps be a meaningless collection of items.

Jasper Johns's assemblages generally employed less variety, and their paint surfaces emphasized Abstract Expressionism's heavy textures more than its brushstrokes. Johns is known mainly for his elaboration of such flat images as targets or flags which he would form with thick paint, wax, and bits of paper. One such painting, *Target with Plaster Casts* (fig. 11-8), combined a large

11-7
Robert Rauschenberg,
Winterpool,
1959.
Combine painting,
88½" x 58½".
Collection
Mr. and Mrs. Victor W. Ganz,
New York.

target with a series of plaster casts of parts of the human body set in tiny boxes above the bull's-eye—a mildly unsettling juxtaposition reminiscent of those found in the paintings of Magritte (fig. 10-19).

In discussing their work, Rauschenberg and Johns have tended to discourage the search for special meanings for their objects and images. Yet their inspired combinations do breed interpretations: Rauschenberg's rapid flux of images and surface effects can easily be seen as a reflection of hectic times; Johns's quieter, often ironic images are suggestive of contemporary myth. The works of both artists implicitly challenged the premises of Abstract Expressionism without entirely breaking away from the movement; hence they are looked on as transitional between it and some of the major developments of the next decade.

Not all assemblagists, however, reflected the turbulent side of post-war abstract painting. Louise Nevelson's works, like those of Rothko and Tàpies, tended to emphasize order and calm. Although she utilized discarded objects, Nevelson imposed order on an otherwise random assortment by restricting her materials mostly to wood, painting them a single color, and structuring the assemblage with repeated forms (usually the rectangular shapes of boxes).

11–8
Jasper Johns,
Target with Plaster Casts,
1955.
Encaustic collage on canvas,
with wood construction
and plaster casts,
51″ x 44″ x 3½″.
Collection
Mr. and Mrs. Leo Castelli,
New York.

11–9
Louise Nevelson,
Royal Tide I,
1960.
Gilded wood,
96" x 40" x 8".
Private collection.

These very frontal works are open to the viewer and filled with simple shapes and fragments such as chair legs, knobs, and scrap lumber (fig. 11-9). The series of niches often creates a subtle interplay between surface and depth, positive and negative. By themselves, neither the niches nor the objects have any particular meaning, but together in the assemblage they generate images suggesting cluttered cupboards or medieval altarpieces.

Pop Art   The sixties, one of the most tumultuous decades in American history, were also the scene of tumultuous changes in art. The rather sudden success of *Pop Art* in the early part of that decade had a profound impact on the art world. Simply stated, Pop Art celebrated popular culture—particularly the most banal and debased aspects of that culture. Because of America's prominence as an originator of popular artifacts—from soft drinks to Hollywood movies—it was probably natural that American artists were the most successful of the Pop Art movement. But English artists also figured strongly, for England had also become an important source of popular culture, expecially in the field of music. In fact, the earliest works of Pop Art were created by London-based artists who were particularly interested in the connections between popular culture and art. Many of the hallmarks of Pop Art—humor, parody, imitation of advertising art—were already present in their experimental works of the fifties.

Many works of Pop Art appear to be so different from those of Abstract Expressionism that Pop Art is often thought of as a total break with the past. But there is an ambiguous continuity between the two. Pop Art was certainly a part of the total modern movement, for many of its traits—ready-made images and irony, to mention two—had precedents in earlier art movements, expecially Dada and Surrealism. Furthermore, many Pop artists had begun as Abstract Expressionists, and, even though they were reacting against the older school, their vison of the world was at least somewhat affected by it.

The striking differences between Pop Art and Abstract Expressionism are demonstrated by the American artist Roy Lichtenstein's series of paintings of brushstrokes. *Little Big Painting* (colorplate 27) is an image of the marks that a painter like de Kooning (colorplate 26) would make with a few sweeps of his large brush, right down to the "accidental" drips. But in Lichtenstein's smooth-surfaced, hard-edged product, such personal touches as drips or spills are completely eliminated. He even used enlarged Ben Day dots—a mechanical method of indicating tones—as the background. To an Abstract Expressionist, a brushstroke was the spontaneous mark of an artist's feelings, the stamp of a personality. To Lichtenstein, it was another shape to be transformed by huge scale and the mechanical means of commercial art. And by his deadpan use of comic-strip methods to *represent* (rather than to create spontaneously) the Abstract Expressionist brushstroke, Lichtenstein was making a mockery of the cherished Expressionist belief that art can be a direct and true revelation of inner feeling.

Abstract Expressionism was a closed aesthetic system that rejected all references to everyday culture. It preferred instead to pontificate about the human condition with emotional brushmarks. The Pop artists turned all of this inside out. Their painting methods were deliberately cool and their themes were often taken without modification from the familiar commercial culture that previously had not been considered worthy enough for art. Lichtenstein himself openly imitated comic strips. In an interview titled ''What is Pop Art?'' he stated:

> Well, it *is* an involvement with what I think to be the most brazen and threatening characteristics of our culture, things we hate, but which are also powerful in their impingement on us. I think art since Cézanne has become extremely romantic and unrealistic, feeding on art; it is utopian. It has had less and less to do with the world, it looks inward . . . . Pop Art looks out into the world; it appears to accept its environment, which is not good or bad, but different—another state of mind.

Pop Art's vision of the world was not so cool that it precluded any judgment of what it saw. It is full of implied social commentary in its choice and its treatment of subject matter. The whole question of American themes that had been a major problem for earlier generations of artists (Chapter 8) never even arose for the Pop artists, who plunged gleefully into the consumer society around them for their material. Just as Lichtenstein expanded the comic-book look into an art form that accurately reflected the emotional and intellectual level of the nation, Andy Warhol used mass-production techniques to emphasize the shallowness of American sexual myths (colorplate 28). The implied commentary of Claes Oldenburg's *Yale Lipstick* (fig. 11-10) touches on art, education, and the military in addition to commercialism and sex. The twenty-four-foot-high sculpture was intended to mock those sculptures that are large in scale and noble in theme and are constructed in public squares to inspire a sense of grandeur and tradition. Although the lipstick sculpture is large, it is hardly noble and only inspires a sense of the absurd. Instead of a public figure or commemorative obelisk, Oldenburg created a gigantic version of a very common object; and instead of building a solid base, he mounted the form

11–10 Claes Oldenburg, *Yale Lipstick,* 1969. Steel, aluminum, Fiberglass, and paint, 24′ high. Yale University Art Gallery (gift of the Colossal Keepsake Corporation).

on a set of bulldozer treads that suggest that the sculpture could be moved from one place to another. The monumental treatment of the commonplace and the mobility of the public work are only the beginning of this work's contradictions, however. Viewing it, we become aware that this object designed for women has a very suggestively masculine shape, and, set on treads, it also bears a close resemblance to a cannon. These simple variations on the traditional object lead us to reinterpret a symbol of sexual desire as a symbol of aggression.

Oldenburg's visual games were well suited to the confusion of the times. The lipstick piece became such a focal point of controversy on the Yale campus in 1969—at the height of the Vietnam War—that it became a victim of graffiti and radical posters and was eventually moved to a less conspicuous location.

Pop Art may have established closer relations between art and the ordinary world, but at the same time it raised questions about the nature of art. If Roy Lichtenstein could copy a frame from a comic strip and call it art, then what was the original? Were the Sunday papers full of little works of art? If Warhol could reproduce Brillo boxes, did it mean a supermarket was a kind of art gallery? The distinction between art and nonart had become less and less meaningful.

Color-Field Art

At about the same time that Rauschenberg, Johns, and the English Pop artists were restoring subject matter to painting and sculpture, others were continuing to explore the potentialities of abstract art. But unlike the Action Painters, they did not work in bold gestures. Even at the height of Abstract Expressionism, the desire to express one's inner feelings spontaneously was not universal among those painters. Many had chosen less dramatic ways to work, preferring to concentrate on the investigation of problems of color and space.

The luminous and atmospheric qualities of Helen Frankenthaler's stained canvases (colorplate 29) have much in common with the paintings of the Chromatic Abstractionists, particularly Rothko. But the shapes in Frankenthaler are far more irregular and tend to suggest natural forms. Frankenthaler's methods were supposedly influenced by the staining techniques of Pollock, but unlike him, she used fast-drying, water-based acrylic paints on raw canvas rather than slower-drying oil paints on sized canvas. Frankenthaler was the first to concentrate on staining, allowing the fluid color to soak into the fabric and sometimes to run and form unex-

11–11 Morris Louis, *Dalet Kaf,* 1958. Acrylic on canvas, 100¼" x 142½".
Estate of the artist. Courtesy André Emmerich Gallery.

pected shapes. She has since expanded her range of working methods to include practically every way that paint can be spread on canvas—pouring, sponging, even brushing—and has found many ways to create the sensation of depth through staining. Over the years, her work has been in the forefront of the advances of *color-field painting*.

Morris Louis discovered the staining technique when he met Frankenthaler. He then went on to develop a style of his own that involved pouring acrylics in broad, smooth floods to create overlapping "veils" of color (fig. 11-11). Later, he poured the paint to form separate stripes of color that stood out against the bare canvas. Although they were somewhat irregular, these stripes did introduce to his style a certain amount of simplicity, repetition, and symmetry—qualities not usually found in color-field paintings. Meanwhile, the shift in sensibility away from the subjective and gestural painting style of the Abstract Expressionists was beginning to be reflected in the work of more and more artists.

Minimal Art

Minimal Art was the major branch of abstract art in the sixties. In painting it was a continuation of the work begun by artists like Rothko and Newman, but the focus was on form and structure with an emphasis on simple, geometrical shapes. Although it seemed to hark back to the paintings of Mondrian (colorplate 24), Minimal Art reflected a very different approach to geometrical abstraction. Minimal artists did not share Mondrian's mystical ideas about order and harmony and were not at all opposed to making straightforward, symmetrical compositions. The dry and simple patterns of Frank Stella's painting *Itata* (fig. 11-12) resemble the cool, unemotional images of Pop more closely than those of other abstract art—whether by Mondrian or the Abstract Expressionists. Just as the previous generation had been influenced by the subjective views of Existentialism, the new generation of abstract painters was influenced by the objectivism of analytical philosophy, especially the branch led by Ludwig Wittgenstein, who championed a common-sense view of the world through a disciplined analysis of language. This approach was reflected in the matter-of-fact, disciplined character of Minimal art.

Stella aimed at consolidating a painting into a single, indivisible image and employed several devices to accomplish this: his works

11–12 Frank Stella, *Itata,* 1964. Metallic powder in polymer emulsion on canvas, 77" x 122". Private collection.

11-13
Donald Judd,
Untitled,
1965.
Galvanized iron and aluminum,
seven boxes measuring
9" x 40" x 31"
with 9" intervals.
Private collection.

were usually symmetrical, limited to two unmodulated colors, painted on raw canvas to increase the flattening effect, and structured in narrow bands that ran parallel to the edges of the frame to echo the overall shape. His intention was to make paintings that would not refer to anything else. They were only about themselves—an ultimate step in the exclusion of content; as Stella himself once put it, "only what can be seen there is there." In its metamorphosis from window-to-the-world to self-referring object, painting had attempted to divest itself of content and the ability to trigger emotional reactions.

Minimal sculpture was based on essentially the same sensibility and philosophy as Minimal painting, rejecting dynamic compositional effects and preferring the most elementary arrangements of forms. The extra dimension of sculpture, however, greatly multiplied the number of relationships between elements that the artist might work with and helped to reinforce the sense that the artwork was an object. Some Minimalist sculptors attempted to develop these aspects by creating works of several elements in which the space between parts became almost as important as the solid structures. The fluorescent-light sculptures of Dan Flavin (colorplate 7) were among the first and most radical experiments in changing the space and making the viewer more aware of it. Donald Judd's wall sculptures, sets of metal boxes that were attached to the wall one above the other, presented a similar idea on a smaller scale, stressing a single form through a persistent repetition of that form and equal intervals of the same dimensions (fig. 11-13). Other artists carried the spatial-relationship aspect even further, exhibiting their work in ways that made the viewer aware of relationships between the individual sculptures; as in the case of Carl Andre (fig. 11-14), between the sculpture and the shape of the floor; or, in still other cases, between the sculpture and the shape of the room it was in. Just as Minimal painting was far removed from the idea of the painting as window, Minimal sculpture aimed at playing a role quite different from that of the traditional statue isolated on top of a pedestal.

11-14   Carl Andre, *8th Reversed Steel Corner,* 1978. Hot rolled steel, each piece 19⅝" square. Courtesy Sperone Westwater Fischer Gallery, New York.

Op and Kinetic Art

Technology pervades all of art—whether the work is a sculpture of polyester resin and fiberglass or a painting from the fifteenth century using oil as a medium. Some artistic products, however, make particular use of recent scientific and postindustrial technology.

Op Art, its name derived from the word *optical*, enjoyed the public limelight just after Pop Art (hence the journalistic alliteration between the names). While using the traditional medium of paint on canvas, the Op artists were notably skillful in applying a scientific understanding of optics. Like Minimal Art, Op Art was abstract, geometric, and hard edged, but differed principally in that it presented an active rather than a passive visual field.

Op Art grew directly out of the works of Mondrian and the artists and designers of the German Bauhaus and was influenced by the studies of visual perception that were being carried out by many psychologists and scientists from the 1920s onward. The recognized pioneer of this style was the Hungarian-born Victor Vasarely, whose work in Paris in the forties and fifties set an example for many other artists. It was a movement dominated by Europeans and South Americans living in Europe, although a few artists from the United States such as Richard Anuszkiewicz (colorplate 3) did develop related styles. Vasarely's experiments have covered all of the visual elements, from color to line, and tend to apply the principles discovered to the creation of illusions of space. He is skilled in the art of making a flat surface appear to advance or retreat, or establishing a number of levels within a picture with simple, rhythmic abstract patterns and color variations that establish their own nonlinear systems of perspective (colorplate 30). Vasarely has also been a leader in the search for a more useful social context for art. Like the American Minimalists, he has rejected the idea of art as an expressionistic gesture of the individual. Going a step further, he has attempted to find ways to place this art at the service of the public—through murals, industrial design, and mass production. For a time in the mid-sixties, while Op Art was considered fashionable, some designs were adopted, stolen, or invented for the decoration of clothing, but other than that, the movement and its social ideas have had little impact in America.

Bridget Riley, a British Op artist, has been the most succesful in creating the sensation of motion, which she achieves with compact patterns spread over large areas (fig. 11-15). Systems of curving lines or other related shapes do not allow the eye to come to rest,

11–15 Bridget Riley, *Current,* 1964. Synthetic polymer paint on composition board, 58⅜" x 58⅞". The Museum of Modern Art, New York (Philip C. Johnson Fund).

an effect that can be both tantalizing and annoying. Riley has experimented extensively with color as well and is unique in her studies of graduated tone variations (with which she can add effects of depth to those of motion).

Kinetic art, which was discussed in Chapter 3, underwent an interesting new period of development during the fifties and sixties as well, its aims being very closely linked to those of the Op artists. Many of the most impressive of these artists did work in Paris with Vasarely, or at least were very much aware of what he had done. The Argentinian Julio Le Parc's dazzling murals of light (fig. 11-16) were typical of the approach of the European-based artists of the 1960s, who favored extremely simple means and tended to shy away from mechanical devices. Le Parc's Continual Mobiles were

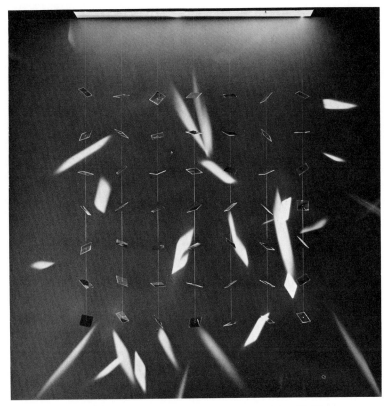

11-16 Julio Le Parc, *Continual Mobile, Continual Light,* 1963.
Steel and nylon, 63" high. The Tate Gallery, London.

descendants, as the name suggests, of the works of Alexander
Calder (fig. 3-19) and were constructed of nothing more than
pieces of polished metal hung on nylon threads. But in spite of
their simplicity and geometric elements, the reflections these mobiles cast on walls and ceiling ironically recalled the slashing
brushwork of the Abstract Expressionists.

More advanced kinetic sculpture has not been as common as
one might expect in this modern era, and what has been done is
not as respectful of the machine as was the painting, sculpture,
and architecture of the early part of the century. The impudent
contraptions of Jean Tinguely (fig. 3-20) offer more to laugh about
than to think about, pumping away and achieving absolutely nothing or performing such tasks as drawing ''abstract'' pictures.

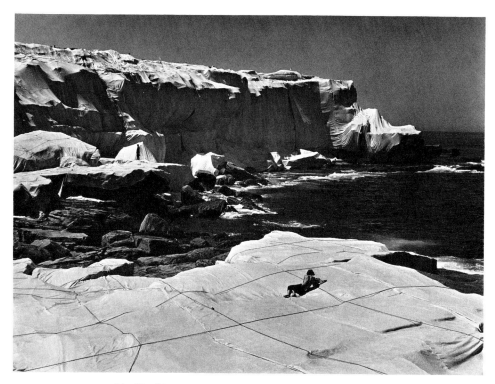

11–17 Christo, *Wrapped Coast*, Little Bay, Australia, 1969.
Cloth and rope, 1,000,000 square feet.

Art as Activity and Idea

One of the more interesting developments of recent years—and an important element in the general ''opening up'' of art—has been the revival of live performances by artists. This phenomenon began with the Futurists in the early years of the century and first attracted interest in the United States with Happenings (Chapter 3). In the late sixties and seventies, new forms evolved that attracted a great many artists. The range of these activities can be extraordinarily broad, from an intensely individual work to monumental operations involving hundreds of people. One example of such an event was the wrapping of one million square feet of Australian coastline by hundreds of volunteers in 1969 (fig. 11-17). The project was the idea of the Bulgarian-born American artist Christo, who began wrapping objects in cloth in the early sixties. He slowly worked his way up, covering public monuments and buildings, until he reached the super scale of the Australian enterprise. His two major projects in the seventies were a 200,000-square-foot curtain suspended over a Colorado canyon and a 24½-mile white fence erected in northern California—both of which, for all their materials, labor, and impressive results, were temporary.

Performances   *Performances* are the principal result of art's expansion into theater. They usually involve only the artist (and perhaps an assistant)
who presents a prepared activity or carries out some form of experiment. One of the most prominent performers has been Joseph
Beuys of Germany, who has bridged the gaps between art and life,
the visual and the theatrical by becoming a sort of living, walking
work of art (fig. 11-18). Beuys became an avid promoter of Happenings in the early 1960s. His own *Actions*, as he called them,
are usually performed alone and often involve a wide assortment of
materials—wood, metal, rope, tape recorders, skeletons, dead or
live animals, and cooking fat. They are also rich in symbolism and
invented ritual, and many have political overtones as well—sometimes rather provocative ones. One performance in Aachen literally
caused a riot.

Another type of performance, sometimes referred to as *Body
Art,* makes use of the artist's own body as the medium. This form
of art differs from theatrical performance largely in terms of its
focus. If any kind of story is represented, it is usually autobio-
graphical; more often, the concerns are conceptual. Perhaps the
most extreme—and possibly the most fascinating—of the Body

11–18   Joseph Beuys, *I Like America and America Likes Me,* **1974. Performance, three days long.
Courtesy of the René Block Gallery and Ronald Feldman Fine Arts, Inc., New York.**

11–19 Chris Burden, *White Light/White Heat,* 1975.
As exhibited at Ronald Feldman Fine Arts Inc., New York.

Artists has been Californian Chris Burden, who has risked death a number of times and has subjected himself to a great deal of pain. One of his less spectacular works, *White Light/White Heat,* reflects just how personal an experience Body Art can often be (fig. 11-19). It consisted of the artist's lying hidden from view in a shallow space close to the ceiling of an art gallery for a period of three weeks. During this time he did not eat, exercise, or speak with anyone. Burden designed the piece largely as an experiment in the effects of isolation and fasting. Thus the arrival of each visitor was important to him as an escape from the boredom and pain and as an examination of the variety of sensations (heightened by the effects of fasting) he experienced. The encounter with the visitor was not a one-sided affair, Burden claimed, for a kind of "energy" existed between them that both could sense. But even if this were not the case, such works certainly do leave the visitor with a number of unusual ideas and issues to ponder.

Conceptual Art   *Conceptual Art* is another major approach to art as idea that developed in the late sixties. Indeed, Conceptual artists have argued that the creation of art is possible without the use of objects or events. Just as Duchamp has challenged the definition of art by designating certain random, manufactured objects as artworks (fig. 10-16), these artists were prepared to challenge the need for anything but the idea itself.

Conceptual Art was partly an outgrowth of the expansion of art into events and performances. Some projects took up such a large geographical area that the participants were only able to communicate by letter or phone, so that the object itself—or any kind of contiguous visual form—no longer existed. Other projects, like some of Burden's, were reduced to such a degree that the idea seemed to overshadow the visual form and the event. In still other projects, the expense or other considerations made the work impossible to create or perform and left the whole thing in the proposal stage.

Yet in spite of their emphasis on the idea, Conceptual artists have made concessions to the physical world—since it is impossible, short of telepathy, to communicate an idea without some kind of a medium. They therefore provide a document of some kind for each piece, usually something as simple as a photograph, a tape recording, or even a postcard. John Baldessari's *Cremation Piece*, for example, was documented with a printed statement (fig. 11-20)

11–20   John Baldessari, *Cremation Piece,* 1969.
As shown at The Jewish Museum in the exhibition *Software,* 1970.

"One of several proposals to rid my life of accumulated art. With this project I will have all of my accumulated paintings cremated by a mortuary. The container of ashes will be interred inside a wall of the Jewish Museum. For the length of the show, there will be a commemorative plaque on the wall behind which the ashes are located. It is a reductive, recycling piece. I consider all these paintings a body of work in the real sense of the word. Will I save my life by losing it? Will a Phoenix arise from the ashes? Will the paintings having become dust become art materials again? I don't know, but I feel better."

that described the process of the work and even some of its ramifications; photographs of the studio; the paintings that were burned and the act of cremation; the ashes themselves; and a plaque that read *John Anthony Baldessari, May 1953–March 1966*.

The ways in which art has been practiced as idea or as activity have helped to expand the range of artistic possibilities and, of course, make definitions even more impossible to establish. Some forms rely on performance as the medium, others on writing, still others on normally undetectable means such as radio waves passing through a room; and the objectives of such art are nearly as numerous as the artists. Rather than leading to a dead end, the de-emphasis of the art object has produced a seemingly endless number of possibilities.

Entering the Eighties

Trying to understand the immediate past is like trying to make sense out of the blur of sights from the rear of a fast-moving train. Everything is passing by too rapidly to see clearly and is too close in time and space to determine at first which object is important enough to focus on. This analogy is especially true for recent art, because our present train of thought seems to be passing through an unusually profuse and exotic landscape and picking up speed as it goes.

Yet in spite of—or perhaps because of—this incredible variety and speed, no new schools of art have appeared on the scene since the decade of the sixties. Pop, color-field, Minimalism, and other styles did not continue as movements into the seventies—although many of the artists who developed them have continued to work in those styles. Apparently the developments of the sixties left artists with enough ideas to develop and explore for some time to come.

Since there are no longer any constraints about the materials to use in an artwork—dirt, garbage, animals, fat, ashes, radio waves, even the artist's body—there seem to be few significantly new materials left for an artist to introduce. But one can always find new ways to look at the old materials. Alice Aycock's sculptures are as new as Earth Art and as old as architecture. Using traditional construction materials such as wood or concrete, she builds untraditional structures. Typically, they invite the viewer to enter a space that is inaccessible or uninhabitable. Some are very low and partly built into the ground; some are set high above the ground; others

11-21 Alice Aycock, *The Beginnings of a Complex . . .* , 1977. Wood and concrete, tallest tower approx. 30′ high. Documenta VI, Kassel, Germany.

are merely facades. Because of its interesting spatial relationships, its clean lines, and even its freshly milled lumber, *The Beginnings of a Complex* . . . (fig. 11-21) appeals to us as an abstract sculpture. But as a shelter, it challenges the imagination. In this context, we tend to associate it with our own bodies, comparing it to other shelters. Where do the steps lead? Can we sit in it? Stand in it?

Sam Gilliam's materials—paint and canvas—are about as traditional as any an artist can use, and even some of his more unusual techniques were anticipated by painters and sculptors working in other styles. But if Gilliam began with traditions, he soon revised them to the point where they seemed to be radical innovations. In a long and intriguing series of works through the late sixties and most of the seventies, he combined the stain and spatter techniques of acrylic painting with the free shaping of soft sculpture (colorplate 31). His canvases were rarely framed; most often they were tacked to the wall, hung from the ceiling, or draped across corners. While other artists argued about the relative importance of the picture plane, Gilliam resolved the problem by doing away with it altogether.

Other kinds of recent art involve neither new materials nor particularly novel ways of using old materials. Instead, their novelty has to do with the radicalness of the idea behind them— meaning that a Conceptual Art sensibility is involved even though a traditional medium was used to make a relatively conventional painting or sculpture. One type of sculpture, like traditional realistic sculpture, entails making objects that represent things in the real world. But it goes so far in its imitation of the appearances of things that it manages to challenge reality itself. The creators of these ''false objects'' tend to reproduce everyday articles in their original size, shape, and color, but in an alien material—strawberries of painted bronze or a motorcycle of carved wood. Among the most fascinating examples of this type of art are the ''leather goods'' of Marilyn Levine. A viewer is almost forced to touch *Trent's Jacket* (fig. 11-22) to realize that the material hanging limply on the coat rack is hard ceramic rather than supple leather.

Closely related to Levine's false objects are the paintings of the Photo-Realists, whose work often resembles photographs. *Kent*

11-22 Marilyn Levine, *Trent's Jacket,* 1976. Ceramic, wood, and metal hooks, 35″ x 18″ x 8″. Private collection. Courtesy of the O.K. Harris Gallery.

11–23 Dan Graham, *Opposing Mirrors and Video Monitors on Time Delay*, 1975. Installation at the Sperone Westwater Fischer Gallery, New York.

(colorplate 32) by Chuck Close even simulates photographic focus, blurring the subject's nose—which is too near—and his neck and shoulders—which are too far away. While Close prefers to make large blowups of his friends with acrylic paints and an airbursh (fig. 3-1), others, like Ralph Goings, prefer to reproduce banal scenes of modern life (fig. 8-13) with oil paints and ordinary brushes. Photo-Realist paintings became popular in the early seventies, when the art world finally realized that they were not simply another wave of traditional realist painting, but an attempt to make use of the unique characteristics of the camera. By prodigiously copying photographs in paint, artists like Close and Goings are calling attention to the surface effects of pattern and color peculiar to the camera's special way of seeing.

One of the most intriguing new media to become available to artists in recent years is *video*—a self-contained television unit that can transmit or record images and sound. More versatile and convenient than film, it has become very popular with many artists. A large part of the work being done with video has concentrated on its "live" aspect and its ability to involve the viewer in the creation of the work. In a work called *Opposing Mirrors and Video Monitors on Time Delay*, Dan Graham made very interesting use of both the live and the tape factors (fig. 11-23). Two units, each consisting of

11–24 Luis Jimenez, *Progress, Part I,* 1973. Fiberglass and epoxy, 7'7" x 8'8" x 9'9".
Collection the artist. Courtesy of the O.K. Harris Gallery.

a camera and a monitor (standard television receiver), were set up
in front of mirrors at opposite ends of a room. Each camera faced
the mirror on the wall but was connected to the monitor at the
other end of the room, where the recorded image was screened
after an eight-second delay. The entering viewer saw nothing but
the empty room at first; then, after sixteen seconds (the time
required for the image to be transmitted to the other end, recorded
by that camera, and retransmitted), his own approach to the set
and subsequent actions. By running to the other end of the room,

he could see an image of himself standing beside an image of himself and then running away from it. Viewers, fascinated by the discrepancies between time and action in this magic mirror, unwittingly became part of the work as they tried to comprehend it.

Materials, concepts, and technology undoubtedly still offer the artist a great deal to work with, but the oldest field may yet prove to be the richest. Subject matter, which was virtually abandoned during the modern period, is now slowly beginning to attract attention again. In an age in which the boundaries between the arts have been erased and anything goes, the only rules left to break are those that Modernism itself established. Most of the avant-garde artists who turned to subject matter seem to have felt a bit self-conscious, afraid perhaps that they would be rejected by their peers. But in the end they have realized that it was the only way that they could say what they felt they had to say.

Sculptor Luis Jimenez attempted to work without images when he was a student, but found that they were the only adequate means to express the ideas that interested him. Divided between two cultures, he has found ample material to work with: the clash of the old and the new, Mexican and American, tradition and technology. Working with polyester resin and fiberglass, and coloring his works with garish sparkle-paints and exaggerated hues, Jimenez produces ''contemporary icons'' that record and rework traditional images of the Southwest. Some of their sources are to be found in both pre-Columbian and popular Mexican art, others in the vulgarity of plastic dime-store souvenirs. In *Progress I* (fig. 11-24), he created a monument to the spirit of the Old West, a huge pyramid of a sculpture that joins hunter, horse, and buffalo in a single dynamic swirl of mass and color. It is both heroic and satiric, a work that nudges our emotions in two directions at once. It is a post-Pop vision of the cowboy-and-Indian sculptures that Frederic Remington and other artists once created to record the myths that progress was rapidly destroying.

On the other side of the country, New York-based artist Dottie Attie has experimented with the restoration of content in a more direct and literary way. Her love of drawing and of the great art of the past—particularly that of the period from about 1600 to the early 1800s—inspired her to develop an unusual form of *Narrative Art*. Attie begins by meticulously drawing a miniature version of an Old Master painting, usually isolating such details as a face, a pair

> She frequently
> slipped into his
> room at dusk to
> receive the
> comfort and
> instruction he
> alone was
> capable of
> providing

11–25 Dottie Attie, *Carolina and Her Father,* 1978. Pencil on paper, each drawing 2″ square. Installation and details at the A.I.R. Gallery, New York. Collection the artist.

of hands, or some form of contact between two people. She then frames each of these tiny sketches and alternates them with brief fragments of stories that she invents or borrows from books. Mounted on a wall, these miniature narratives sometimes stretch more than forty feet (fig. 11-25). Typically, the events they suggest are vaguely erotic or perverse, yet she never openly represents such activities in the pictures or explictly states them in the texts, but leaves it up to the viewer to draw conclusions. Attie's droll stories are crisp and elegant understatements that stimulate curiosity and imagination.

Conclusions Although recent art has been dominated by developments in the United States, it is important to remember that they are part of the aesthetic revolution that began over a century ago with Manet's *Luncheon on the Grass*. Each major work of art throughout history has inspired changes in the works that followed, but this particular painting seems to be the logical choice as the launching point of the enormous series of changes that have marked the period we call "modern art."

The modern movement was never a unified or orderly progression. Viewed broadly, certain general patterns can be identified. One movement, centering on an interest in form, began with Cézanne and linked the Cubists and Mondrian with the recent geometric art of Minimalism and Op. Another movement, concentrating on color, began with the Impressionists and connected Seurat, Matisse, and Kandinsky, as well as such color-oriented abstract artists of our own day as Newman, Louis, and Frankenthaler. The Expressionist tradition of Van Gogh and Munch was still present in the abstract painting of Pollock and de Kooning in the 1950s. The radical experimentation and ironies of Dada re-emerged in Happenings and Pop Art and were continued by events, performances, and Conceptual Art. None of these divisions has been clear-cut; many artists might be grouped under several headings. Indeed, the present situation defies categories.

Art in the eighties—and, presumably, beyond that—is heir to an aesthetic freedom and variety Manet could never have conceived of. Entering a gallery today, a viewer is likely to find abstract art side by side with Photographic Realism, the hard edge of steel next to a formless sculpture of latex, an object alongside an idea.

Picture
Credits

Chapter 1   p. **12,** right, **13,** left, Alinari-E.P.A.

Chapter 2   p. **19,** top, William Dyckes; **23,** photo courtesy Leo Castelli Gallery; **25,** from "Information Theory and Figure Perception" by R.T. Green and M.C. Curtis, *Acta Psychologia,* vol. 25, 1966, pp. 12–36, Elsevier Excerpta Medica, North Holland Publishing Company; **27,** Kate Morgan Guttmann; **28,** William Dyckes; **29,** A.J. Wyatt, staff photographer; **33,** top left, Museum of Modern Art; **38,** Alinari-E.P.A.; **39,** top, Robert E. Mates, bottom, Edward Peterson.

Chapter 3   p. **49,** William Dyckes; **51,** top, Schopplein Studio; **59, 60,** Alinari-E.P.A.; **61,** D. James Dee; **64,** Charles Uht; **66,** New York Times photo; **67,** eeva - inkeri, New York; **68,** right, Marta Sentis; **69,** W.S. Stoddard; **73,** Gianfranco Gorgoni.

Chapter 4   p. **75,** top, Marburg-Art Reference Bureau; **76,** bottom, Photo Draeger, Paris; **77,** HBJ photo; **78,** British Architectural Library, Riba, London; **79,** Ezra Stoller © ESTO; **80,** Australian Tourist Commission; **81,** Canadian Consulate General, New York; **83,** American Airlines; **84,** Alison Frantz; **85,** The Public Archives of Canada; **86,** Wendy V. Watriss-Woodfin Camp & Associates; **87,** from "The Dogon People" by Fritz Morgenthaler, © 1969 Barrie and Jenkins, Ltd., London. Reprinted from *Meaning in Architecture,* Charles Jencks and George Baird, eds., George Braziller, Inc., New York, 1970; **88,** from *Art Through the Ages,* 6th edition, by Helen Gardner, © 1975 by Harcourt Brace Jovanovich, Inc. Reproduced by permission of the publisher; **89,** General Research and Humanities Division, The New York Public Library, Astor, Lenox and Tilden Foundations; **90,** Art and Architecture Division, The New York Public Library, Astor, Lenox and Tilden Foundations; **91,** New York City Housing Authority; **92, 93,** Alinari-E.P.A.; **94,** Robert Stefl; **95,** Doug Long, Photocraft; **97,** from *The Japanese House* by Heinrich Engel, Charles E. Tuttle Co., Inc., Tokyo, Japan; **98,** Sekai Bunka; **99,** Chicago Architectural Photographing Co.; **100,** Hedrich-Blessing, Chicago; **101,** Colorado Office of Tourism; **103,** Architekten "Atelier 5," Bern, Switzerland, photo by A. Winkler.

Suggestions for Further Study

Chapter 1   Arnheim, Rudolf. *Art and Visual Perception: A Psychology of the Creative Eye.* Berkeley and Los Angeles: University of California Press, 1954.

Barr, Alfred. *Picasso—Fifty Years of His Art.* New York: Museum of Modern Art, 1955.

Fast, Julius. *Body Language.* New York: Simon & Schuster, Pocket Books, 1971.

Goodman, Nelson. *Languages of Art: An Approach to a Theory of Symbols.* Indianapolis, Ind.: Bobbs-Merrill Co., 1968.

Kubler, George A. *The Shape of Time: Remarks on the History of Things.* New Haven: Yale University Press, 1962.

Langer, Susanne K. *Philosophy in a New Key; A Study in the Symbolism of Reason, Rite, and Art.* 3rd ed. Cambridge, Mass.: Harvard University Press, 1976.

Segall, M. H., Campbell, D. T., and Herskovits, M. J. *The Influence of Culture on Visual Perception.* Indianapolis: Bobbs-Merrill Co., 1966.

Chapter 2   Arnheim, Rudolf. *Visual Thinking.* Berkeley and Los Angeles: University of California Press, 1969.

Bloomer, Carolyn M. *Principles of Visual Perception.* New York: Van Nostrand Reinhold Co., 1976.

Clark, Kenneth. *Looking at Pictures.* Boston: Beacon Press, 1968.

Eitner, Lorenz. *Introduction to Art.* Minneapolis: Burgess Publishing Co., 1961.

Ehrenzweig, Anton. *The Hidden Order of Art: A Study in the Psychology of Artistic Imagination.* Berkeley and Los Angeles: University of California Press, 1967.

Gibson, James J. *The Perception of the Visual World.* Boston: Houghton Mifflin Co., 1950.

————. *The Senses Considered as Perceptual Systems.* Boston: Houghton Mifflin Co., 1966.

Gombrich, Ernst H. *Art and Illusion: A Study in the Psychology of Pictorial Presentation.* 2nd ed. Princeton: Princeton University Press, 1961.

Gombrich, E. H., Hochberg, J., and Black, M. *Art, Perception and Reality.* Baltimore: Johns Hopkins University Press, 1972.

Gregory, R. L. *Eye and Brain.* New York: McGraw-Hill, 1966.

Hogg, James, ed. *Psychology and the Visual Arts.* Baltimore: Penguin Books, 1970.

Kepes, Gyorgy. *Language of Vision.* Chicago: Paul Theobald & Co., 1945.

Kohler, Wolfgang. *Gestalt Psychology.* New ed. New York: Liveright, 1970.

Russell, John. *Seurat.* New York: Praeger Publishers, 1965.

Chapter 3 Celant, Germano. *Art Povera.* New York: Praeger Publishers, 1969.

Craven, George M. *Object and Image.* Englewood Cliffs, N.J.: Prentice-Hall, 1975.

de la Croix, Horst, and Tansey, Richard G. *Gardner's Art Through the Ages.* 7th ed. New York: Harcourt Brace Jovanovich, 1980.

Dyckes, William. *Contemporary Spanish Art.* New York: Art Digest, 1975.

Encyclopedia of World Art, 15 Vols. New York: McGraw-Hill, 1959–68.

Ivins, William M., Jr. *Prints and Visual Communication.* Cambridge, Mass.: M.I.T. Press, 1969.

Kirby, Michael, ed. *Happenings: An Illustrated Anthology.* New York: E. P. Dutton & Co., 1965.

Martindale, Andrew. *Gothic Art.* New York: Praeger Publishers, 1967.

Mendelowitz, Daniel M. *Drawing.* New York: Holt, Rinehart & Winston, 1967.

Popper, Frank. *Origins and Development of Kinetic Art.* Greenwich, Conn.: New York Graphic Society, 1969.

Read, Herbert. *The Art of Sculpture.* 2nd ed. Princeton: Princeton University Press, 1961.

Seitz, William. *The Art of Assemblage.* New York: Museum of Modern Art, 1961.

Sontag, Susan. *On Photography.* New York: Farrar, Straus & Giroux, 1977.

Wollheim, Richard. *Art and Its Objects: An Introduction to Aesthetics.* New York: Harper & Row, 1968.

Chapter 4 Engel, Heinrich. *The Japanese House: A Tradition for Contemporary Architecture.* Rutland, Vt. and Tokyo: Charles E. Tuttle Co., 1964.

Evenson, Norma. *Le Corbusier: The Machine and the Grand Design.* New York: George Braziller, 1969.

Furneaux Jordan, Robert. *A Concise History of Western Architecture.* New York: Harcourt Brace Jovanovich, 1970.

Giedion, Sigfried. *Space, Time and Architecture: The Growth of a New Tradition.* 5th rev. ed. Cambridge, Mass.: Harvard University Press, 1967.

Huxtable, Ada L. *Will They Ever Finish Bruckner Boulevard?* New York: Macmillan, 1970.

Jacobs, J., ed. *The Great Cathedrals.* New York: American Heritage, 1968.

Jencks, Charles, and Baird, George, eds. *Meaning in Architecture.* New York: George Braziller, 1970.

Nishihara, Kiyoyuki. *Japanese Houses: Patterns for Living.* Tokyo: Japan Publications, 1967.

Norberg-Schulz, Christian. *Existence, Space and Architecture.* New York: Praeger Publishers, 1971.

———. *Meaning in Western Architecture.* New York: Praeger Publishers, 1975.

Rudofsky, Bernard. *Architecture Without Architects: A Short Introduction to Non-Pedigreed Architecture.* Garden City, New York: Doubleday & Co., 1969.

———. *Streets for People.* Garden City, New York: Doubleday & Co., 1969.

Scully, Vincent. *American Architecture and Urbanism: A Historical Essay.* New York: Praeger Publishers, 1969.

———. *Modern Architecture.* Rev. ed. New York: George Braziller, 1974.

Wright, Frank Lloyd. *When Democracy Builds.* Chicago: University of Chicago Press, 1945.

Zucker, Paul. *Town and Square: From the Agora to the Village Green.* New York: Columbia University Press, 1959.

Chapter 5 Carter, Dagny. *Four Thousand Years of China's Art.* New York: Ronald Press, 1948.

Clark, Kenneth. *Landscape Into Art.* London: John Murray, 1966.

———. *Leonardo da Vinci.* Baltimore: Penguin Books, Pelican Books, 1968.

Giedion, Sigfried. *The Eternal Present: The Beginning of Art.* Princeton, N.J.: Princeton University Press, 1964.

Hartt, Frederick. *History of Italian Renaissance Art.* New York: Harry N. Abrams, 1969.

Kahler, Heinz. *The Art of Rome and Her Empire.* New York: Crown Publishers, 1963.

Klingender, Francis D. *Animals in Art and Thought to the End of the Middle Ages.* Ed. by Evelyn Antal and John Harthan. Cambridge, Mass.: M.I.T. Press, 1971.

Michalowski, Kazimierz. *The Art of Ancient Egypt.* New York: Harry N. Abrams, 1969.

Peacock, Carlos. *John Constable: The Man and His Work.* Rev. ed. Greenwich, Conn.: New York Graphic Society, 1972.

Richter, Gisela M. A. *Perspective in Greek and Roman Art.* London: Phaidon, 1971.

Shepard, Paul. *Man in the Landscape.* New York: Alfred A. Knopf, 1967.

Willets, William. *Foundations of Chinese Art.* New York: McGraw-Hill, 1965.

Chapter 6   Berger, John. *Ways of Seeing.* New York: Penguin Books, 1977.

Clark, Kenneth. *The Nude: A Study of Ideal Form.* Garden City, New York: Doubleday & Co., Anchor Books, 1956.

Crespelle, Jean-Paul. *Chagall.* New York: Coward, McCann & Geoghegan, 1970.

Hodin, J. P. *Oskar Kokoschka.* Greenwich, Conn.: New York Graphic Society, 1966.

Honour, Hugh. *Neo-Classicism.* Harmondsworth, England: Penguin Books, 1968.

Lal, Kanwar. *Immortal Khajuraho.* Delhi: Asia Press, 1965.

Powell, Ann. *The Origins of Western Art.* New York: Harcourt Brace Jovanovich, 1973.

Richter, G. M. A. *A Handbook of Greek Art: A Survey of the Visual Arts of Ancient Greece.* 6th rev. ed. London: Phaidon Press, 1969.

Schefold, Karl. *Myth and Legend in Early Greek Art.* New York: Harry N. Abrams, 1966.

Sewter, A. C. *Baroque and Rococo.* New York: Harcourt Brace Jovanovich, 1972.

White, Christopher. *Rubens and His World.* New York: Viking Press, 1968.

Chapter 7   Clements, Robert J. *Michelangelo: A Self-Portrait.* New York: New York University Press, 1968.

De Tolnay, Charles. *The Art and Thought of Michelangelo.* New York: Pantheon, 1964.

Friedman, B. H. *Jackson Pollock: Energy Made Visible.* New York: McGraw-Hill, 1972.

Hauser, Arnold. *The Social History of Art.* New York: Alfred A. Knopf, 1961.

Hibbard, Howard. *Michelangelo.* New York: Harper & Row, 1974.

Lubin, Albert J. *Stranger on the Earth: A Psychological Biography of Van Gogh.* New York: Holt, Rinehart & Winston, 1972.

Muller, Joseph-Emile. *Rembrandt*. Trans. by Brian Hooley. New York: Harry N. Abrams, 1969.

O'Connor, Francis V. *Jackson Pollock*. New York: The Museum of Modern Art, 1969.

O'Hara, Frank. *Jackson Pollock*. New York: George Braziller, 1959.

Ramsden, E. H. *Michelangelo*. New York: Praeger Publishers, 1971.

Rosenberg, Jacob. *Rembrandt: Life and Work*. New York: Phaidon Press, 1964.

Schapiro, Meyer. *Vincent Van Gogh*. New York: Harry N. Abrams, 1970.

Tralbaut, Marc E. *Van Gogh*. New York: Viking Press, 1969.

Van Gogh, Vincent. *Letters of Vincent Van Gogh*. Ed. Mark Roskill. New York: Atheneum, 1963.

Chapter 8   Driskell, David C. *Two Centuries of Black American Art*. New York: Alfred A. Knopf, 1976.

Fine, Elsa H. *The Afro-American Artist: A Search for Identity*. New York: Holt, Rinehart & Winston, 1973.

Goodrich, Lloyd. *Edward Hopper*. New York: Harry N. Abrams, 1971.

McCoubrey, John W., ed. *American Art 1700–1960: Sources and Documents*. Englewood Cliffs, N.J.: Prentice-Hall, 1965.

McLanathan, Richard. *The American Tradition in the Arts*. New York: Harcourt Brace Jovanovich, 1968.

Owings, Nathaniel A. *The American Aesthetic*. New York: Harper & Row, 1969.

Rose, Barbara. *American Art Since 1900*. New York: Praeger Publishers, 1967.

Taylor, Joshua. *America as Art*. Washington, D.C.: National Collection of Fine Arts, 1976.

Tighe, Mary Ann, and Lang, Elizabeth E. *Art America*. New York: McGraw-Hill, 1977.

Whitney Museum. *200 Years of American Sculpture*. Boston: David R. Godine, 1976.

Wilmerding, John. *American Art*. New York: Penguin Books, 1976.

Chapter 9   Arnason, H. H. *History of Modern Art: Painting, Sculpture and Architecture*. Englewood Cliffs, N.J.: Prentice-Hall; New York: Harry N. Abrams, 1968.

Badt, Kurt. *The Art of Cézanne*. Trans. by Sheila A. Ogilvie. Berkeley and Los Angeles: University of California Press, 1965.

Balakian, Anna. *The Symbolist Movement: A Critical Approach*. New York: New York University Press, 1977.

Bell, Clive. *Art*. New York: G. P. Putnam's Sons, Capricorn, 1959.

Boudaille, Georges. *Gauguin*. Trans. Elisa Jaffa. New York: Tudor, 1964.

Champigneulle, Bernard. *Rodin*. Trans. by J. Maxwell Brownjohn. New York: Harry N. Abrams, 1967.

Duret, Theodore. *Manet and the French Impressionists.* Trans. J. E. Crawford Fitch. Freeport, N.Y.: Books for Libraries Press, 1971.

Hamilton, George H. *Manet and His Critics.* New York: W. W. Norton & Co., 1969.

Harris, A. S., and Nochlin, L. *Women Artists, 1550–1950.* New York: Alfred A. Knopf, 1977.

Hess, Thomas B., and Ashbery, John, eds. *Avant-Garde Art.* New York: Macmillan, 1971.

Kubler, George A. *The Shape of Time: Remarks on the History of Things.* New Haven: Yale University Press, 1962.

Loengren, Sven. *The Genesis of Modernism.* Indianapolis: Indiana University Press, 1971.

Rewald, John. *Post Impressionism: From Van Gogh to Gauguin.* New York: Museum of Modern Art, 1962.

Slocombe, George. *Rebels of Art.* Port Washington, N.Y.: Kennikat Press Corp., 1969.

Chapter 10   Barr, Alfred. *Matisse: His Art and His Public.* New York: Museum of Modern Art, 1951.

Bowness, Alan. *Modern European Art.* New York: Harcourt Brace Jovanovich, 1972.

Chipp, Herschel B. *Theories of Modern Art: A Source Book by Artists and Critics.* Berkeley and Los Angeles: University of California Press, 1968.

de la Croix, Horst, and Tansey, Richard G. *Gardner's Art Through the Ages.* 7th ed. New York: Harcourt Brace Jovanovich, 1980.

Diehl, Gaston. *The Fauves.* New York: Harry N. Abrams, 1975.

Douval, Bernard. *The School of Paris.* Trans. Cornelia Brookfield and Ellen Hart. New York: Alfred A. Knopf, 1977.

Haftmann, Werner. *Painting in the Twentieth Century.* Vol. 1, *An Analysis of the Artists and Their Work.* New York: Praeger Publishers, 1965.

Jean, Marcel, and Mezei, Arpad. *The History of Surrealist Painting.* Trans. by Simon Watson Taylor. New York: Grove Press, 1960.

Madsen, Stephan T. *Sources of Art Nouveau.* Trans. R. I. Christopherson. New York: McGraw-Hill, 1967.

Mondriaan, Pieter Cornelis. *Plastic Art and Pure Plastic Art.* New York: George Wittenborn, 1945.

Neumeyer, Alfred. *The Search for Meaning in Modern Art: Die Kunst in Unserer Zeit.* Trans. by R. Angress. Englewood Cliffs, N.J.: Prentice-Hall, 1965.

Penrose, Roland. *Picasso: His Life and Work.* Rev. ed. New York: Harper & Row, 1973.

Read, Herbert. *The Art of Sculpture.* 2nd ed. Princeton: Princeton University Press, 1961.

Rickey, George. *Constructivism.* New York: George Braziller, 1967.

Rosenblum, Robert. *Cubism and Twentieth-Century Art.* New York: Harry N. Abrams, 1968.

Rubin, William S. *Dada, Surrealism and Their Heritage.* New York: Museum of Modern Art, 1968.

Selz, Peter. *German Expressionist Painting.* Berkeley and Los Angeles: University of California Press, 1974.

Chapter 11   Amaya, Mario. *Pop Art . . . and After.* New York: Viking Press, 1972.

Ashton, Dore. *A Reading of Modern Art.* Cleveland: Press of Case Western Reserve University, 1969.

————. *The New York School: A Cultural Reckoning.* New York: Viking Press, 1973.

Battcock, Gregory, ed. *Idea Art: A Critique.* New York: E. P. Dutton & Co., 1973.

————, ed. *Minimal Art: A Critical Anthology.* New York: E. P. Dutton & Co., 1968.

————, ed. *The New Art: A Critical Anthology.* Rev. ed. New York: E. P. Dutton & Co., 1973.

————. *Super Realism: A Critical Anthology.* New York: E. P. Dutton & Co., 1975.

Burnham, Jack. *Beyond Modern Sculpture.* New York: George Braziller, 1968.

Gottlieb, Carla. *Beyond Modern Art.* New York: E. P. Dutton & Co., 1976.

Hunter, Sam, and Jacobus, John. *American Art of the Twentieth Century.* New York: Harry N. Abrams, 1973.

Leymarie, Jean, ed. *Art Since Mid-Century.* Greenwich, Conn.: New York Graphic Society, 1971.

Meyer, Ursula. *Conceptual Art.* New York: E. P. Dutton & Co., 1972.

Muller, Gregoire. *The New Avant Garde.* New York: Praeger Publishers, 1972.

Popper, Frank. *Origins and Development of Kinetic Art.* Greenwich, Conn.: New York Graphic Society, 1969.

Rose, Barbara. *American Art Since 1900.* Rev. ed. New York: Praeger Publishers, 1967.

Sandler, Irving. *The Triumph of American Painting: A History of Abstract Expressionism.* New York: Praeger Publishers, 1973.

Sontag, Susan. *Against Interpretation and Other Essays.* New York: Farrar, Straus & Giroux, 1966.

Index

309

A 9
B 0
C 1
D 2
E 3
F 4
G 5
H 6
I 7
J 8